# DAD'S ARMY GOES TO WAR

# DAD'S ARMY GOES TO WAR

MELODY FOREMAN

FRONTLINE
BOOKS

First published in Great Britain in 2024 by
Frontline Books
An imprint of Pen & Sword Books Ltd
Yorkshire - Philadelphia

Copyright © Melody Foreman, 2024

ISBN 9781399092821

Typeset by Lapiz Digital
Printed and bound in the UK by CPI Group (UK) Ltd,
Croydon, CR0 4YY.

Printed on paper from a sustainable source by
CPI Group (UK) Ltd, Croydon, CR0 4YY

Pen & Sword Books Limited incorporates the imprints of Archaeology, Atlas,
Aviation, Battleground, Digital, Discovery, Family History, Fiction, History,
Local, Local History, Maritime, Military, Military Classics, Politics, Select,
Transport, True Crime, Air World, Claymore Press, Frontline Publishing,
Leo Cooper, Remember When, Seaforth Publishing, The Praetorian Press,
Wharncliffe Books, Wharncliffe Local History, Wharncliffe Transport,
Wharncliffe True Crime and White Owl.

For a complete list of Pen & Sword titles please contact
PEN & SWORD BOOKS LTD

47 Church Street, Barnsley, South Yorkshire, S70 2AS, England
E-mail: enquiries@pen-and-sword.co.uk
Website: www.pen-and-sword.co.uk

or

PEN & SWORD BOOKS
1950 Lawrence Rd, Havertown, PA 19083, USA
E-mail: uspen-and-sword@casematepublishers.com

# CONTENTS

# ACKNOWLEDGEMENTS

These real-life wartime stories about the wonderful *Dad's Army* cast were originally going to form part of a previous non-fiction book, *From the Battlefield to the Big Screen*, which was published by Frontline/Pen & Sword Books in 2022. However, as I soon realised there was so much to write about the unique military experiences of the legendary *Dad's Army* stars, it only seemed right they had a book purely devoted to them.

I was fortunate to have access to various biographies – some written by the wartime heroes/actors themselves about their time in real uniform, others by their proud relatives, and noted co-authors. There were rare interviews too that I managed to track down and watch, listen to and absorb in a bid to build up a well rounded tale. Eminent historians and their studies helped me to add authenticity and background to each reminiscence. For example, when I wrote about Clive Dunn I turned to author John Carr and his superb book *The Defence and Fall of Greece 1940–1941*, while David Croft's experiences at Bône airfield in Algiers, North Africa, led me to Hilary St George Saunders' book published in 1950, *The Red Beret, The Story of The Parachute Regiment at War, 1940–1945*.

A brilliant study of the Home Guard was supplied by Penny Summerfield and Corinna Peniston-Bird in their volume, *Contesting Home Defence: Men, Women and the Home Guard in the Second World War*. Jerry Murland's book *Retreat and Rearguard: Dunkirk 1940: The Evacuation of the BEF to the Channel* assisted my study of Arnold Ridley's little known service as an army captain and press officer in the Second World War.

The stars of *Dad's Army* – Arthur Lowe, John Le Mesurier and Clive Dunn – and the producers Jimmy Perry and David Croft mentioned their wars and yet were as ever modest, sometimes comical, as was their way, and the general attitude for the old soldier to 'just get on with life as the past is the past' was employed by them all, judging by the light-heartedness of some of their narratives.

I'd like therefore to thank Nicolas Ridley (author of *Godfrey's Ghost, From Father to Son*) for his special contribution to this book about his father Arnold (Private Charles Godfrey), who served in both conflicts. John Laurie, as far as I know, never wrote an autobiography and I had only the noted memories of his pals, like Bill Pertwee and Ian Lavender, and war archives to work from.

To help build a picture of the military experiences connected to the actors I was able to use the eye-witness accounts of men who had served either in the same regiment or in the same battle. I owe a huge heap of thanks to Dr Julian Brock for allowing me to use his late grandfather George Taylor's recorded interview about his time as a lance corporal serving in the trenches with the Somerset Light Infantry. The quiet and talented Ridley was in the same regiment in the First World War. Dr Brock's skill as an indexer is superb and I'm tremendously grateful for his assistance.

A big thank you, of course, must go to the late, great *Dad's Army* star Ian Lavender (Private Frank Pike), who a couple of years before he died in February 2024 kindly agreed to write the Foreword of this book. Ian was as always a keen supporter and is much missed.

Stephen Lowe and his son the brilliant photographer Jack Lowe (who shares his celebrity grandfather Arthur's passion for the sea, the RNLI in particular) have been a great help. And to artist Jessica Dunn, daughter of the wondrous Clive – thank you!

Frontline publisher Martin Mace has been full of encouragement for this book and is a *Dad's Army* fan of note!

Like so many millions of people across the world, my family love *Dad's Army*. Thanks to Hattie and Henry Cats, Helen and Lucy. Also I am grateful to Madeline and Geoff Usherwood for allowing me the use of Mrs Brenda Usherwood's wartime ATS (Auxiliary Territorial Service) picture and story which I have included in the chapter about Jimmy Perry.

A heap of thanks goes out to the excellent Christine who accompanied me on a lively research trip to the marvellous Dad's Army Museum in Thetford, Norfolk, and it's hats off to all those smashing and welcoming volunteers there who recreate the memory of the show so well. Thanks and ever thanks, Christine and I had a ball!

I also want to thank Elizabeth at Boutique 44, High Street, Charing, Kent, for the supportive chats, book sales, and for running the box office for my literary talk events. Also, a big salute to Helen and Martyn at Nine Oaks Vineyard in Kent, and also thanks to my supportive pals Ann-Marie Finn, Paul Finn and the poet Mims Sully. To the Tenterden & District Local History Society, Charing & Local District History

Society, Bentley Priory Museum, and the many noble organisations which book me for lectures – I'm forever grateful.

And to all *Dad's Army* fans across the world who are keen to learn more about those epic cast members who really went to war, then this is book is for you.

Melody Foreman, April 2024

Author's note: Every effort has been made to establish the rightful copyright owners of photographs in this book.

# FOREWORD
# BY IAN LAVENDER

DURING the early days of the writing of this book I was lucky to receive the following thoughts, memories and support from the actor Ian Lavender, who starred in *Dad's Army* as the nation's favourite young innocent, Private Frank Pike. It came as a great sadness to learn that kind and thoughtful Ian had died aged 77 on 2 February 2024. His words are here, though, as he wrote them. *Author.*

***

I AM now two years older than both Arnold Ridley and John Laurie when we assembled at the then BBC Television Centre at Shepherd's Bush for the start of a few weeks' work in 1968.

David Croft and Jimmy Perry sailed off with not too much wind in their sails, followed by a motley crew who became known privately as 'The Magnificent Seven' but who in reality, when joined by vicar, verger and air raid warden, were 'The Magnificent Ten'. David always said it was just unfortunate that films with Ten in the title were few and far between and usually unusable.

We spent, over the next ten years, somewhere around 1,000 days together making TV, radio, film and stage versions of the show, plus, of course, other radio, pantomime and theatre ventures in various other combinations. I even did cabaret with Clive Dunn in Weston-super-Mare!

This is a long winded – I apologise – way of telling that we got to know each other extremely well over a considerable time in deliciously varying circumstances.

I cannot remember during those times and happily for several years afterwards ever having sat and discussed each other's war.

My experience was, of course, non-existent. The stories and experiences that I listened to from them were made up of snippets of information and, more often than not, humorous observations of what they went through in their different wars.

I was particularly close to John Laurie and the stories of his and Arnold's first war experiences had to be teased out from them almost as though they were remembering them for the first time. Both he and Arnold were in daily pain from their First World War experiences. John certainly found nothing brave or romantic in the stories he told me. Some he told me only with the promise that I would never repeat them. The pair of them were on occasion to be found sitting in the corner of a room or restaurant deep in their own conversation. I know not what they were talking about, except that sometimes John would be wiping a mote from his eye as they rejoined the rest of the group.

John's way of showing he liked something or someone was to show how much he didn't like them. At one of our regular location dinners (one each series), he famously complained of being the finest Hamlet of the 1920s but having become 'famous for doing this crap!' He wouldn't have missed it for the world.

We all learned each others' ranks and achievements as we went along. No one banged on about their various jobs and positions. The stories were as much about all the things that happened after their real wars as well as during. Spike Milligan's role in Hitler's downfall was not funny at the time, but how else were all these men and women, known and unknown, actor and bank clerk, writer and reader, going to get through the rest of what had been left of their lives?

Prisoner of war camps, concerts in the desert, Home Guard platoons after work, fire watching, all were talked of, and these real experiences were, of course, a shorthand that they all had and that I tried to learn.

I have always likened those ten summers of making *Dad's Army* to being paid to go back to a glorious summer school each year. I was given the chance to go away and learn something new from this amazing group of teachers. If you couldn't learn something from them, then where could you?

I like to think I was close to all of them. I was particularly close to John and Arthur; Clive and John le Mes were very special too; Billy Pertwee, him as well; I played Arnold's 'Ghost Train' four times.

Oh yes, I do think they were special most of the time, and when you put them all together in the same room, or the same book . . .

Ian Lavender, 2020

# INTRODUCTION

ON 14 May 1940 Britain's Secretary of State for War Sir Anthony Eden broadcast the following announcement to millions of people listening to the BBC:

Since the war began the Government has received countless enquiries from all over the Kingdom from men of all ages who are for one reason or another not at present engaged in military service, and who wish to do something for the defence of the country.

Now is your opportunity. We want large numbers of such men in Great Britain who are British subjects, between the ages of 17 and 65, to come forward now and offer their service in order to make assurance doubly sure. The name of the new force which is now to be raised will be the 'Local Defence Volunteers'. This name, Local Defence Volunteers, describes its duties in three words. It must be understood that this is, so to speak, a spare-time job, so there will be no need for any volunteer to abandon his present occupation.

Part-time members of existing civil defence organisations should ask their officers' advice before registering under the scheme. Men who will ultimately become due for calling up under the National Service (Armed Forces) Act may join temporarily, and will be released to join the Army when they are required to serve. Now a word to those who propose to volunteer. When on duty you will form part of the Armed Forces, and your period of service will be for the duration of the war. You will not be paid, but you will receive uniform and will be armed. You will be entrusted with certain vital duties, for which reasonable fitness and a knowledge of firearms are necessary. These duties will not require you to live away from your homes. In order to volunteer, what you have to do is to give in your name at your local police station; and then, as and when we want you, we will let you know.

This appeal is directed chiefly to those who live in small towns, villages and less densely inhabited suburban areas. I must warn you that, for certain military reasons, there will be some localities where the numbers required will be small, and others where your services will not be required at all. Here then is the opportunity for which so many of you have been waiting. Your loyal help, added to the arrangements which already exist, will make and keep our country safe.

***

ALMOST thirty years later this speech, which had galvanised men and women to join volunteer defence forces across Britain, went on to inspire *Dad's Army* – one of the world's greatest comedic phenomena ever to hit our television screens, cinemas and stages too. The show was even described by the late Her Majesty The Queen as 'one of her all time favourites', and Buckingham Palace insiders revealed HM The Queen Mother was also a keen follower of the wartime antics of the Home Guard unit of Walmington-on-Sea. Even today, and decades after its first broadcast in 1968, *Dad's Army* continues to entertain audiences old and new. This ongoing success across the world has also led to the publication of important cultural theories written and debated by a raft of notable academics.

So what makes this legendary series about Britain's valiant Home Guard so memorable, so durable? The power of the storylines, motivated by the authenticity of the cast and writers' real-life military experiences, provides many answers. Indeed, the autobiographical energy contained within each of the eighty episodes places *Dad's Army* uniquely at the forefront of televised comedy. Its characters are constructed of a certain quality which only honest human endeavour in times of conflict could create and then represent.

The actors in this series, which regularly gained audiences of eighteen million viewers, had served during the First World War, the Second World War or even both. And out of the dark in the mind of the entertainment artiste often comes the light of comedy, while beyond the humour of the gallows so associated with the British penchant for resounding understatement arrived a broadcasting event that touches hearts and minds whenever and wherever it is experienced. Put simply, *Dad's Army* is magical.

Analyse the reasons behind the popularity of the show and we'd all agree that it feeds off the real oral and written histories of life on the Home Front. It is these tales, which live in museum archives, books and old documentary film reels, which provide us with an awareness of the men and women who served valiantly in the Home Guard and Local Defence Volunteer groups.

In November 1940 Anthony Eden told MPs in the House of Commons: 'No one will claim for the Home Guard that it is a miracle of organisation . . . but many would claim that it is a miracle of improvisation, and in that way it does express the particular genius of our people. If it has succeeded, as I think it has, it has been due to the spirit of the land and of the men in the Home Guard.'

In the book *Contesting Home Defence: Men, Women and the Home Guard in the Second World War*, co-author Penny Summerfield wrote: 'The humour in *Dad's Army* is generated by a combination of farce, slapstick, wordplay and innuendo, but is derived above all from the strong characterisation of the seven key members and their relationships with one another and with those outside the unit.'[1]

When a survey was carried out in the 1980s and 1990s seeking viewers' comments on the show, all of them paid tribute to its authenticity and true-to-life representation. One fan, Nigel Grey, was 16 years old in 1940 when he joined the Home Guard. But two years later a medical examination revealed he had a heart condition that left him unfit for any sort of war work. He described himself as 'reject' material and he was 'devastated' not to be able to help Britain at a time of crisis. He never forgot his two years with the Home Guard, however, and greatly admired *Dad's Army*. He wrote:

> One feels the authors of the series must have had first hand experience, or at least have done much in-depth research into the subject. There was so much I could relate to even allowing for comedy having to be larger than life to project itself from the small screen.
>
> On one occasion our Company Sergeant Major (CSM) was endeavouring to emulate a Regimental Sergeant Major of the Guards Brigade, and as I recall doing a very good job of it. However, the raucous barking got too much for the poor man's dentures, which suddenly ended up on the road. I always expected this incident to be repeated in *Dad's Army*, as there was so much I could identify with in that excellent show.[2]

And in 2000 Bill Trueman, also a former member of the real Home Guard, said:

> The researchers of that show certainly depicted the events and characters. I enjoy them every time, as memories flow back, and can laugh at events that you experienced and was associated with. The characters are typical of the Home Guard as I knew it.
>
> In my own platoon we had the officer who was the one who thought he knew best, the young one who had mother behind him looking after his well being. Then the 'spiv' always able to get the unobtainable item from the Black Market. The jittery sergeant. I can put names to most of them.[3]

However, fears were regularly expressed by BBC bosses back in 1968 about the show being seen to 'mock' the hearty endeavours of the British on the Home Front. Head of Light Entertainment Tom Sloan, who was a stickler for 'old fashioned BBC standards', backed up by the National Viewers' and Listeners' Association championed by Mary Whitehouse, gave a lecture in 1969. He concluded that while the show was indeed 'funny' (about the war), it redeemed itself because it was also 'true' and that characters like those created by Jimmy Perry really did exist in those 'marvellous' days. 'The possibility of defeat did not enter our minds,' he said.[4]

Indeed, Perry never allowed his characters to express the thought of giving up. The only time doubt about the situation crept into the script was when Private Frazer (John Laurie) uttered his 'we're all doomed!' prophecy, which no one took seriously. Maybe the actor's comical eye-rolling had something to do with that.

It's true, however, that there was reluctance among some of the characters to stress and strain over their duties too much. Sergeant Wilson and Private Walker often expressed their dismay about any orders which involved physical exertion.

The generally upbeat attitude of the show, though, is brilliantly evident in the episode 'Sons of the Sea', in which Captain Mainwaring and his men find themselves floating out to sea in a rowing boat having gone astray during a river patrol. Towards the end of a long night bobbing about, Mainwaring is stoically bright:

> *Mainwaring*: Pay attention, men. It will be light soon. We shall be spotted by a boat.
> *Wilson*: Suppose it's a German boat, sir?
> *Mainwaring*: I don't want any of that sort of talk here. There are no German boats in the English Channel.

'While such sentiments were sincere and even laudable, they were, as in this example, exaggerated to the point of absurdity,' explains academic Penny Summerfield, who also described how 'combining a loyal representation of Britain's part in the Second World War with a comedy about a wartime organisation was not easy to achieve'.

> 'Perry's Home Guard characters were not only ineffectual soldiers, but some (Private Walker and even Sergeant Wilson) were not averse to shirking. Churchill's noble speech . . . "Make no mistake, it was our finest hour" could be read ironically, especially in view of jokey references in early reviews to the thirty-minute show as 'comedy's finest half hour'.[5]

And while *Dad's Army* does not espouse an anti-war agenda, there are similarities to the lampooning of patriotic military officers akin to those who appear in the musical film based on Joan Littlewood's play *Oh What a Lovely War* (1969). Even earlier, in *The Life and Death of Colonel Blimp* (1943), a romantic drama and war film created by the awesome Michael Powell and Emeric Pressburger, we see the motivations of the Home Guard and the blustering main character Clive Candy (played by the actor Roger Livesey) exposed as honourable and sincere, if not somewhat outdated. The inner workings and complications of the organisation are not totally revealed as the story unfolds in a series of flashbacks that cover Candy's life, including his military service in the Boer War.

In 1995 *The Life and Death of Colonel Blimp* was deemed to be among the most popular one hundred films of all time and remains a steadfast member of the legendary Powell and Pressburger Archers' company classics. 'Blimp' was created by the legendary wartime *Evening Standard* newspaper cartoonist David Low. However, the film proved to be Churchill's least favourite. He failed to see through the layers of the story and believed the British military high command was being unfairly lampooned by the film's creators.

Another representation of the Home Guard is a George Formby comedy film co-starring Dinah Sheridan called *Get Cracking* (1943). Once again the honest and good patriotic intentions of the Minor Wallop and Major Wallop platoons are embedded in this picture and the comic rivalries between them provide the essential action. It is mostly set in a pub and evolves around the drinking culture of the time and the chirpy rapport between the characters.

Ealing Studios' *Whisky Galore* (1949), based on Compton Mackenzie's novel of 1947, is set on a tiny Scottish island in the Second World War. In it we see the Home Guard appear as an influencing structure among a community of Hebridean islanders who believe a cargo of whisky stranded on a nearby shipwreck belongs to them. The men of the island Home Guard are determined to outfox the English commander of their unit. Such is the everlasting appeal of *Whisky Galore* that it was remade in 2016.

Penny Summerfield writes: 'In the film the main theme is not to deride the Home Guard but to combat the bureaucratically-imposed austerity of the time. The drama lies in the islanders' collective efforts to thwart official shortages, imposed by an alien officialdom, of the commodities that make life worth living, rather than the Home Guard's contribution to the war effort.'[6]

By the time Jimmy Perry wrote his fledgling script of *The Fighting Tigers* (retitled *Dad's Army*) in 1967 there had been very little else featuring the Home Guard since *Whisky Galore* almost twenty years previously. The organisation had been stood down towards the end of 1944 as the Allies continued their united push through the German defences. All Home Guard platoons were officially disbanded on 31 December 1945.

But this didn't mean such a brilliant Home Front force should be forgotten, and thanks to *Dad's Army* the memory of its endeavours lives on . . . and on. A lifelong fan of the show is the popular British comedian Andy Hamilton, who explained: '*Dad's Army* is the most perfect example of writing and casting. The whole thing had been triggered by the real experiences of those men in a real war. I thought that was really effective.'

And when describing the cast, the writer and co-creator of *Dad's Army*, Jimmy Perry said: 'We're talking about seven tough old pros – all of them been there and not quite made it. And suddenly they're stars – every time they stop in the street they hear 'there he is!'

Indeed, it truly was so much more than a television show. In his book *Different Times, A History of British Comedy*, David Stubbs writes:

> When the series was first aired on July 31, 1968, however, it was quite out of keeping with the incendiary spirit of the times. Fire raged everywhere, from cities up in flames in the wake of Martin Luther King's assassination to the rocket burners of Apollo 8, to Jimi Hendrix's guitar set alight, to a Czechoslovakian student who burned themselves alive in protest at the Russian invasion of their country.
>
> 1968 was a year of growing, angry militancy, including the May demonstrations in Paris, London, New York and West Germany. The sixties were at once experiencing a violent death and instigating a violent birth of who knows what. It was impossible for anyone with a television set not to be buffeted by these inflammatory events. *Dad's Army* ran counter to all this. For all the presentation of arms and Corporal Jones's thrusting bayonet, it was a fundamentally gentle series. None of the characters die. It was a wartime series and yet in the very best sense it was cosy, reassuring and, despite its aged characters, ageless. In the late 1960s when the social historians might think the country's mind would have been preoccupied with more contemporary issues, its television viewers warmed immediately to this platoon of famous but elderly duffers standing to attention with broomsticks in readiness for an invasion which, with happy comic relief, we knew would never happen.[7]

In the following chapters of *Dad's Army Goes to War* I aim to retell and explore the stories of the cast whose own experiences of battle are as vast as they are varied. From what we know, they appear to have survived the memories of deadly conflict by throwing themselves into the cut-and-thrust world of show business. Any small insights into secret inner hauntings from their lives during wartime often arose in a quiet sentence or two from controlled memoirs or were overheard in conversations which burst through the iron-clad and rigid stoicism bred into a generation long gone. For the *Dad's Army* cast of war veterans the idea of getting therapy for post-traumatic stress disorder was unimaginable. Back then, for a sense of comfort, survivors of psychological distress often fell back on the hope of 'time healing everything'.

Entertainers with their talent to engage with an audience excelled at upholding the myth of normality. 'Struggle and survival!' yells the rumbustious all-knowing actor/manager 'Sir' before he marches on stage during the Blitz as King Lear in Ronald Harwood's hit play and film *The Dresser* (1983). 'We all bloody struggle . . .' hisses the fragile embittered backstage dresser Norman, who dares speak the truth, albeit through gritted teeth.

Nicolas Ridley, son of *Dad's Army*'s own Arnold Ridley (Private Charles Godfrey), told me his father never discussed his appalling experiences in the First and Second World Wars in case it raised in Arnold a trauma of inner demons. Clive Dunn's (Corporal Jones) own perceptive memoir *Permission to Speak*, published in 2002, is a straightforward account of his years as a prisoner of war but there is little mention of those dark memories which threatened his sense of inner peace in the days, weeks, months and years after the war. For Dunn the idea of utter soul-baring was not the order of the day. The *Dad's Army* cast and its creators were truly honest troopers, encapsulating Captain Mainwaring's sterling advice to 'gather round . . . and get on with it'. In reality, most of them had seen war and knew war, and yet always completely and generously realised and understood how the power of laughter is the ultimate triumph.

*Melody Foreman*
*April 2024*

# JIMMY PERRY OBE

*I'll never forget the day I was issued with my rifle.*

WHEN the sound of the first air raid siren wailed across the streets of Watford, 16-year-old Jimmy Perry and his sister Mary pulled on their gas masks, sat down and, with their eyes tight shut, waited to be 'obliterated'. But when the noise stopped and they heard the all-clear from the local warden, they began to fully realise that while they were still very much alive, their futures were about to become very different from how they'd imagined. So as the early autumn of 1939 marked the arrival of the phoney war, Jimmy, like so many young men, had to accommodate the idea that he'd have little choice but to put on a uniform and become part of it all.

That day all his hopes of becoming an actor and comedian disappeared into the mists of uncertainty. He now faced a dour saturnine life very far removed from the jollity of a stage career. It seemed to the teenager that the new reality was a real and frowning party-pooper. Perhaps his father Arthur had been right after all in calling him a 'stupid boy' for having theatrical ambitions. 'When I was young I often asked him if I could go to a special school just for comedians. That's when I heard him call me a stupid boy!', recalls Perry in his memoir. (Decades later, of course, this wounding comment from Perry senior would become a famous funny catchphrase thanks to actor Arthur Lowe's unforgettable admonishments of the teenage character of Private Pike in *Dad's Army*).

But in the late 1930s who could blame the lively-minded young Perry for being bored working in his father's carpet shop in Watford. It was hardly a fulfilling role for a young man with a passion for the cut, thrust and slapstick fun of the live stage and the magic of the big screen. No doubt some of the customers provided opportunities for a joke or two in the stockroom among the carpet samples but it wasn't the same as the real thing – entertaining an audience.

Perry had been mad on the cinema and theatre since he was old enough to buy his own tickets. His favourite comedians were stars

1

of the day like Will Hay and he was crazy about live Variety shows too. There was nothing finer or more electric for him than to spend his days languishing at the Ranelagh, his favourite local picture house. Here, nestled among the plush seating in an atmosphere wreathed in cigarette smoke expelled by the shadowy strangers around him, the impressionable boy could watch his heroes – a notable favourite was Ronald Colman starring in *A Tale of Two Cities*. And, many decades after relishing the 1931 films *Frankenstein*, starring Boris Karloff, and *Dracula*, played by the awesome Bela Lugosi, the veteran comedian Perry chuckled loud and long at the knowledge that Karloff's real name was Bill Pratt from Camberwell.

*** 

JAMES Perry was born 'with an erection to show he was ready for action' at 2am on 20 September 1923 in Barnes, South London. As a newborn in his cot at 20 Nassau Road, it appears his gift to portray the funny side of life had already made itself apparent before he even uttered his first word.[1]

His timing for mirth was spot on. He had arrived at a time when there was a great need for humour. The population was trying desperately to forget the horrors of the First World War and certain areas of the capital were a social whirl. However, as young James began to toddle about and explore his little world, the General Strike hit the country in May 1926 and shops began to close in every high street. The Trades Union Congress (TUC) had called upon the government to stop wage reductions and do more to improve conditions for more than a million coal-miners. Sure enough, that year thousands of businesses went bankrupt.

His father Arthur Perry ran an antiques shop in Brompton Road, Knightsbridge, in those days and noticed a depressing decline in his sales. It seemed the 1920s weren't so roaring after all. Then, out of the blue, Arthur's hand-wringing ceased. There came good fortune for the Perry family thanks to a grand and wealthy customer named Lady Tollemache. She knew Perry senior well enough to call him whenever she was in a panic over a domestic issue. This time she needed his help because her cook was sick and unable to prepare the food for an important dinner party at the Tollemache residence.

Young Perry's mother Dolly was called in to step up to the plate and save the day. Within a week or two, news of Dolly's culinary rescue was circulating among the wealthy upper-middle classes. Then, with Lady Tollemache's support, Dolly decided to run a series of popular and entertaining cookery classes for the wives of rich and powerful men. These lessons showed all those who were keen to learn how to impress the great and the good with successful and glamorous social events, which, of course, included the various scrumptious dishes and wines of the day. Thanks to Dolly, the Perry family didn't go bankrupt after all.

Dolly's financial prowess and social skills as the entrepreneurial head of the prestigious 'Barnes School of Cookery' also had a downside, however. It meant her son, to his complete and utter dismay, had to remain at the dreaded Colet Court, a fee-paying prep school in Barnes, which he hated with every inch of his little body. Not only was he bullied by fellow pupils, who cruelly dubbed him 'Pisspot Perry' and 'Mouse', but there was always a caning from sadistic masters who punished anyone caught telling jokes and making frivolous use of their time. Decades later Perry wondered how he survived the rigours and tyranny of such a terrible place.[2]

Back home, he soon realised he'd have to tolerate more disappointing behaviour. This time he discovered that his parents, especially his father, could be outlandishly snobbish. Arthur Perry wore starched collars that left a welt mark on his neck, and often professed a dislike of 'ugly' people, especially beleaguered German prisoners of war still living in Britain just after the First World War. Both Arthur and Dolly Perry made an issue of people who were 'common', especially if they had bad habits. Jimmy remembers being told not to talk with his mouth full, or to hold a dinner knife like a pen 'because that's too common'.[3]

But life wasn't all grim, as living in the grand house opposite the Perry family in Nassau Road was the American-born actor, comedian, singer, writer and Vaudeville star Fred Duprez (1884–1938). Perry obviously admired Duprez and having a star so close by must have cheered his little theatrical heart. Now here was a fine fellow who'd made a life in films. Why shouldn't I, thought young Perry the son of naysayer Arthur, do the same?!

During the 1930s the twice-married and distinctive-looking Duprez appeared in almost thirty films and his comedy farce *My Wife's Family* was a hit in Britain in 1931. He was also the father of the glamorous actress June Duprez, who at 21 years old starred in the great director/producer Alexander Korda's 1939 film about the Mahdist War, *The Four Feathers*. (This film was one of Winston Churchill's favourites because he claimed it represented his own experiences as a young soldier serving in the Boer War.)

Korda, who went on to become Churchill's cinematic propaganda man in Hollywood during the Second World War, managed June

Duprez's career, which had begun with the Coventry Repertory Company followed by small roles in various black and white British films. When A.E.W. Mason's book *The Four Feathers* was turned into a film it sky-rocketed June to stardom in Britain.

By then, of course, Perry's only chance of seeing the gorgeous Miss Duprez was on the big screen as by 1940, when *The Four Feathers* was proving a hit at the box office, the Perry family were on the move to Watford. The decision to relocate almost 30 miles from his beloved Ranelagh Cinema wasn't, of course, of young Jimmy's making. Neither was it his fault that he'd never see Miss Duprez skipping along the street again. But the air raids on London had begun to intensify and his mother Dolly persuaded her elderly Uncle Tom to surrender his shop at 237 High Street, Watford, so the family and their business could move in. There was a house attached to the property, which in Jacobean days had served as one big house to a wealthy family. The move from Barnes to Watford took three trips. There was also lots of antique furniture to transport which had been sitting in Arthur's Brompton Road shop. Perry recalls: 'A few days after we left Nassau Road in Barnes a bomb fell on the street and blew out all of the windows of our home, making it uninhabitable.'⁴ It was a narrow escape, but as with so many families and the generations which preceded them the Perrys had survived all sorts of adventures and experiences. Perry recounts in his memoir how he came from a long line of tough sailors, including one William Perry who was in charge of the 'rope's end' (flogging) on HMS *Ganges*.

Arthur Perry's father had served in the Royal Navy on HMS *Victory* before it was taken out of service in 1812, and he became the butler to Admiral of the Fleet Sir Thomas Cochrane. When he was discharged from the Navy he took up the same job at a large house in Belgravia, where Arthur was born. Stories of a butler's life, which often had a madcap, comedic flavour, were regularly included in the conversation at the Perry dinner table. Such tales of servitude exposing the misdemeanours of the Edwardian class system went on to inspire Perry and Croft's hit BBC sitcom *You Rang, M'Lord*, which ran from 1990 to 1993.

However, one experience, often recounted by Arthur with relish over mouthfuls of the roast beef, was how in 1868 his own father was in the crowd in London to see the last man hanged in public. Fenian Michael Barrett was executed at Newgate Prison for mass murder, having taken part in the Clerkenwell explosion that killed a dozen people. Whenever Arthur started to mention the gallows and the grim sight of the criminal Barrett hanging by his neck, Dolly would sigh and roll her eyes as if to say 'not again', but she let her husband continue, hearing him polish the story some more as she finished her dinner. If the cheeky young Jimmy had thoughts of adding sound effects like choking noises to the tale then he knew he'd be for the high jump and a scolding from Arthur. It would be 'too common', after all, to interrupt an adult's conversation, albeit a one-sided one!

In the early 1920s Arthur Perry at 47 years old was twenty-three years older than Dolly Govett, who had married him following the death of his first wife. She bravely agreed to take on him and his three children, Eddie, Arthur and Cissie, much to the horror of her own sisters, who made sarcastic comments about 'marrying an old man with a ready-made family of his own'.[5] But in his memoir Perry writes of wholesome family holidays spent in the rural countryside of Eastry, near Sandwich, Kent. He recalls picnics and walks, and moments when his uncles would stop suddenly in their tracks, and stare into the distance, perhaps reliving the haunting events of their lives in the trenches of the First World War. In the 1920s and 1930s, explains Perry, it was a common sight to see men in the street with limbs missing.

But while he was deeply respectful of the heroic and wounded men in his family, he also looked at entertainers as his idols. Among them were Tommy Trinder, Ken Roberts, and Flanagan and Allen; the latter both served in Flanders during the First World War, and decades later Bud Flanagan went on to perform the theme song to *Dad's Army*. The legendary Bob Hope from Eltham, south-east London, also came out tops, but when Perry became famous and was quizzed about whom he admired the absolute most as a laughter-maker, he always replied 'the comedienne Hylda Baker'.

When Hylda Baker from Farnworth, Lancashire, was 10 she had followed her father Harold Baker's footsteps into the music hall. Whilst he was only on the stage part-time, at 14 his daughter set out to make it her full-time career. Comedienne Baker's famous catchphrase, delivered with a wobble of her famous jowls, was: 'Oooh, she knows, y'know!' Her hilarious performance with the bulldog-faced entertainer Arthur Mullard in a jokey version of the hit 1970s musical film *Grease* was comedy gold. Later in her life Baker had a run of misfortune, and lost a lot of money after her chauffeur absconded with her savings. Even though she managed to get the courts to award her most of her money back (totalling around £ 4,000), she had become difficult and upset a lot of people. Only six people attended her funeral when she died aged 81 in 1986.[6]

Perry's choice of the growly-voiced Baker as his top comic indicated his preference for northern entertainers which continued throughout his life and in particular showed in his enormous respect for the acting talents of Derbyshire's Arthur Lowe.

But there was a war for Perry to go through before he ever got to champion his idea that Lowe would be just the right actor for Mainwaring. His chance to meet with the 'snobbish' BBC to promote Lowe wouldn't arrive until 1968 – twenty-three years after both men had racked up a variety of experiences as soldiers serving their country.

\*\*\*

IN January 1940, with snow covering rooftops and front gardens and ice frosting the windows, the Germans still had not arrived in Britain. The films at the cinemas began showing French troops boasting how their Maginot line was impregnable, but the Germans boldly marched into the Netherlands and Belgium in April of that year – they had simply avoided the Maginot Line and laughed loudly at the idealistic French. Perry would later write: 'A typical Nazi trick!' – as Captain Mainwaring can often be heard saying in *Dad's Army*.

When the raids really began and knocked the idea of a 'phoney war' into a cocked hat, it was time for Perry and so many others to hunker down in the Anderson shelters on many an occasion. The Luftwaffe's blitz on the capital had begun. At one time Perry was near Oxford Street when it was bombed and he remembered the grand John Lewis and Peter Robinson department stores being blasted to pieces. 'I never felt a shred of fear,' he remarked. 'I was cracking jokes. Jokes! But then what do boys of sixteen know about death? But as the war went on I soon found out!'[7] His memory of being 16 is a pertinent reminder of Private Pike's character in *Dad's Army*. Pike's naivety and wide-eyed demeanour are brilliantly portrayed by actor Ian Lavender, who delivered each line in the show true to Perry's own youthful attitudes of the time.

In real life, however, and long before *Dad's Army* was conceived, Dolly Perry was terrified that her son would be called up to 'serve the Colours'. She'd watched three of her brothers march off to the trenches in the First World War, with one of them being seriously wounded, a fact she was always reminded of during the family holidays. She knew that the psychological scars of war seldom healed, and the idea of her own boy facing a German bayonet, bullet, shell shock and cannon fire was too much.

At this point of Perry's real life story we note how his own teenage experience in the newly formed Watford Company of the Home Guard stayed with him for the rest of his life. It was these times of comedy and drama which flooded back to him the moment he sat down on a train in 1967 and began thinking about writing a situation comedy. He commented: 'So many people ask me, "What was the difference between the real Home Guard and *Dad's Army*?" Strangely, not a lot. *Dad's Army* was based firmly on fact and the truth of the situation, in common with many other popular television shows, including *Steptoe and Son* and *Yes Minister*.'[8]

Perry argued that while some programmes attempted to belittle the spirit of the British people during the war, they had mostly been written by a younger generation with little real knowledge. *Dad's Army*, he totally believed, was intended to promote the British people and their stoicism during a time of war.

As a young man he joined the Home Guard in 1941, partly to please his mother and therefore to stay at home until his official call-up papers arrived. The organisation itself had been formed nine months previously, on 14 May 1940. Its aim was to prevent panic in the face of invasion and ensure that communication routes would not be blocked by refugees. The doughty Home Guard was to provide a back-up to the regular military forces and patrol the coastal areas of the United Kingdom. This fact provided Perry with the inspiration to base *Dad's Army* in a fictional place known as 'Walmington-on-Sea'.

In the early days of the Home Guard some men laughably paraded like scarecrows armed only with brooms, wooden rifles and shovels. By the time the 17-year-old Perry was in their ranks in Watford, he was thrilled – 'thanks to President Roosevelt' – to be issued with an old American Ross rifle of the type used by US troops serving in the First World War. He recalled: 'I'll never forget the day I was issued with my rifle – after all the muck had been removed it was mine to be kept with me at all times – but no ammunition; we teenage boys were not allowed to take that home. If the church bells rang to signal an invasion we had to jump on our bikes and pedal like hell to the headquarters to get our fifty rounds.'[9]

A man who would inspire Perry's talent for characterisation soon appeared to him in real life. The Commanding Officer of the Watford Platoon was in fact the manager of a local building society and, like the actor Arthur Lowe, who was cast in the show as Captain Mainwaring, was 'short and round'. Mainwaring, of course, was a bank manager in Walmington-on-Sea.

Perry was unable to recall the name of the fellow, but he wrote in his memoir: 'This CO gave us a lecture about the responsibility of carrying arms. He was always fussing and inspecting things. His famous expression, after we'd been on night patrol, was "You boys had better stop mucking about! I'm in no mood for jokes at six o'clock in the morning!"' It's difficult to read these words and not hear the voice of Arthur Lowe at his pompous best.[10]

Perry's first CO had served in France in the First World War but many in the platoon believed the man had a lesser rank than the 'major' he became in the Home Guard. Perry explained:

> He was delighted to be in charge and was always buying extra bits for his uniform – a dress forage cap, smart shirt and tie, and a brown leather Sam-Browne belt – all these items were, of course, for officers only. When he was told he couldn't wear the Sam-Browne belt with battledress, he was heartbroken; it was for wearing with a dress uniform and, unfortunately, he didn't have one. But if it had come to the push of course he'd have been as brave as anyone else.

These observations went straight into the character of Captain Mainwaring and were wonderfully absorbed and portrayed by actor Lowe in *Dad's Army*. There's an episode where Mainwaring's vanity went so far as him wearing a toupée, only to be met by sniggers from Sergeant Wilson (John Le Mesurier) and the platoon, especially when it moved across the indignant captain's bald head on its own.

The Home Guard CO once told Perry: 'Your rifle should be as vital to you as a third limb; keep it with you always, clean it and cherish it. You could even take it to bed with you!' This apparently was the only joke the man ever made. Although the anonymous major had no sense of humour at all, the memory of him had a lasting effect on the talented young Perry, who was promoted to lance corporal in the Home Guard.

During the research for this book I happened to discover in an old friend's collection some genuine Home Guard report books compiled by the busy Bromley branch of the organisation in south-east London. Perry himself admitted in his autobiography to have become immersed in research while writing *Dad's Army*. He said he found disappointingly little material in library archives and gleaned most of what he learned from newspaper archives. Much of the following – which I discovered – would no doubt ring true to him.

Indeed, the well-thumbed report books my friend had kept locked away until I asked to see them were authentically bruised and battered from their heady days of active service. They are full of notes written in ink and pencil by the diligent hands of lofty officers of the Home Guard Watch from so long ago. Some pages are stained with tea, perhaps slopped upon when the hand holding a tin mug was jolted by a shout of urgency ringing through the Church House, Bromley, where a platoon was stationed with the Royal Observer Corps. Each entry in these rare volumes of record is as illuminating as it is honest, right from the very first note in the sloping blue-inked handwriting of a Captain Roberts, 'May 21, 1940 – 23.50hrs – Plane spotted in easterly direction and picked up in searchlights. Plane dropped two red lights', to the final diary entry on 2 October 1941 which is simply a pencilled line from the Commander of the 2nd Platoon that 'at 6am the Guard was dismounted'. However, by the time the last entry was made in the second volume in the autumn of 1941, the Home Guard and Royal Observer Corps had already been bombed out of Church House, which was hit in the April of that year.

The diaries, having survived the Luftwaffe raids and hourly battering of the heavy-handed on duty, are life-affirming. It's hard not to smile now at the handwritten evidence of some long ago friction between the two Home Defence forces revealed by a ditty in pencilled scrawl on 14 October 1941:

> Goodbye ROC we must leave you
> Though it breaks our hearts to go
> Hospitality has been lacking
> So we have had to pack you know
> Others more appreciative are calling
> So we go on our way
> Though unpaid but always willing
> With guard last night,
> And off to work today.

Apologies are then made to 'Dolly Gray' (a wartime song) from 'No.16 section' of the Home Guard!

Judging by the content of the Bromley Home Guard records, it's no surprise that the creators of the famous *Dad's Army* television comedy series were inspired to come up with such an array of hapless but well-meaning characters, attracting millions of viewers from 1968 to 1977. During wartime, of course, rules were seriously important if we were to beat the enemy, and some of the Home Guard records show the emotional force of angry Captain Mainwaring types that now seem hugely comical. For instance, there's a specific and detailed complaint about 'livestock' (bugs) being left in the blankets and demands of 'Who is to blame?'! And when the Home Guard was based in the Old Telephone Exchange, Bromley, on 26 May 1941, a Major Shepheath was appalled about the lack of coffee, tea and milk for 'A' Company and wrote that 'a strong word must be had with Mrs Derby'. One can only assume 'Mrs Derby' was the supplier of refreshments. Although women were not permitted to join the Home Guard, since government policy ruled that women must not be in combat or front-line units, there is every chance 'Mrs Derby' was a member of the Women's Royal Voluntary Service. However, later that year the Labour MP Dr Edith Summerskill created the Women's Home Guard Auxiliary Unit to assist with administrative duties. The only uniform they were supplied with was a small Bakelite brooch bearing the initials 'HG'.

It's important to remember that in 1939 the idea of home defence was not really a new one. For generations the people of Kent especially had lived with the chance of invasion from across the Channel. This was particularly so in the sixteenth century when Elizabeth I, in fear of hordes of Spanish invaders arriving on our coastlines, created the role of Lord-Lieutenant. It was then their job to muster a force of men of any age to stand united against potential marauders. Their weapons? – pitchforks, spades, sharp sticks, slingshots and muskets. Defence was all.

During the Second World War the Lord-Lieutenants once again were expected to play their part in defending the realm and Churchill suggested they assist in recruiting 500,000 men over the age of 40 for home defence training. Within a few months the Local Defence Volunteers (also known as Parashots) were formed as official units.

An announcement about the formation of LDVs was broadcast on 14 May 1940 by the Secretary of State for War, Anthony Eden. All those men interested in joining were to report to their local police station. Within a few days 250,000 men stood ready to help the war effort. By July 1940, and at the height of the Battle of Britain, more than 1.5 million men aged between 16 and 65 volunteered to take up arms should German armies attempt to invade Britain. By the end of 1940 most Home Guard platoons had been issued with Enfield rifles and Bren sub-machine guns.

What's so wonderfully characteristic of the British is how some communities had decided to take their own course of action long before the politicians made it 'official'. In Essex, for example, there was a lively Legion of Frontiersmen practising their drill with borrowed shotguns and pitchforks. Communities throughout the land were keen to protect Britain. The name 'Home Guard' was originated by Churchill, who believed the idea of the LDV had not been properly formatted; keen to abolish any grey areas, he announced the name change on 22 July 1940.

During the intensity of community defence practice in 1940, Churchill proclaimed that Britain was ready to 'fight on the oceans, on the landing grounds, in the fields and streets – we will never surrender'. With the Royal Air Force and the Luftwaffe locked in aerial conflict during the Battle of Britain that year, the activity on British soil was just as fierce. The people of Britain, especially the populations of Kent and Sussex, watched aircrews and aircraft from both sides fall to the ground from the skies each day. Death and destruction was everywhere. Homes were destroyed, hundreds of civilians were killed and aircraft wreckage was scattered far and wide or mangled itself down deep in furrowed fields.

The Home Guard had an important job to do. Many units were sent to man anti-aircraft guns, with the Royal Artillery being posted along the coast for this very purpose. Aircraft spotting was also vital, along with the manning of searchlights.

One of the first jobs of the Home Guard was to help construct roadblocks, using anything they could find – including oil drums, old beer barrels, sawn-down trees and reconstructed fences – to act as barriers. Road signs were also removed. Even Kent locals travelling from one town to the next who asked the way anywhere would be abruptly told to 'clear orf 'cos we ain't telling yer'. The Home Guard was very alert to the idea of clandestine Fifth Columnists in our midst who might be acting as spies for Hitler.

On 22 July 1940 a Captain R. Halland, No.3 section leader of 3 Platoon 'A' Company of the Home Guard in Bromley, wrote: 'There is a complaint the Guard Room lights could be discerned, the Black Out arrangements are not too effective. Gave first aid for the remainder of the night by hanging mackintoshes over offending windows'.

At 1.10am he noted: 'Plane reported high – flying North North West – searchlights made short attempt to connect but 'plane retraced by sound of engine. Believed to be enemy plane. 3.10am – About six bombs in quick succession dropped many miles away – direction North North East. 5.20am – Returned six rifles, sixty rounds and seven helmets, plus three whistles.'

The stoic attitude of our communities at this time is recorded in refreshing detail by Henry Roy Pratt Boorman MA, CBE in his book, first published in 1940, *Hell's Corner: Kent Becomes the Battlefield of Britain*. Mr Boorman, then owner of the Kent Messenger Group newspapers and a member of the Home Guard, wrote about the RAF Hawkinge aerodrome which became known as 'the drome where something happens every day.' He describes how the Home Guard platoon was on constant red alert in the Folkestone area, with Hawkinge on constant high alert for bombing attacks. One particular tale stuck in his mind:

A sergeant pilot with a DFM [Distinguished Flying Medal] and Bar, with fourteen enemy aircraft to his credit when I was there at Hawkinge (this pilot was a bank clerk before the war), used to fly one aircraft in which he took particular pride. Then a Jerry came over and bombed it. He was furious, he saw it happen and he saw red. He rushed out and jumped into the first aeroplane which was ticking over, waiting – found when he was in the air it was in fact the Commanding Officer's – followed the Jerry over the Channel and shot him down. That was one more!

One particular Home Guard action during the Battle of Britain took place on Sunday, 18 August and involved a Dornier 17 flying close to the ground near Biggin Hill aerodrome. Already damaged, this German aircraft was further hit by 111 Squadron's aircraft and ground defences, plus a fusillade of shots fired by the Home Guard. Coming over Leaves Green, the aircraft burst into flames and crashed just short of the airfield. As the four crew members scrambled out, the local Home Guard were celebrating the fact that they'd played their role in shooting the Dornier down. The platoon commander pointed out proudly that he had given the order to fire and they pumped 180 rounds into the belly of the bomber. When the German crew got out, they were described by the platoon commander as 'most arrogant'.

One must not forget the serious contribution to the downing of this Dornier 17 by heroic 111 Squadron Hurricane pilot Flight Lieutenant Stanley Connors DFC (sadly killed during this attack on Dornier 17s over Kenley). Other 111 Squadron pilots also engaged the Dornier, including Sergeant Pilots William Laurence Dymond (killed in action on 2 September) and Ronald John Walker Brown.

The following day, Monday, 19 August 1940, the *Kent Messenger* reported: 'One of the many Nazi pilots to land in Kent was captured by Home Guard Platoon Commander E.F. Talbot in Maidstone. He rounded up the German pilot, disarmed him and then said 'Spitfire got you. Spitfire good!' The German, still in fighting mood, replied 'No, Messerschmitt better!' What the commander did after that is not reported!'

Throughout the war the Home Guard and its millions of men in army-issue khaki carried out a vast multitude of essential jobs which kept the communities of Great Britain together in times of hardship. For all those who served, a certificate was issued to them by King George VI which read: 'In the years when our country was in mortal danger (*name*) who served (*dates*) gave generously of his time and powers to make himself ready for her defence by force of arms with his life if need be.' The Home Guard was finally stood down on 3 December 1944 and finally disbanded on 31 December 1945.

Whilst we all love the *Dad's Army* television series, it is important to acknowledge that the real Home Guard, including young men like Jimmy Perry, made a serious contribution to the welfare of Britain's communities during the war. Indeed, Perry went on to comment years later: 'Make no mistake, it was our finest hour. To be alive at that time was to experience the British people at their very best and at perhaps the greatest moment of their history. I'm proud to have lived through it.'

He recalled:

> When I joined the Home Guard, however, there were all age groups and they came from every walk of life. The comradeship was amazing and we used pubs as headquarters where we'd often meet after a parade. The plain battledress was a great leveller and young boys like me flocked to join in. We weren't called 'teenagers' then. From the age of fifteen you went from boy to man. Many also smoked so I took up the pipe![11]

In 1943, when Perry was just 19 years old, the comedian and actor George Formby starred in *Get Cracking* – a film about the Local Defence League, which, just like *Dad's Army*, started with Eden's radio broadcast about volunteers being needed to join the war effort on the Home Front. The film, made twenty-five years before the show created by Perry and Croft, is arguably a forerunner to their hit comedy and also involved a group of bumbling and very different characters all thrown together to defend Britain if there was an enemy invasion.

Perry couldn't forget his own experiences with the Home Guard when in 1967 he searched for inspiration 'out of desperation' to write the characters for *Dad's Army*.

\*\*\*

IN 1941 the organisation had men in its ranks who had served in the First World War and even earlier conflicts. The observant Perry never forgot one particular character who had taken part in the battle of Omdurman in 1898 with General Kitchener and then served on the North-West Frontier in India. The veteran rifleman, whose name Perry could not recall, was in his late 60s during his time in the Home Guard and yet constantly told stories about his time as a young soldier serving in far-flung conflicts.

One day when the old man was talking he mentioned a time when he was in the Sudan. Perry and his comrades heard how the sun rose higher and higher until it was 'like a great burning ball in the sky.' When the rifles became hot during battle and 'the bodies were piling high', Perry heard how the British and Egyptian soldiers in Sudan were told by their CO to 'piss on their rifles' to cool them down. The thing was, explained the storyteller, 'we hadn't any water left to drink and therefore didn't have any piss to pass'. When finally the Mahdi's army stopped charging at the British soldiers, it was deemed a victory and the men, their tongues swollen black because of thirst, received a cursory visit from General Kitchener upon a horse who shouted 'Well done, boys!'

Although Perry adapted the humour out of the old man's tale and related it to *Dad's Army*'s Lance Corporal Jones (Clive Dunn), the history of the battle of Omdurman, which took place on 2 September 1898, makes for serious reading. As Perry pointed out, the conflict was more of a massacre. Kitchener, described as a 'cold and ruthless man', had been waiting for a chance to slaughter the Khalifa's forces for two years.

More than sixty thousand Dervishes were ready and waiting to fight the British and Egyptian armies, which numbered just thirty thousand men between them. The famous charge of the 21st Lancers at Omdurman is known as the last charge of the British Cavalry, and among those who took part was the young Second Lieutenant Winston Churchill. It was an error of enormous magnitude. The cavalry believed they were charging at just two hundred Dervishes but the real figure was more like three thousand. Perry reckoned Churchill saved his own life because he was equipped with a German automatic pistol that could fire twenty rounds at a time. It was much more efficient than the British six-round revolver.[12]

The film famous for including the battle of Omdurman is *The Four Feathers* (1939). The cast as we know included Perry's neighbour June Duprez, with Sir Ralph Richardson and John Clements CBE in the leading male roles. Its screenplay was masterfully crafted by R.C. Sherriff, who was famous for his play about the First World War, *Journey's End*. The film's cast included John Laurie (Private Frazer) playing Khalifa Abdullah, one of the chief lieutenants of the Mahdi. When the Mahdi died, the Khalifa took over control of the Mahdists. Certainly the film shows him in command of the natives in revolt. *The Four Feathers* used the 1st Battalion, East Surrey Regiment, as extras, which inspired Perry and his *Dad's Army* co-creator David Croft to make an episode for their Home Guard characters called 'The Two and a Half Feathers'. The battle scene was shot not in the Sudan but in a sand quarry in King's Lynn, Norfolk! It was a chilly day and the actors writhed and wriggled in their uncomfortable rough Victorian uniforms. The actor Bill Pertwee (Warden Hodges) played a Dervish but struggled to stay aboard when his horse reared up as the loud sound of rifles at full blast began to crack the atmosphere.

But reel back to 1943, when young Perry had yet to see battle and was still waiting for his call-up papers. In the meantime life went on in the Watford brigade of the Home Guard and there was now a new CO in charge. The 'fanatical' Major Strong, who liked to run about waving his revolver yelling 'kill!, kill!' at imaginary Germans, left Perry with many valuable memories. During one 'commando mission' the platoon was issued with wire cheese-cutters, bicycle chains and knuckle-dusters as part of their kit as they 'had to be armed to the teeth'.

But while Perry and the Watford brigade were grappling with survival tactics on the Home Front, his mother Dolly was fretting about the day he would be called up. She urged her son to find work in a munitions factory to help keep him at home. Sure enough, he began training to make scientific instruments. After six months at a factory called Broadhurst, Clarkson & Sons, Perry's old trouble struck him – he was flat bored and the urge to join the war full-time as a professional soldier began to gnaw at him. For Perry, tedium was a killer.

However, his passion to go on the stage never left him and he couldn't believe his luck when he was invited to join a Home Guard concert party. Perry said the invitation to continue his 'larking around' in a theatre was the moment his career really began in show business. The big moment came when the curtain went up on him at the drill hall in Queen's Road, Watford, and the audience applauded his act – even though many there that day were his drunken pals! After this, he appeared on stage at the Gaumont Cinema in Watford in an amateur variety show watched buy a full house of two thousand people. This time his impersonations of Charles Laughton as the hunchback of Notre Dame greatly amused the crowds and an invitation to join another semi-professional concert party soon arrived in his dressing room.

The Perry family enjoyed Christmas together in 1943 but soon enough the day Dolly had dreaded finally arrived. Her son's call-up papers told him to report for duty wearing his Home Guard uniform with its lance corporal stripe on the sleeve. Despite his mother's heartbreak, Perry himself was fully intrigued by the prospect.

On New Year's Day 1944 he caught a train to the British Army training barracks at Colchester, where his life was about to change again. Here he was taught how to run with his rifle and fixed bayonet at 'Hitler' – the motivational name given to the target sacks stuffed with straw. It was here he first heard the phrase 'They don't like it up 'em' delivered by a First World War veteran who was now his sergeant major. Not only was the training basic, it was dangerous, too.

During one particular exercise, which involved the recruits crawling on the ground while machine-gun bullets flew over them, one man stood up too early thinking the exercise was over. He was shot dead in error. Perry and several other witnesses were asked to give evidence at an enquiry, after which the warrant officer in charge that day was exonerated of all blame.[13] The tragedy remained with Perry for the rest of his life and marked the moment when he realised life as an adult could be deadly serious.

From Colchester Perry was posted to Park Hall Camp in Oswestry, Shropshire. This vast site had been donated by Major Wynne Corrie during the First World War and became an official British Army training base. Part of the area was used for explosives and excavating trenches. It had been reactivated for military use in July 1939 and was split up into Birch, Butler, Milne and Wingate Lines, with barrack huts located near the Park Hall rugby club. It became home to 2,500 Royal Artillery recruits and the No. 1 Plotting Officers' School.

On arrival, Perry reported to the 1st 'Mixed' Heavy Anti-Aircraft (HAA) Regiment. He had opted to become a gunner and described his new base as 'very different' from the rough and tumble of the Colchester training barracks. For a start he couldn't believe it when he heard Glenn Miller's music being broadcast over the camp loudspeaker system, and he was most impressed to eat breakfast in a room where a major addressed everyone as 'gentlemen'.

Then came the moment when the dapper major briskly stepped forward, swallowed hard and then said he wanted to 'talk to the chaps about . . . sex'. Perry felt himself blush, as did most of the young men assembled in the room that day, who began to cough and shift about awkwardly. Perry then wondered if it was another lecture of the sort often heard at his loathed prep school about the 'sin and perils of wanking'. But he soon found out the 'talk' wasn't going to be the sort of 'I say!' shocker. The major's talk wasn't as blunt as that. They were simply informed they were now in the 1st 'Mixed' Heavy Ack-Ack Regiment and so, ahem, . . . there were women about the place.[14]

'We are a training unit, but I want you to concentrate on that word – Mixed. For the first time in the history of the British Army, women are on active service, side by side with the men. The ATS [Auxiliary Territorial Service] won't actually be loading and firing the guns, but [will be] manning the fire control instruments, predictors, radar, height finders, etc.,' said the major, who obviously felt he'd said enough about 'sex' via the word 'mixed'. He'd leave lads like Perry to work it out for themselves. Years later, and smirks aside, Perry admitted it dawned on him just how brave the ATS women were as they carried out their duties with the ack-ack guns. Perry recalled that there were four huge Bofors guns in each heavy ack-ack battery and the controlling instruments were all placed near the guns so if enemy aircraft dive-bombed or strafed the guns, the men and women of the ATS would undoubtedly be injured or even killed by flying shrapnel. Equally at risk were those serving in the 93rd 'Mixed' Searchlight Regiment and other associated batteries focused on Home Front defence.

The 435th Heavy Anti-Aircraft Battery of the Royal Artillery, which was the first "Mixed" battery was formed in June 1941 and was based from August of that year at an operational gun site in Richmond Park, south-west London. This soon sparked the creation of hundreds of similar units, with the ATS making up the majority of the human effort. By 1943 the HAA batteries were making their mark as a serious defence force against the enemy, and at least three-quarters of the batteries were mixed. By VE Day in 1945 no fewer than 56,000 out of 190,000 ATS women had served in the Royal Artillery Anti-Aircraft Command. At its peak the ATS had 210,308 serving women on its books. Records show 355 were killed during the six years of war.

One veteran ATS volunteer was Mrs Brenda Usherwood, née Soughton, who talked to the author of this book in 2010 when she was 89 years old. She was a huge fan of *Dad's Army* and knew exactly what Perry was referring to when he remembered his time with the mixed ack-ack unit. Mrs Usherwood, who served in the Luftwaffe's target zone of Kent, recalled:

I was 19 when I had my letter to join up. I had a choice, either serve on the ack-ack guns or go into a factory. I didn't fancy factory work so I made for the anti-aircraft guns and had to report to a camp in Faversham. Then I was moved to Manchester for three months' training and practice shooting. They told us we would spend twenty-four hours spread over four days with the guns.

Then I had cleaning on one day a week, and then a day's leave. It was a busy, hard old routine but I was with some good friends and we always found a way to hop over the wall at night to get fish and chips. Sometimes we used to bribe the sentry at the gate to let us out, too.

I was in 566 Heavy Mixed Ack-Ack Battery and was trained to be a height-finder. I had to sit outside in all weathers at the designated posts where there were the gunsights, sometimes along the coast, and check the distance of enemy planes with a special piece of equipment. When it was lined up correctly I had to shout 'On Target'. This would be heard by the men who could then check the best time with the radar to fire the guns and bring down any German aircraft.

> Some of my friends operated the searchlights at night and sometimes I was in a mobile unit during the V1 and V2 rocket campaigns against southern England in 1944.[15]

However, despite being trained to spot enemy aircraft with crackshot precision and to fuse live weaponry, she wasn't allowed to actually fire the huge AA guns. An order from Prime Minister Winston Churchill forbade ATS girls to take part in any such action because 'they would not be able to cope with the knowledge they might have shot down and killed young German men'. This was a confusing attitude at a time when any woman who became a secret agent with the Special Operations Executive (SOE) was trained how to shoot a gun and risk their own lives to get classified information in and out of enemy territory. The women of the First Aid Nursing Yeomanry (FANY) also supplied SOE agents.

In fact, many of Mrs Usherwood's ATS friends also served in the danger zones of north-west Europe in 1944. As well as home defence, the ATS served in most theatres of war and some mixed anti-aircraft batteries were sent to areas like Antwerp following the Allied invasion. Many women in the armed forces at the time also had to endure the resentment of some men who felt women were not suitable to wear uniforms and take on what they deemed 'men's jobs'.

Mrs Usherwood earned 32 shillings per week. 'We had to line up and salute the captain to collect our wages,' she recalled. 'We had to spend a bit of time keeping our uniform in order. We were kitted out with two pairs of trousers, a battle-dress top, brown boots, leather gaiters and socks. There was also a skirt, shirts and stockings. We had to shine the buttons for inspection.' Working as a height finder (or a predictor, as they were often known), Mrs Usherwood was also given special hand protectors to help with the cold. These were mittens with topless fingers made of sheepskin. 'I still got tremendously cold hands despite wearing those huge mittens,' she added.

'I was only ever frightened once,' commented Mrs Usherwood:

> We were in bed in our barracks near Gravesend when we heard this terrible droning noise. We saw this thing going across the sky. It passed over and we kept listening until we heard a huge explosion. There was a thud on the ground. The next morning we found out it had fallen on the Isle of Grain – just a couple of miles away. We'd heard from other girls how deadly doodlebugs had destroyed parts of London and killed many civilians. I remember they flew faster than Spitfires but, luckily, our guns had a decent score of hits before the doodlebugs reached Kent.

Like many of her ATS friends, Mrs Usherwood left the service when the war ended in 1945. For many decades she kept in touch with her old pals of 566 Battery and they would meet up every year at the Union Jack Club near Waterloo East station. When Mrs Usherwood died in 2012, aged 91, she was the last surviving member of 566 Battery.

It's important to note that shows like *Dad's Army* had not only proved a massive hit with the general audience everywhere but also provided a link to times long gone but very much remembered by veterans across the globe.

During his service with the women of the ATS in the spring of 1944, Perry was a radar operator before he got to know the technology of the big guns. He asked why both sexes were needed to work on radar and was told the men were usually sent abroad with the same skills set while the women operators were needed on the Home Front.

However, he pointed out there was one time when women of the ATS 155th (Mixed) HAA Regiment were deployed to Antwerp to defend the city and help combat the German advance in the Ardennes. The area was being pulverised by the enemy's V1 and V2 rockets. Even then, the efficiency, loyalty and good humour of 'those wonderful women' remained as relevant and vital as ever. They were on duty with the 21st Army Group, which was made up of men from not only Britain and Canada but also the rest of the Commonwealth. Also included were Polish forces, alongside Dutch, Czech and Belgian units, and even the US Army. At this time there was a raft of campaigns aimed at driving out the enemy, including Operation Market Garden, Operation Pheasant and the Battle of the Bulge.[16]

In the spring of 1944 the men in Perry's unit were sent to North Wales for firing practice. This involved them aiming heavy guns at windsocks towed by a brave pilot in a flimsy Tiger Moth just a few feet above them! Being based in the Welsh countryside for ten weeks left him with many happy memories, and there was even a chance for him to tell a few jokes at the local pub and spend the £1 bonus his father had sent him. In early June 1944 Perry challenged the sergeant major because his name had been missed off a list detailing which men of the unit were going on to Normandy. The reply from the tetchy sergeant was: 'How the hell should I know? . . . Count yourself lucky, keep yer fuckin' 'ead down if you don't want to get it blown off.'[17]

When he approached a colonel about the decision to leave him behind he was informed it was because he was 'officer material' and a 'damn clever chap'. Interestingly, it was this CO who went on to inspire Perry to create the character of Colonel Reynolds in *It Ain't Half Hot Mum*.

Through the summer and autumn of 1944 Perry recalls feeling huge guilt about not being with his friends in Normandy. He had also been kept informed by the shouty sergeant major how many of them had been badly injured or killed during the invasion. This particular sergeant major was a bitter man. Mostly he was frustrated about his own lack of promotion, and was irritated to learn that army newbie Gunner Perry had been selected for officer training 'for making people laugh' while he himself had not. The man's behaviour inspired the character of the sergeant major (Windsor Davies) in Perry and Croft's hit television show *It Ain't Half Hot Mum*. And it's worth noting that in one episode of *Dad's Army* Captain Mainwaring gets huffy because former public schoolboy Sergeant Wilson is invited to join the golf club, while Mainwaring, despite being the town's esteemed bank manager, has not! Mainwaring soon tells Wilson not to forget who is captain of the platoon as he has three pips on his shoulder. Wilson asked him gently if he had one chip!

In the autumn of 1944 Gunner Perry packed up his kitbag, said a brief farewell to Park Hall Camp and travelled 26 miles to Chester where he would find out whether he was suited to a commission. He had certainly done his best to fit in with army life and always kept his uniform and kit spruce, clean and tidy. He'd been advised by a wise old show business pal named 'Morry' that looking smart and as crisp as possible always went down well with anyone, not just audiences.

At Chester the potential officer cadets filed into a room to sit various examination papers. It wasn't a time for laughing but Perry couldn't help but daydream when boredom set in. Whatever thoughts made him lose focus were soon interrupted. The glazed look on his face was spotted and the senior officer at the desk reprimanded him for not keeping his mind on the task ahead of him. Then came a shock. A boxing match was arranged 'in order to test the men's aggression levels'.

Perry was ordered to fight a huge man who promptly punched him in the face and on other parts of his body. Thump, thump, thump. When Perry's front tooth pierced his own lip, there was blood everywhere. And all the time the lieutenant who organised the match was yelling: 'Show some aggression and defend yourself, man!' Then another opponent arrived and continued to bash him.[18]

But it wasn't the other boxers the injured Perry wanted to batter: he had his eye on the lieutenant's throat. How he would love to strangle this bully with the big mouth. But the intelligent Perry also understood the army's rules. If a private attacks an officer he is punished and even flogged. But if an officer strikes a private, then he faces a court-martial and this was often the reason why so many of the lower ranks liked to goad anyone beyond sergeant major status.

The boxing match didn't do much to encourage any fledgling ambition to become an officer. When he got back to Oswestry, the sarcastic sergeant major smirked at his sore face and bruised jaw and said: 'I know your act is bad, Perry, but there was no need for them to beat you up.' Perry didn't smile at the lame joke but walked away happy in the knowledge that he had been invited to appear on stage again.

This time the Garrison Theatre was calling. Then came a blow which led to a dramatic turn of events. An unpleasant captain named Dix ambushed Perry's role as compère and left him standing in the wings, unable to take part in the show. On the day before curtain up, Dix turned up drunk – behaviour that Perry deemed unprofessional. Although Dix thought the audience were laughing at his jokes, they were in fact sniggering about seeing an officer slurring his words.

Dix knew Perry thought him incompetent and so he told the angry young Gunner that he would 'fix him'. Sure enough, the jealous captain saw to it that the talented, entertaining Perry was sent to the dreaded Far East. As he sat perched in the back of an army lorry, Perry's only comforts were the jungle greens he wore and the company of pals facing the same journey. The odious Dix waved Perry goodbye from Oswestry by running a finger across his throat. What a charmer!

Now on his way to India, the young Gunner found among his various official documents a letter from the War Office asking him to get back in touch to continue his officer training. No way would that happen as he realised the war would probably be over by the time he returned to England. Besides he was on board a troop ship now on his way to Bombay with the Royal Artillery. There was lots to focus on, all centred on the best way to stay alive. He'd heard many scary stories about the Japanese military and he wasn't keen on his own demise becoming one of their statistics.

It did cheer him up to join the ship's concert party, albeit it was an amateur affair. And he was delighted to see beneath his name on the billing the words 'professional comedian and impressionist'. He formed a double act with another trooper, one Harry Waller. The excited Perry even added a new character to their set, appearing as Clark Gable's Rhett Butler in the Hollywood blockbuster *Gone with the Wind*. According to Perry, his version of Butler's final words to Scarlett O'Hara, 'Quite frankly, my dear, I don't give a damn', went down a storm. Perry's act was cutting edge in those days, as *Gone with the Wind* was proving one of the most popular must-see films of the war. During the five-week journey to Bombay, he had plenty of time to polish up his act and devise some new jokes. He realised that for comedy to be successful it had to be transparent and accessible. It came as some relief that he'd discovered some of the secrets to provoking laughter.

But for now, he would have to mentally park his new-found theatrical enthusiasms. He was about to disembark down the troop ship gangplank into the noisy, spice-smelling busyness of Bombay. The wide-eyed Perry and his unit were then sent on their way to a camp in Kalyan where they would stay for six weeks, having a medical and inoculations, listening to lectures (including a film about 'keeping your private parts safe' to avoid catching venereal disease), and learning how to make the jungle your best pal. In the heat of Kalyan, Perry was promoted to bombardier. Soon enough, however, his unit was sent to relieve the desperate, half-starved and beleaguered men of the 'forgotten army' in Burma. It was time for them to go home to England.

This was, of course, the best news for these brave souls – almost as fabulous as the day in late spring 1944 when the legendary wartime singer Dame Vera Lynn arrived to entertain the troops in the Far East. Known by this time as the 'forces' sweetheart', she had just celebrated her 27th birthday when she heard former BBC man and now ENSA's Colonel Eric Dunstan wanted to welcome her to Bombay. The organisation's liaison officer was the actor and British film star Jack Hawkins. The news that Vera Lynn was coming made Perry happy as he had soon discovered in Bombay that many of the ENSA acts were so bad they attracted not cheers but boos from troops in desperate need of a boost to their morale.

So Miss Lynn flew thousands of miles from the white cliffs of Dover to India in April 1944 on a Lockheed Hudson twin-engine bomber aircraft. Soon enough she managed to shake off her feelings of air-sickness and get on with her next gig – and ready to greet her with cheers and applause was a grateful audience made up of troops on leave from active duty in the jungle. She describes in her memoir how the Bombay performances were like a rehearsal for the big show, as she knew her next journey would be on to Burma to greet the British soldiers of the 'forgotten army'. Despite efforts by the Cabinet Office to keep her away from such dangerous territory, she insisted on carrying on with the tour. Back home, she said, she'd sung her heart out in rough and ready working men's clubs. She saw no reason to not go on and provide cheer to those British lads fighting for their lives and stuck in the jungle so far from home.

After flying 2,345 miles she arrived in Burma and was made to feel as if she'd just popped by to say hello, sing a few songs and share a cup of tea. One soldier told her that 'home can't be that far away 'cos you're here'. It was a short sentence but it meant the world to Miss Lynn. It was a comment loaded with hope in the aftermath of the horrors so many of the men in her audiences had endured while fighting the Japanese.[19] The so-called 'battle of the Admin Box' in the Arakan region, for example, had taken place in February. The fighting was vicious. On one particular day thirty-five sick patients were killed by Japanese soldiers who ran through a hospital tent. Many of them were then cut down by British troops. Hand-to-hand fighting resulted in more deaths and destruction.[20]

By the time Perry's unit arrived in Burma the following year, the fiercest battles had moved towards Malaya. However, the word was out to any soldier in Burma to beware of Japanese spies. Most of Perry's time was spent searching the skies for enemy fighter aircraft, such as the deadly Nakajima Ki-27 (known as the 'Nate'), which could reach speeds of up to 470mph. His aerial recognition skills were spot on but never once did he see 'a single Japanese aircraft'.[21] What he did see was a horror that remained with him for the rest of his life. A group of miserable, flea-ridden, humiliated Japanese soldiers were brought into the camp. Their mantra to 'never surrender' left them refusing offers of water and food from their British captors. They had no wish to live.

By the spring of 1945 the perceptive Perry had begun to wonder why the army instructors continued to lecture the men about aircraft recognition. Surely the war must be coming to an end – all sorts of stories were getting through about the German military being wiped out by the Allies. But meanwhile, in the depths of Burma there was a new operation to deliver. The CO told the men to aim and fire the 'out-of-date' ack-ack guns at the Japanese bunkers. Suddenly, Perry realised to his horror that the Royal Artillery crews had been sitting ducks, especially, as the CO explained, since their weapons lacked the range and the firepower to be of much use in shooting aircraft out of the sky. Never mind, blustered the CO, let's fire the guns at the enemy hide-outs instead, and sharpen up our bayonet practice in case we flush out any Japanese soldiers. Something about this story in Perry's memoir sounds very much like a *Dad's Army* situation. It was all very much 'make do and mend' but there was always comedy to be found in the darkest situation.

News that the war was over arrived in camp soon after 6 August 1945 – the day the Americans dropped a nuclear bomb on Hiroshima, Japan. Another bomb was dropped on Nagasaki on the 9th. Six days later, on the 15th, the Japanese Emperor announced his country's surrender. The men of the Royal Artillery regiment in Burma were overjoyed at the thought of going home within a couple of weeks. As it turned out, Perry had to wait another two years before he could return to see his family in Watford.

In the late summer of that year he reveals in his memoirs how he almost 'bought it'. A burst appendix meant a mad dash back to Kalyan, where he was operated on in a makeshift hospital tent. The surgeon told him it had been a close thing. His recovery took several weeks and he was put in a wheelchair and transported to a special camp in Srinagar in Kashmir to get fit. Evidently, losing his virginity was part of it. According to Perry, he was seduced by a young woman named Edith, who visited him at the camp. Edith was mad about the Kama Sutra and assisted him in detail with his new physical adventures.

Once recuperated, and more aware of the difference between love and lust, Perry was posted to Deolali in the Nasik district of Maharashtra, a place some 100 miles north-east of Bombay. Here theatrical events and concerts were the norm and the artistes hoped to provide much-needed morale-boosting entertainment for the troops waiting to get home. Deolali was a transit camp for British troops, and its name was the origin of the phrase 'doolally-tap', or just 'doolally', to describe the mental disorders exhibited by combat-weary troops waiting to be transported home. Despite the camp's reputation, and the frightening rumours about mad men running amok shooting at everyone and everything, Perry enjoyed the chance to step out on stage as a new member of the resident Royal Artillery Concert Party. He was delighted to meet up again with his pal Harry Waller and they revived their old double act. Also in the programme was a chirpy tap dancer and comedian named Roger Bourne. It was the crafty, clever, wily Bourne who inspired Perry to write the spiv character of Private Walker (James Beck) in *Dad's Army*. Life in India was indeed proving beneficial to the creative mind and Perry's memories were placed firmly in his comedy tool box. In Deolali he was promoted again, this time to lance sergeant, but in 1946 the RA Concert Party was disbanded. Sadly, the new stripe on his sleeve didn't last for long as he was posted to the Gordon Highlanders, based in Coimbatore, in the south of India. He says he wasn't treated well by the Scottish officers, who looked down on 'Sassenachs' and demoted him. The hardy Scots thought little of his value as an entertainer but it was noted that he was a Gunner and so he was put in charge of the armoury at the base. It was yet another boring job, but Perry did his best to get through each day and avoided the temptation to goad the Scots officers, even though there was comical kerfuffle among them over who got to wear the ceremonial kilts.

Life improved rapidly when Perry's pal Harry turned up with some good news. He had heard that a new unit called Combined Services Entertainment was being set up and both men had every right to go to Delhi and audition. Ten days later a date and time came through, much to the horror of the arrogant Scots adjutant, who told them in no uncertain terms to not come back!

In Delhi, under the stage management of RAF Squadron Leader Charles Fletcher, Perry began to flourish. The antics and adventures of each man in every production went on to inspire him two decades later to write what became the hit comedy show, *It Ain't Half Hot Mum*.

Sharing luxury digs with Harry Waller at Delhi racecourse meant life was on the up for them both. Each day they'd be greeted by grateful audiences and mix with the social set who knew and loved Squadron Leader Fletcher. Perry was promoted back to sergeant and so, it seemed, was everyone else in the company. In March 1947 there was a tour of northern India.

Back in Delhi that year Perry and his pal Harry were told it was time to go home. There followed a long trip by train back to Deolali, and from there to the docks at Bombay, where a ship bound for England would be waiting for them, along with so many other men in khaki.

Once aboard the SS *Franconia*, Perry mustered a troupe of entertainers to provide a show each night to help pass the time. More than a month went by before they arrived in Southampton docks in old England. Perry noted that everyone on board was quiet, respectful even, and various goodbyes were whispered soberly. The war really was over; it was a moment he had longed for and now all he had on his mind was home. Now it was time for people throughout blitzed Britain to pick up the pieces and build bright new lives out of the old darkness.

Perry went from Southampton to Aldershot, and there he contacted his parents to let them know he would be arriving in Watford the next day. Any civilians who saw him on the street gave him a smile and a hero's welcome. As he finally sat down to dinner with his parents and the rest of the Perry family on his first day home he couldn't help but notice the twinkle in his mother's eye. Her son really was here to stay at last.

His theatrical ambitions as strong as ever, he wasted no time and auditioned for the Royal Academy of Dramatic Art (RADA), where he trained in classical and modern styles of performance. He was lucky enough to receive a special scholarship grant as he had served in the armed forces. At RADA he met Joan Collins, Robert Shaw and Lionel Jefferies, among many others. In the 1950s, during his holidays from London, he worked as a 'redcoat' at Butlin's holiday camps.

Perry by now was enjoying the opportunity to use humour as a way of exposing the lunacy of the British class system and all it represented, especially when it came to life in the military. Deconstructing stereotypes was always an interesting exercise to him, especially if carried out as a force in the comedy genre. The memories of his early years in the Home Guard enabled him to create the characters and experiences we now know materialised as *Dad's Army*.

When he was asked how and why he wrote the series, Perry confessed in his memoir how it was 'born out of desperation'. By 1967 he was working with Joan Littlewood's famous theatre workshop but after seventeen years in weekly rep his bank balance was still pretty empty. He was growing tired of being hungry and living off the seat of his pants and feeling something of a misfit. Then he had a flash of inspiration – he would write his own show. Why not?! The idea of the Home Guard began to seduce him every day on the train to Stratford East and he would make copious notes and sketches. There would be a vicar, and he'd cast Frank Williams in the role, then how about a spiv? Perry, who recalled the antics of his old army pal Roger Bourne, fancied that role for himself. Then he wondered about having a 'pompous old man in charge of the platoon', then a young boy in the show . . . and so it began to come together. His research and his own memories merged into a complete and brilliant vision. One day, when he had come to the end of his first ever script, he talked to his agent Anne Callender about it. She happened to be married to David Croft, the television producer.[22]

Once Perry had an opportunity to show Croft the script, history was made and the show began to grow arms and legs and characters and plots. The location was tremendously important to the success of the series as it had to be somewhere near the Channel, where in reality for the Home Guard the risk of invasion was always high on the emotional agenda.

All the decisions about the characters and their day jobs were made between Perry and Croft. One area they both fully agreed on was that the sergeant (John Le Mesurier) should be posh and the commanding officer less so. The duo wanted to show how the Home Guard was an equalising force and, as Perry pointed out, there did come a time during the early days of his life in the military when he was one of the first to serve alongside the women of the estimable ATS, whose most famous recruit, of course, was Her Majesty the Queen (then HRH Princess Elizabeth). Another recruit was Mary Churchill, the youngest daughter of the wartime prime minister. In the most recent film of *Dad's Army*, released in 2016, there are several scenes involving the women of the ATS. Perry died that year but there's little doubt he would have been happy to know about the ATS's inclusion in the film.

When he had first started scribbling down his ideas for the show Perry himself had wanted to play the 'spiv' role in *Dad's Army*, but to his initial disappointment the part was given to the actor James Beck. The decision was made by Croft and the BBC Head of Comedy Michael Mills, who thought that having the writer in the cast would irritate the other actors.

The character of Private Godfrey (Arnold Ridley) was created by David Croft. Godfrey's gentleness stood out sharply against the harsh, dour nature of the Scotsman Private Frazer (John Laurie). Laurie's rolling eyes and voice of doom made him perfect for the role of the pessimistic old Celt who ran the local undertaking business. The character's catchphrase 'Doomed! We're all Doomed!' lives on today. Ian Lavender was cast as the idiotic young Private Pike and the role of the highly charged Warden Hodges went to Bill Pertwee. The verger was played by Edward Sinclair and the redoubtable Clive Dunn was superbly cast as Lance Corporal Jones. Perry explained: 'David (Croft) and I had put in all these peculiar ingredients, mixed them carefully, and when the pudding came out of the oven it was beautifully cooked – in other words, it was perfect.'

Filming began, ironically enough, on April Fool's Day 1968. Snow fell and heralded the beginning of a magical legacy in the history of British comedy. Some of the actors, including Arthur Lowe, sat waiting in Croft's Rolls-Royce with a flask of tea. They appeared to be happier sitting in the car than doing their job when an excited Perry ran over, opened the door and suggested they get cracking. He told Croft he thought they told him to 'shut the door' and they all seemed like 'a right miserable lot of old sods!'[23]

At first the show faced a rocky period. Market research carried out by the BBC had suggested it wasn't going to be popular, and an audience that didn't laugh could kill off any idea of a second series of *Dad's Army*. There was a frustrating three-day wait before Croft's constant campaigning and arguing for the show to continue was accepted and the audience ratings began to rise into the stratosphere. Perry recalled: 'When the market research crowds gave it a thumbs down I felt like Bizet who, after the opening night of *Carmen* when the critics had torn the production to pieces, distraught, went away and walked about in the rain, got soaked through, caught pneumonia and died.' Ever grateful, Perry later said that without Croft's determination, *Dad's Army* would never have made it.

Perry died in 2016, aged 93. Tributes rightfully poured in from all over the world. In his later years he remained loyal to his achievements and always defended his shows against anyone who claimed they were 'politically incorrect'. In a newspaper article published just before his death, he said: 'I believe *It Ain't Half Hot Mum* is as equally funny as *Dad's Army*, and full of characters just as memorable – the blustering sergeant major, the camp drag-artiste and the Indian orderly who was more British than the Brits. That role was played by the actor Michael Bates, who wore a light tan for the part, but in reality spoke fluent Urdu and had been a captain in the Gurkha Rifles during the war. Perry went on: 'I believe today too many executives at the BBC have rather too little idea what reality looks like. They are Oxbridge graduates trained by other Oxbridge graduates who learned what they know from still more Oxbridge graduates. The real world doesn't get a look-in at today's BBC.'

# DAVID CROFT OBE

It has long been a favourite saying of mine that it takes no talent
whatever to be uncomfortable.

AS a commissioned British officer who served in the Second World
War, the man who steered *Dad's Army* to success had already lived a
life of varied experiences, some dangerous and some just plain funny.
Major David Croft was no fool, and many of the events which erupted
during his long war, both in training on home shores and serving in
the Far East, were often cushioned by baffling fateful situations which
were brilliantly recreated in the show.

Even his childhood recollections of rifle drill at his independent
school, Durlston Court in Swanage, Dorset, in the early 1930s provided
a significant funny story and forty years later he was able to describe
perfectly to the cast of *Dad's Army* just what military parading was
all about, including the lunacy that followed when someone put the
wrong foot first! Now remembered as a pale-skinned, red-haired, shy
but determined man, he told the actors on a day in 1968 how the school
embraced a First World War method that forced recruits to 'form fours'
in army drill. He said:

> There then ensued a complicated dance-like series of steps while
> shouting 'One – one two' and us boys would all bump into each other
> prior to finding ourselves in four ranks. Having sorted ourselves out,
> this would be followed by our schoolmaster yelling, 'Form two deep'
> and after shouting 'One – one two' again, we scrambled once more into
> two ranks.
>
> It continued to be a shambolic way of forming a neat parade until a
> bright spark at the War Office decided it would be better if men formed
> up into three ranks instead. The chaos certainly lessened, although it still
> needed concentration as there was always the issue of left arms going
> forward at the same time as the left leg thus creating a penguin-like
> movement.[1]

When Croft first became involved in the creation of *Dad's Army* he completely understood Captain Mainwaring's frustration when the rifle drill turned into a shambolic mess resembling a pure jumble of men! While some of the actors had already served in a war and had some knowledge of the procedure, the younger ones including Pike (Ian Lavender) and Walker (James Beck), had to start from scratch.

All this went to prove how Croft's life, especially his war years in the Royal Artillery, would continue to provide him with experiences which he could press into use as superb comedy material. As a young Gunner, for example, he suffered the traditional military baptisms of fire, including the maintenance of hyper-neat rows of beds in the barrack room, yelling and aggressive sergeant majors, square bashing, incessant polishing of boots and buckles, and how could he forget the regular humiliation of having an army doctor examine the 'wedding tackle'.

Serving in the British Army was tremendously different from his civilian life, which was bohemian in nature and ordained in theatrical social whirls. He was used to show-business people, the happy-go-lucky who searched relentlessly for work, the whimsical charade of networking, trusting the fates and the Gods, and all the highs and lows that went with a life on stage. There was a 'hey fiddle-de-dee' attitude alluding to the idea the actor's life really was the best.

Croft's youth was unlike that of his eventual *Dad's Army* cohort Jimmy Perry. Indeed, the baby David Sharland (Croft) had been more or less born in a costume basket backstage in a theatre. In later life, when he was famous, he often told reporters how he was just a toddler when he first made up his mind to tread the boards and serve 'Dr Greasepaint'. His mother was Annie Croft (1892–1959), the famous theatre actress and first ever female company manager in the West End, while his father Reginald Sharland (1886–1944) from Southend, Essex, had become a well known actor about Hollywood in the 1920s, appearing alongside stars such as John Barrymore, Joel McCrea and Constance Bennett. In the last ten years of his life Sharland had also forged a career as a successful radio artiste.

In 1922 Annie was so fanatical about her career as a doyenne of the theatre scene she told her son he had cost her £ 1,500 in lost earnings during her pregnancy. Within weeks it became more and more difficult for her to perform on stage without her gamine figure to fit into small-sized costumes.

By 1930 Reginald returned to Hollywood alone. Croft and his brother Peter were still small boys, but it would be the last time Croft ever saw his ambitious father. A year later in 1931 his mother, who had many admirers, filed for divorce.

At some time in his early theatrical life a decision had obviously been made to make the most of his mother's fame and David used her surname, Croft. His father went on to marry again in 1939 in Hollywood and remained with the Austrian-born actress Herta Lynd (best known for her appearance in the 1938 film *You and Me*) until his death aged 58 in 1944.

Back in England his youngest son David was enrolled at Durlston Court, a traditional independent school in Dorset. Interestingly enough, and no doubt to Croft's relief, it boasted a long tradition of excellent drama productions. When the school was founded in 1903 its crest was a Roman eagle and its motto was 'Erectus Non Elatus' ('Proud but not boastful'). When money got tight, Croft was removed from Durlston but his intelligence enabled him to be accepted for Rugby School in Warwickshire where he would complete his basic education. He learned a new school motto: 'Orando Laborando' ('By praying, by working').

By now, however, showbusiness was deeply ingrained in his genetic make-up and he loved its friendly familial appeal which seemed to extend beyond the miseries of academic competition. Despite all of its financial trials, disappointments, heartache and near-misses, the entertainment world was where he felt most at home. As a boy, and well into his teens, he often appeared in various plays and concerts and mingled with his mother's theatrical friends. He came to know the ins and outs of various venues of entertainment as if they were his living room. Once, as a very young child, he made a comical appearance by just showing his skinny bare leg out at the audience from the stage left curtain. The sight of a small knobbly knee and a big boot obviously provided much mirth in those days.

Money was at times low and Croft grew up in awe of how entertainers lived on their wits and learned how it was often just through sheer luck that they might win a part in a production or earn a few shillings because a friend of a friend told them there was a walk-on going at the Wyndhams or the Palace Theatres. He learned how it was important always to keep an ear to the ground and an eye on the main chance. When the going was good it was good and when riding high on her fame his mother would take risks – she had to.

During the depression of 1931 the popular Annie made a big decision to transfer a whole show to the Shaftesbury Theatre in London, relying on the philosophy that people would need entertainment to help them forget their troubles during tough times. Her gamble paid off and her light production of *The Chocolate Soldier*, in which she starred, drew in the crowds. She had proved she could put food on the table and pay for the family lodgings.

Annie, like many artistes, always claimed she had an affinity with the 'other side' and would consult any mystic claiming a connection with spirit guides. It was after such a consultation that she decided to divorce Reginald Sharland, who had been gone from her life for some years. Her son David was then 9 years old and had always kept in postal contact with his father; Reginald had obviously earned enough at one point to send home £100 for his sons – some of which the diligent Annie spent on sending David to typing and shorthand lessons. No doubt she sensibly believed he should have a 'second string to his bow' if he couldn't find an acting job in the future to pay the bills.

After the divorce came through, she married her boyfriend Hugh Gough, a show business investor who owned a country house in Kingsdown, north Kent, and a hotel. Well into his 40s, Gough married the pretty actress and life was steady and calm. But Gough was accustomed to the life of a carefree bachelor and he seemed to be unable to shake off his independent and pedantic attitudes to life. Croft observed comically how his step-father carved the Sunday roast into 'such thin slices you could read *The Times* newspaper behind them!'[2] Not long into the marriage the Goughs decided to part company. Annie thought she'd be happier to go her own way again and she knew that as well as the steady stream of ready male admirers, there was always her faithful assistant Olive to turn to if she needed emotional support.

Croft was 16 years old when he made history as the BBC's youngest juvenile lead. He was cast as the hero of the musical *Charing Cross Road*. The production was directed by Roy Speer.

When war broke out on 3 September 1939 the 17-year-old Croft discovered that many of his actor friends, including Ronnie Waldman, were being called up. Waldman, who went on to become a leading light at the BBC in the 1960s and 1970s, joined the RAF. Croft became an ARP warden as he was laughingly considered 'too old' to join the Home Guard. Then, on a bright May morning in 1942, he left the family home in Boscombe, Dorset, to walk to the railway station. Like so many young men, Croft had been called up. His first taste of life in the British Army was to report to the Royal Artillery army barracks 20 miles away at Blandford. His brother Peter had already joined RAF Bomber Command as a wireless operator. Annie and the loyal Olive, like so many other women, had to manage without a man about the place.

Blandford Camp had been a training centre for Royal Naval reservists since 1939. But following the Dunkirk evacuation in 1940, the British Army was reorganised and this led to Royal Artillery anti-aircraft units being trained at the site. The reconnaissance battalion of the Royal Northumberland Fusiliers was also in residence until

Blandford became mostly a battle training camp for officers and non-commissioned officers. Many of the Blandford men were posted to North Africa in 1943 or Normandy in 1944. In the late summer of 1944 the site was turned into a US Army hospital complex. When it closed in 1945, a special Roosevelt Garden and Memorial was created in honour of those who had died fighting for liberty.

When the young Croft arrived at Blandford Camp in 1942 he faced an aggressive bombardier who was very much alive, and with his fellow new recruits he was marched off to find some food. 'It was a stew of some sort and an atrociously watered down cup of tea,' Croft recalled. The living quarters were seriously basic, too. The barrack room was 'full of beds which had three rough grey blankets apiece' and Croft was kept awake by the sounds of boys sobbing for home.[3] In his memoir *You Have Been Watching,* he writes candidly of the survival tactics which helped him steer a course through the rough and tumble, and occasional brutality, of military life.

From the bleakness of Blandford, he was soon posted to Buxton, Derbyshire, to join the Light Anti-Aircraft Training Unit. As soon as he arrived he discovered there was no bed at all and he was forced to sleep on a straw-covered floor in a crumbling old hotel. Only the horses were missing in this stable-like dwelling, the style of which features in an early episode of *Dad's Army.* In the fresh air of the Derbyshire dales Gunner Croft was taught everything there was to know about the Bofors 40mm gun. His ability to operate the mighty Bofors was impressive – a military skill he learned just like regimental colleague Gunner Jimmy Perry, who was 80 miles away in Oswestry in an RA ack-ack platoon. The Bofors was akin to a giant machine gun and fired sixty exploding bullets, each weighing 2lb or so, per minute. Its aiming/sighting system had been designed by Colonel Kerrison, and Bofors was the name of the Swedish company which built this huge military weapon.

Croft recalled: 'It was operated by a team of ten men, whose task it was to unhook it from the truck that towed it and, in two minutes or less, put the damned thing together and use it to shoot down low-flying enemy aircraft.'[4] This frenzied activity lodged in his mind. There was always comedy involved, especially as Croft and the men had to shout loudly each time they carried out their individual task to get the Bofors ready to fire. All the noise and furore of so many young Gunners yelling at once was 'like nothing he'd heard since', and years later the power of this wartime memory energised the heart of *Dad's Army.* The sight of the characters bumbling and fumbling around with weapons of war became a set piece.

Croft again:

The loader would yell things like 'I am now placing the level foot pedal held to the position "Held"' and reporting "Held"', following which the unfortunate lad would turn his head in the director of the Sergeant Instructor and yell 'Held'. This was basically the same as saying 'I've put the safety catch on!' The Geordie who was deputed to put the hefty side girder into its socket was once heard to yell 'I'm putting this fookin heavy fookin iron thing in this fookin hole and trying to put this fookin retaining pin in this fookin little socket and it won't fookin go.'

Such banter added colour to the proceedings, which became typical of *Dad's Army*, albeit without the language!

The Gunner's life was proving a busy one for Croft, who was glad to read a letter from his mother telling him not to worry at all as she and Olive were coping well at home without him.

After about a month serving the needs of the mighty Bofors, and successfully taking part in relevant training experiences, Croft was approached by a senior officer about joining an officers training unit in India. But the idea didn't sit well with him and he turned down the offer. In hindsight, he believed his decision, whilst unpopular at the time, probably saved his life, as had he gone to India, he would no doubt have been sent on to serve in the dangerous territories of Burma. Eventually he was posted to Penhal, near Newquay in Cornwall, where he continued training under the watchful eye of a sergeant whom Croft described as 'exceedingly intelligent and civilised'. And while there was leisure time to swim in the deep blue Atlantic and sunbathe on the Cornish sands, there were also intensive days of heated activity when the Bofors guns blasted away at targets of imagined enemy aircraft. It was an identical exercise to that recounted by Gunner Jimmy Perry. Ironically enough, and decades later, both men became known as the big guns of situation comedy.

Early on, Croft noted that whilst his training was going well, the war was not: 'General Auchinleck was barely holding Rommel at El Alamein, Hitler was hammering at Stalingrad, and the British raid on Dieppe had been a fiasco,' he wrote in his memoir.[5]

Then, from the charms of Cornwall the skilled young Gunner was posted to the 285th Battery, 64th Light Anti-Aircraft Regiment, at Birmingham, where it soon became clear the unit was being prepared for service abroad. While based in Birmingham, Croft encountered a Scottish major by the name of Wilson, a man described at best as 'sinister'. It was this character who told Croft there wasn't a chance he'd ever make an officer as he didn't have the drive and initiative.

Croft replied: 'You're wrong about that,' to which the major responded with 'I don't give a damn what you think.'[6]

At this point all Croft could do was wait it out in the cramped barracks and get to know some of the men around him. He recalls members of Glasgow gangs who were good at standing up for themselves, and it was fun to be posted with them to the old Butlins' camp at Clacton-on-Sea, Essex. The place had become a firing range and the chalets had been converted into billets. Croft was delighted when he discovered there were 'no bugs in the rugs' – an interesting observation when compared to the Home Guard officer who wrote in the daily report how 'livestock has been found in the beds'.

After the recruits had settled in to their new accommodation, they were summoned to a hall which was home to the former Butlins boxing ring. That day every man was in full uniform to welcome the bristling, overweight colonel of the 64th Regiment, who would make a speech to the assembled troops. The giggling among the men began to ripple through the hall as the colonel squeezed himself and his officers through the ropes around the ring in order that he might place himself above the men for the address. Without further ado, the colonel puffed out his chest and told his audience they were 'conscripted raw material' and he and his staff were going to turn them into 'real disciplined soldiers, come what may!'

Life from that day was always 'at the double', and Croft recalled how the men continued to 'bang off their guns', more often than not missing the targets! Among his crew of amiable young Gunners was a fierce red-headed Glaswegian named Joe Postlethwaite. Then there was Peter Wyper, whom Croft described as tall and exceptionally strong; although he was a quite straight-laced character, Wyper's muscle power was useful when it came to hauling the Bofors around.

Croft's other new friend, Frank Lock, was a footballer in civilian life before he became a gun loader in the Royal Artillery. After the war in 1945 Lock's then CO in the Army persuaded Jimmy Seed, the manager of first division Charlton Athletic FC, to sign Lock as a full-back. Seed was impressed with Lock's performance and he went on to play two hundred games with the south-east London club. By 1947 Lock was being written about in the sports sections of national newspapers, and he became one of football's most popular stars. In 1953 his fame led Lock to be snapped up by Liverpool FC for a two-year contract. Here, at the club's famous Anfield ground, the sturdy Lock made his debut against West Bromwich Albion. After Liverpool, he played for Watford, Cambridge United and Clacton Town until he hung up his boots in 1960.

***

Soon Lock, Croft and Postlethwaite were on the move again 'at the double' as another military training goal was in sight. This time they were sent to Packington Park in Meriden, near Birmingham, where in the bleakest of winters they shivered in bell tents and had no option but to huddle together for warmth at night. A small compensation for Croft came in the form of a stripe as he was made into a full Bombardier, earning him £ 2 a week. It meant he could send some of that sum home to Annie and Olive in Dorset to help out with the family finances.

When it was time to leave the canvas city of Packington Park, the newly promoted Bombardier Croft journeyed to Clacton in Essex, only to find his barracks were in the village hall at Wishaw. Floorboards, though, were better than wet grass anytime. He said: 'It has long been a favourite saying of mine that it takes no talent whatever to be uncomfortable.'[7] But the Royal Artillery boys soon discovered the climate would be far from chilly for their next posting. They were issued with khaki drill shirts and shorts and a raft of kit which meant only one thing: they were bound for the hot tropics, but exactly where remained a secret. There were also new Bofors with shining brass screws available to them, and Tommy guns with large quantities of bullets to lug around. 'I felt like a Chicago gangster,' noted Croft in his memoir, 'and it was an awkward thing to carry about.'

That Christmas Bombardier Croft took some leave in London to meet his brother Peter, who, looking smart in his RAF uniform, was staying at the Ritz Hotel in Piccadilly. Now aged 20, Croft went home to Dorset to enjoy Christmas Day with his mother and Olive, and revelled in a soft bed to sleep in. He made the most of such luxury in the full knowledge that the new year was going to be very different indeed.

Back at the barracks at Birmingham, he learned that he was in for a rare treat . . . there would be a bed for him as he travelled to his new posting, although it was only a smelly canvas hammock aboard the newly built 494ft troopship *Empire Pride*! Croft and his pals also found out their station on the vessel was right next to one of the Bofors guns on the bridge. Talk about a busman's holiday!

Croft was glad of the chilly weather at sea in those early weeks of the new year as the freezing and rough conditions kept the German U-boats away, but he didn't enjoy the seasickness and dehydration and was pleased enough when *Empire Pride* and her human cargo docked at Bône in Algeria. After disembarking, Bombardier Croft and his pals discovered they were about to join Operation Torch, which had begun on 8 November 1942 with the intention to drive Erwin Rommel's troops out of North Africa.

Croft's unit was part of the First Army. Their role was to operate the Bofors and defend the small RAF airfield at Bône, some 250 miles east of Algiers, near the border with Tunisia. It was essential that Bône be held because, following the capture of Casablanca, Oran and Algiers, the Allied armies were planning to push eastward to capture Tunis and Bône was on the route of their advance.[8]

On 12 November 1942 the heroic men of the 3rd Parachute Battalion, 1st Parachute Brigade, commanded by Lieutenant General Geoffrey Pine-Coffin, were flown in Dakotas from Gibraltar by American pilots and dropped over the area of Bône close to the airfield. A quick reconnaissance flight had confirmed to Pine-Coffin that the area was unoccupied. He knew the mission would be a close-run thing as German paratroopers at Tunis were waiting to carry out a similar operation. But the 3rd Paras got there first, and safe in the knowledge that No.6 Commando unit would soon arrive, they seized the airfield – but only just held on as they came under attack from the Luftwaffe's merciless Stuka dive-bombers. The quick-thinking Commandos rapidly went about installing old anti-aircraft guns seized from sabotaged ships in the harbour to protect the airfield from future enemy attacks.[9] Soon after their arrival, the 3rd Paras linked up with an Allied armoured force from the First Army and took up a ground role as infantry before moving forwards to secure other strongholds earmarked for Allied invasion in North Africa.

Thus, during the few months before Croft and the gunners arrived in Algeria, the airfield at Bône and its harbour had already seen a great deal of action. Rare film footage of the area in early 1943 shows RAF Spitfires and American P-43 aircraft in dramatic action against Me109s and Ju88s over Bône. At night tracer bullets shot into the dark sky like small bright rockets at marauding Luftwaffe bombers, and in daylight anti-aircraft gun crews are shown blasting away at the enemy aircraft overhead. Boom, boom, boom. Dramatic evidence of the gunners' success is revealed in the film in the form of the smouldering wreckage of Luftwaffe aircraft. Debris is scattered around Bône airfield as the crash and burn ritual continued day after day. Meantime, on the palm tree-lined streets of Bône people are seen at first walking and getting on with their daily lives, shopping and talking, and then running for cover to hide in various doorways as the aerial conflict between the RAF and the Luftwaffe begins to kick off in the clear skies overhead.[10]

One pilot of 32 Squadron RAF recalled being posted to a place called Tingley near Bône in April 1943. His squadron was equipped with Beaufighters to carry out night-time sweeps against the Luftwaffe. In July there was much joy when speedier, more agile Spitfires arrived to bolster the squadron. Many men living in tents pitched on the sands of Bône complained about scorpions wandering about; to keep the deadly arachnids away at night the men stood the legs of their beds in empty tin cans. Another problem facing many men in North Africa was malaria, which debilitated its victims and could kill if not treated in time.

By the time Croft and his unit arrived at Bône, they discovered the airfield was very much in the hands of Anglo-American forces, with the RAF's 657 Squadron backed up by British Army anti-aircraft units. As part of an Air Observation Post, the squadron flew twin-engined Vickers Wellington bombers and mighty four-engined Short Stirlings from the airfield in the weeks from 22 September to 16 October 1943. There were a number of RAF rescue launches patrolling the waters around Bône, too.

Rare photographs of the airfield during the war show us the building that housed the RAF headquarters. It was around this building that the men of the Royal Artillery, including Croft, would have had to pitch their tents. This time they put planks of wood on the floor to help ease the discomfort. Let's hope the RAF had tipped them off about the empty bean-can trick to prevent scorpions joining them in bed! Food was of the tinned variety, and other inedible offerings did not help motivate fair-haired Englishmen in the blistering heat. There was also the curse of mosquitoes. Each day Croft forced a Mepacrine pill down his throat to ward off the dreaded malaria. Meantime the Bofors and anti-aircraft guns were at the ready day and night.

From December 1943 until March 1944 Bône was home to 293 Squadron RAF, which had been formed in the late autumn of 1943 at RAF Bilda, North Africa. Its mission was to provide air search and rescue, and the aircrews flew twin-engined Vickers Warwicks and Supermarine Walrus seaplanes.

Once the Luftwaffe attacks had begun to fade in the autumn of 1943, there was little work for the gunners and after a few months at Bône the dutiful Croft and his unit received orders to head 60 miles westward to the small township of Philippeville, where they were to join 657 Squadron RAF. Here the Bofors gun was placed on a hill offering a grandstand view of the docks below. Soon enough Croft realised the theatre of war he was involved in was very, very different from his civilian life on the West End stages back home. His days in Philippeville, though, allowed him to experience a town typical of French colonial rule. The architecture was grand, almost opulent, and the tree-lined avenues were interspersed with small cafés providing a heady whiff of nostalgia, made even more poignant by the 1942 film *Casablanca* starring Humphrey Bogart and Ingrid Bergman. This legendary example of film-noir was set in Morocco and reveals so enigmatically the French cultural influence in a climate heavy with heat, exotic aromas and repressed sexuality. And despite the desolation in parts of North Africa caused by the Luftwaffe's bombing attacks, the film offers us a good idea of Croft's Algiers of 1943 – although instead of visiting, as Rick (Bogart) drawls, 'one of all the gin-joints in all the towns in all the world', Croft found himself in a seedy bar drinking what he described as 'rough red wine' straight off the local vines. There were no glamorous Ingrid Bergman types ready to gaze into his eyes, and he and his pals soon learned not to gulp the wine down like a pint of beer as the resultant hangovers proved to be intense and long-lasting.

Evidence of Croft's witty observations of military life showed up well in his memoir about his time in Philippeville:

> From our gun site we could see the comings and goings of the town and the port. Royal Navy corvettes driven with great panache would arrive in impressive style. They would approach the entrance to the port very fast, conduct a couple of wiggles to get inside and then slam on the brakes, producing a froth of white water, before tying up in no time at all. Naval officers are quite different from army officers. An army officer can lead his troops into the valley of death, lose half of them and emerge with a medal. If a naval officer bashes into a jetty rather vigorously, he is likely to lose his job.[11]

When enemy forces began to attack Philippeville and its port, the men of the Royal Artillery stood their ground and gallantly brought down many Luftwaffe bombers. The gunners' success rate usually occurred during the daytime when aircraft were easily visible. However, it was some months before the Luftwaffe gave in, and their bombardments could be expected to last for hours every day. These vigorous attacks drew to a close once the big friendly Americans arrived with their giant tents, bulldozers (to increase the size of the gun pits) and vital extra equipment to take over the defence of the area.

Almost before they could begin to swap stories with their US allies, Bombardier Croft and his men were sent back to Bône. On arrival, he was unexpectedly reunited with his brother Peter, who wanted to celebrate David's 21st birthday. It took just one look at his rake-thin younger sibling to convince Peter Croft that the birthday boy was ill. Peter was also horrified to note his brother's skin was ravaged by impetigo. One day, when the aching Bombardier Croft was unable to stagger in and out of the gun pit without assistance, the Medical Officer decided to send him to the military hospital, where he would be placed under observation.

Diagnosed as suffering from rheumatic fever, Croft was given medication to bring down his blood sedimentation rate and his aching knees were soothed by the warmth of two light bulbs placed beneath a prop on his bed tended by women of the Queen Alexandra's Nursing Yeomanry. Peter artfully persuaded the medical staff to transfer the patient to a bigger hospital in Algiers, which would mean he was safely out of the way of any aggressive enemy troops. After a few nights of professional care, and a good helping of fresh oranges, Croft's health improved enough for him to be sent home to England for recuperation on a hospital ship. On arrival at Liverpool docks, he was quickly transferred to Clatterbridge Hospital just outside the city.

***

IN mid-December 1943 the recovering Bombardier Croft was given leave to return home to a delighted Annie and Olive in Dorset. But once the Christmas festivities were over and the new year approached, he was ordered to report to nearby Bournemouth Hospital and await further instructions. It's easy to imagine the conversations at home. There's little doubt his mother hoped her son would be too frail to continue with his military service and he could soon get back into show business and take up some of the many theatre and screen roles available for men on the home front.

No one could blame the 21-year-old Croft for thinking the same. As he admits in his memoir, he fully believed he would receive a medical discharge and expected to get a march on his future career again, back beneath the theatrical spotlight. He even visited an agent who told him he would be snapped up for work as it was difficult to find any actors under the age of 55 since most eligible young men were in the armed forces.

Alas, from the moment he stepped into Bournemouth Hospital all hopes of a rapid return to the civilian life he loved disappeared and the scary suspicious nursing sister in charge of a special recuperation ward kept him in. His bed was placed near a draughty window in order for him to get fresh air to continue his bounce back to peak condition. This same sister, explained Croft, decided there was 'nothing wrong with this patient' and he was swiftly moved to a convalescent hospital in the countryside near Wareham in Dorset.[12]

Another recuperation experience followed and sure enough Croft found himself in an army camp in Taunton, Somerset. 'It was a much more rigorous affair which began with five-mile walks extended to 25-mile route marches,' he wrote, 'and on top of that we had to throw tree trunks around as if they were made of balsa wood. It made a very funny sequence for Jones and Godfrey in *Dad's Army*.'

By the end of spring 1944 he was back at the Royal Artillery depot at Woolwich, where the attitude to 'soldier on' at all costs and regardless of how bad you felt was never so prevalent. Any man who complained of illness was put through such an embarrassing procedure that Croft said it was considered best to keep quiet as reporting sick was so frowned upon in most cases it 'wasn't worth the candle . . .' Privately, he went to Harley Street to get his health checked out and was given an A1 rating to continue his duties at Woolwich, some of which included the dreadful duty of escorting deserters in handcuffs back to barracks.

But it wasn't all doom for the young bombardier, as he was the proud wearer of an Africa Star medal, which in those days was a rare sight. In the pubs he was treated to free drinks and described as a hero, with even senior officers offering him a salute. Croft was also proud to learn that Hitler's troops had been driven out of North Africa and Italy by the heroes of the Eighth Army (which included 'Desert Rats' like my own father, David Felix Foreman of the Royal Engineers and the 7th Armoured Division – author).

Although Croft proudly wore a First Army clasp, anyone seeing his Africa Star seemed to assume he was a member of the Eighth Army, and showed him the respect the Eighth had earned. Soon enough he received notification to attend a War Office Selection Board. Whereas his future writing partner Gunner Jimmy Perry received nothing but a battering in a boxing ring at this stage, followed by a kick in the teeth and a 'you'll be hearing from us' letter after officer training, Croft had a successful experience. There was also a wealth of material for him to log in regard to lunatic tasks and events which years later inspired some *Dad's Army* episodes. He'd only been back at Woolwich for a few days before the Selection Board passed him ready and he was ordered to make his way to Sandhurst to train as an officer in the infantry.

Any thoughts of a glamorous lifestyle of smartness, efficiency and riding a white prancing horse soon evaporated as Croft found himself in a leaking tent with a number of fellow baffled cadet officers. Among them were Johnny Spittal and Barry Stewart-Fisher (actually Czechoslovakian, with an unpronounceable real name, who had fled his country just before Hitler's army marched in) who became his friends. But these three musketeers did not remain at Sandhurst, as they failed to pass the test about infantry knowledge. Croft explained: 'In my case I knew absolutely nothing about infantry soldiering . . . in spite of my leading the patrol against the German commandos along the African coast – an adventure I thought it best not to mention.'[13]

On the move again, the trio found themselves at a pre-officer cadet training unit at Wrotham, Kent. Here in the deep valleys they often saw Spitfires flown by keen-eyed pilots shooting down doodlebugs bound for London. Occasionally Croft and his pals watched as brave RAF airmen flew close enough to a deadly flying bomb in order to use the tip of the Spitfire's wing to nudge it off its course.

After a month the three men were posted on to the 164th Officer Cadet Training Unit in Barmouth, North Wales, where they lived in a small hotel by a bleak grey sea. Who could blame Croft for feeling like he was a rookie recruit again as he came face to face with an aggressive sergeant major from the Grenadier Guards?:

> This man's name was Copp and his favourite threat to us fearful cadets was 'I'll give you a wet shirt' – a threat he frequently carried out by the simple means of doubling us up and down with rifles at the slope. His other favourite comment spat out with malice was 'I'll have you on the 7.18' – which was the morning train to London.

Croft wrote to his father in Hollywood about the extremes of officer selection training. 'My father wrote back and was at a loss to understand how times had changed since his day when a couple of good recommendations from senior officers resulted in a subaltern's pip on the shoulder a few weeks later. Now we were trained to virtually Commando standard and watched all the way.' Fortunately Croft, Barry and Johnny managed to shed the aggressive Copp and instead found a cultured Welshman of a commanding officer named Jack Edwards, who was a 'brilliant leader' and 'the embarrassed owner of a George Medal'.

It was the kindly Edwards who allowed Croft two days' leave when he received a telegram from his brother Peter to inform him their father had died as a result of rheumatoid arthritis. Reginald Sharland's young widow Herta was left to handle the funeral arrangements and she informed her husband's sons that he had been buried at Forest Lawn. Their friend the film star Herbert Marshall had stood at a lectern and spoke eruditely about Reginald's life and career.

Croft's mood lightened, however, when he learned he was about to be promoted to the rank of lieutenant and he felt motivated enough to stage a concert with the platoon in North Wales. It was a good time for collecting memories of performance hilarities which would later serve him well during the creation of his television comedy hits.

In December 1944 Lieutenant Croft arrived at the station to catch, ironically, the 7.18 train to London. This time, in the full military dress uniform of an infantry officer in His Majesty's British Army, he could really wave goodbye to the bombastic brow-beating Sergeant Major Copp. When it came to a choice of which regiment to join, he plumped for the Warwicks but was assigned to the Dorset Regiment. This meant Croft would be part of the 105th Light Anti-Aircraft Regiment, Royal Artillery, which had been stationed in North Africa since 1942 as part of the British First Army. Croft's pals Johnny and Barry had also chosen the Warwicks but only Barry got his regiment of choice. Johnny Spittal joined the frontiersmen of the West African Rifles.

Lieutenant Croft's next move was to a 'battle school' at Attleborough, Thetford. Now he was sharpening up his military organisational skills in an area which was, ironically, not far from where he would find himself, more than twenty-five years later, filming *Dad's Army*. During the war Norwich Castle had miraculously survived the Luftwaffe's Baedeker raids, which had devastated the British cities listed in the famous tourism book. In June 1942 Norwich Cathedral had been seriously damaged, along with parts of the city centre and several streets of Victorian houses. The Baedeker Blitz was Hitler's retaliation against the RAF's massive bombing of the large German coastal city of Lübeck and other historic German cities.

In the spring of 1945 Lieutenant Croft found himself aboard the troopship SS *Empire Deed* sailing through the Mediterranean and the Suez Canal bound for India. His job was mostly to check how the men were coping with a trip which he claimed in his memoir was made 'much more bearable because there were women on board who were part of ENSA (the forces entertainment services)'. He passed the time learning to speak Urdu, playing poker, and celebrating the news that the Japanese were on the retreat. When the ship arrived in Bombay some weeks later, everyone discovered the war in Europe had finally come to an end. The Germans at last had surrendered. Morale among the men had been given a massive boost and yet Lieutenant Croft and his unit were told to remain at the Kalyan transit camp – a place he described as a 'fly-blown settlement' in a desert about 25 miles east of Bombay.

Croft tried not to complain as there were various civilised amenities on hand, including shops, a restaurant, a barber and a tailor. His memories of the characters and events in Kalyan went on to inspire the hit television comedy *It Ain't Half Hot Mum*, as he discovered there was no better situation to explore and expose the juxtaposition of comedy and tragedy. Croft discovered the beauty of turning the raw facts in front of him into powerful fiction. As the BBC producer John Lloyd CBE once said about Croft: 'All comedy is truthful – no matter how silly . . . it's trying to get out some universal truth.'

In Kalyan the young lieutenant received an order to jump on a train and travel across the dusty Indian plain to join the 2nd Battalion, Essex Regiment, at Ranchi. The regiment was part of the 29th Independent Brigade Group, which in turn was part of the 36th Division (Burma). Orders were then received and Croft's battalion was on the move again. This meant a trek with thirteen trucks across a thousand miles of the busy main route to Poona, which sits 100 miles south-east of Bombay. Never before had Croft seen such a cacophony of human and animal life, carts and carriages on their travels.

At the hill station of Poona, which was a British Army garrison, Croft and his unit set themselves up at Uruli camp. Once again sweating under canvas, every man lined up to be vaccinated against plague, yellow fever and beriberi disease. Croft wrote:

> Shortly after our arrival the unit was renamed 2nd British Division and I was made Liaison Officer to the battalion. I was given a motorcycle and told to become good at riding it as soon as possible, so I swanned around the countryside riding it on all available surfaces and falling off it a couple of times.
>
> It appeared I was quick on the uptake and I was made station staff officer, brigade entertainments officer (ENSA) and brigade intelligence officer, and promoted to Captain. I had only been commissioned a little more than seven months ago, and the Brigadier – a regular officer – pointed out he had been a Lieutenant for seventeen years.[14]

Croft's memories of his time in India continued to include perfect examples of the British military, with its strict ranking system and class snobbery. One day when he was producing a show, he wanted the audience seating to be arranged in a more egalitarian way. In 1945 he leaned towards socialism politically and was a huge fan of the Beveridge Report which advocated a National Health System and a welfare state. What a good idea then, thought Captain Croft, to place the officers in the third row from the front. Why not let the Tommies sit in the front row for a change?

What ensured was a near riot as a colonel kicked off about the idea and various sergeant majors were called in to reorganise the seating and put it back to having officers at the front: Croft recalled:

> It was an ugly scene. The colonel was incandescent. Sergeants and sergeant-majors stormed up and down shouting until order was restored, whereupon the pianist played like mad and the entertainment proceeded with a very lively and not very sympathetic audience.
>
> The next debacle occurred when the members of the ENSA cast discovered they were being entertained in the Sergeants' Mess instead of being able to hobnob with the officers. Apparently they felt insulted. Perhaps the girls had hoped to entrap some rich chinless wonder. There were one or two chinless wonders numbered among us, but I don't think they were rich . . .[15]

While the ENSA troupe was in Uruli under the watchful eye of Captain Croft, there came the news that a few other entertainers just along the road in Poona were planning to produce the 1943 play *While The Sun Shines* by Terence Rattigan. This three-act comedy by one of Britain's most popular writers was one Croft had been keen to introduce to his audiences at the camp.

The production is set during the war in a posh apartment at the Albany in Piccadilly and among the cast of characters are three men who are keen to marry the same woman. We see the wealthy Earl of Harpenden as an ordinary seaman who is engaged to the female lead. The laughter begins when two rivals in the form of an American airman and a Free French officer arrive to challenge Harpenden's claim on the girl. All this becomes even more farcical when an angry potential father-in-law and a former girlfriend of the Earl are dropped into the mix. It's classic Rattigan and was ideal in its appeal not only to the troops but to audiences back home in Britain. It had premiered at the Globe Theatre in 1943 and research reveals it enjoyed 1,154 successful performances, proving itself to be Rattigan's longest-running West End play. Its original cast included Douglas Jefferies, Hugh McDermott, Ronald Squire, Jane Baxter, Brenda Bruce OBE and Eugene Deckers. The reviews of this ever-popular play (still being produced in theatres in 2020) were glowing and in 1947 it was turned into a film directed by Anthony Asquith.

However, before the big screen production got under way, Captain Croft was greeted by 19-year-old Robin Nash, who was running what was known as the Combined Services Entertainment in Poona. Croft had no idea why Nash wasn't in the Army, but invited him to join in the fun at Uruli and soon discovered the young man had a gift for set building. *While The Sun Shines* was to have its Indian premiere at Uruli.

Their shared experience in India turned in a lifelong friendship between the two men and Croft's initial private query about Nash's status was soon explained: Nash suffered from a rare bone disorder which meant he was unfit for military service. Despite this, Nash went on to become Head of Variety at the BBC, and joined Croft more than once at auditions and on stage during their struggle for work just after the war. 'Robin fought many battles for me when he was at the BBC,' added the loyal Croft.

In Uruli in 1945, however, the applause for the Rattigan play was enthusiastic but it could hardly stamp out the prospect of the unit's next foray into the seriousness of war. Word at the time was that the loyal men of Croft's 2nd Battalion would soon join in the British invasion of Malaya and face fierce combat against the Japanese. The Japanese were known for their ferocious fighting spirit and Captain Croft worked diligently to figure out the best and most effective attack plans. He wrote:

> We did a certain amount of land training in which, as brigade intelligence officer, I stuck a lot of flags on maps and made china-graph lines where I thought the troops were dug in. The seaborne training was to come later.
>
> Unexpectedly, but to my intense delight, we heard on the radio the atom bomb had been dropped on Hiroshima. Let there be no mistake about our attitude to this event. We were facing another two years of most intense fighting.
>
> The Japs were a cruel and ruthless enemy whose war record was atrocious. The bombs made us wild with delight and immense relief. Now there was every chance that we would all survive this war.[16]

Within a day or two everything changed for the men at Uruli. Orders came through that they were to be posted to Singapore, and the bureaucratic headache of moving a complete brigade was handed to Captain Croft, who was then promoted acting major. Thanks to his organisational skills, the men successfully boarded the aircraft carrier HMS *Colossus* with their military vehicles and kit. The transportation was then taken over by the Royal Navy and Major Croft could relax a little during the journey, despite suffering from sunburn. His new job in Singapore was to take charge of 90,000 Japanese prisoners of war and, with the help of Japanese interpreters, the Royal Navy and a high-ranking Japanese officer called Colonel Naito, to find those suspected of war crimes.

Croft recalled how the Chinese in the area couldn't understand why the British Army were transporting Japanese prisoners in heavy trucks. Had not those same ruthless Japanese only a few months before the surrender made Australian soldiers crawl on their hands and knees for 80 miles along the road from the hills to the city?

Looking back on his time in Singapore, Croft admitted it was a tough call on many occasions when it came to decision-making and it was a case of taking it a day at a time. After the brigade headquarters was moved to what he described as a 'really luxurious house', it's no surprise Major Croft began to feel rewarded for his efforts. He even had air conditioning. Then, just as he got used to waking up refreshed and ready for the next day's decisions, he learned his boss had been sent home to be demobbed, and he was rapidly promoted to Deputy Assistant Adjutant and Quartermaster General (DAAQG) to the 4th Independent Brigade Group.

During these weeks in Singapore Croft's administrative skills were once again noted by his bosses and he was offered a post at division headquarters with the rank of Deputy Assistant Adjutant-General (DAAG), which in reality was a lieutenant colonelcy. If not this job, then he was offered one of the same rank sitting on the War Crimes Committee in Kuala Lumpur. But he didn't have to think for long, telling the brigadier who had made the offer of promotion that both positions were far beyond his capabilities. 'I wanted out of the army as quickly as possible and I thought that if I were to take on either of these posts, I would be bound to stay in at least another year,' he recalled.

In the event, fate had other plans in store for the young officer. He was needed at home to help his brother Peter cope with their mother's mental health problems. Croft admitted he had been alarmed for some time about her letters, with the scrawled capital letters and accusations which were marked signs of schizophrenia. He flew home on a small aircraft on a £ 195 ticket to Poole, Dorset, to see his mother and then followed orders to report to the War Office, where for some weeks, still in uniform, he worked at a civilian job assisting on a project about the Far East known then as 'Operation Madhouse'. The Chief of the General Staff was the notable war hero General Sir Alan Brooke KG, GCB, OM, GCVO, DSO, who met Croft only once . . . in the urinal! Croft joked: 'I had gone inadvertently in the wrong lavatory to spend a penny. To my alarm I was joined at the next Thomas Crapper piece of porcelain by the General (also nicknamed Colonel Shrapnel). Having fulfilled the purpose for which he came, he did up his flies and said, "Cor! That's better!"'[17]

The days were slow and Croft spent his time doing *The Times* crossword. While he waited to be demobbed, he made the most of every opportunity to get out and about in London to see agents and check out the latest news in theatre-land. On 17 January 1947 he received his demob suit, mackintosh, hat and shoes and was discharged with a letter from the adjutant-general's department thanking him for his invaluable services during the emergency: 'So much for four and a half years of my life! To be fair, however, and taking a longer view, nobody has profited more from their wartime service, except possibly the Krupp family, who owned munitions factories. Those years gave me *Dad's Army*, *It Ain't Half Hot Mum* and *'Allo 'Allo*, so I mustn't be ungrateful,' he wrote.

Lady Luck was smiling for the next few years as he made contacts and appeared in various plays in London, including at the Q Theatre – famed for its outlook and opportunities for playwrights to present new works to modern audiences. Various appearances on the stage followed, including a run at Butlins venues where the manager was often an 'ex-British Army major' and this went on to inspire Croft and Perry's hit show *Hi-de-Hi!* Despite the welcome regularity of work, Croft soon realised his life experiences were turning him into a writer.

In 1952 Croft married Ann Callender and his career moved towards production. By the early 1960s he was working for Tyne Tees television, until he landed a job in London at the BBC. When his wife Ann, then an agent representing the actor Jimmy Perry, introduced them to each other, it was a significant moment in entertainment history. Perry, whom Croft described as 'very much the actor-laddie', showed Croft his script called 'The Fighting Tigers: The Confessions of a Home Guard Sergeant'. And boom! Croft recalled:

> It was a welcome departure from the usual television comedy which was always set in a living room with a sofa, two chairs and the next-door neighbour popping in. I told Jimmy I fancied the general idea of his show and I got the BBC Head of Comedy Michael Mills to look at it.
>
> Michael too then saw the comedic advantages of a little seaside Home Guard unit without proper weapons, or even ammunition, preparing to take on the might of the German military machine. He suggested that, since Jimmy was not experienced in television, we should write a pilot episode together . . . and Jimmy readily agreed.[18]

Firstly they decided to bounce off the initial episode from cabinet minister Anthony Eden's famous speech of 14 May 1940 which appealed to people all over the land to help in the defence of the country. This powerful address (quoted at the start of this book) contained everything Perry and Croft needed to form a structure for the show, as well as its purpose, which fed into the motivations of the characters.

It was brilliant for absolute coherence, thus ensuring its validation as an instrument of entertainment success – it beautifully communicates the essentials of who, why, what, where, when and how. The magical ingredients were in the bowl and now they needed a cast to season the mix and cajole the recipe to life.

Evidence of the comedy duo's full understanding of the *Home Guard Training Manual* is evident in many episodes. The *Manual* forbids the misuse of power by those with rank and prohibits any sort of bullying or intimidation. It clearly states: 'The worst fault you can show is to give the impression that you regard your job as a splendid opportunity for bullying and ordering people about. We want no little Hitlers or Gestapo imitators in the Home Guard.'

In contrast, ARP Warden Hodges is the ultimate jobsworth everybody recognises and tries to avoid. His wartime role *is* to make heavy demands and threats against people who don't follow the blackout rules. The antagonism only adds to the comedy.

In *David Croft and Jimmy Perry: The Television Series*, the author Simon Morgan-Russell writes:

> Hodges makes a steady stream of mockery pointing to the platoon's follies and inabilities and challenges Mainwaring's authority at every turn. His nickname for Mainwaring ('Napoleon') attacks the Captain's diminutive size, his grand military aspirations and his dictatorial manner.
>
> Despite the fact that Hodges, the Vicar and the Verger (a trio often allied against the platoon) offer challenges to Mainwaring's authority, however, their threats are hardly as serious as those brought to bear by the regular army – largely because, of course, these individuals possess very little power over the Home Guard. Most of Hodges' mocking remarks have very little effect as they are mostly momentary. Hodges is often proven wrong or otherwise disgraced by the episode's events.
>
> He is quick to pour scorn on Mainwaring's abilities in the episode 'The Deadly Attachment', for example, but is put in his place when held hostage by the Germans and saved by Mainwaring's surrender. Then in 'The Test' we see Hodges' attempts to disgrace the platoon thwarted by Private Godfrey's success at the wicket during a cricket match.[19]

The verger and the vicar, who regularly complain about Mainwaring using the church hall office, find themselves at odds with the platoon as it strives hard to 'rightfully defend the public at large' and reach a compromise with fellow volunteers on the home front. The audience laughs at the song and dance of a way to go about it, only to realise fate takes a hand and no one expects the outcome. Tension coupled with the threat of a Nazi invasion makes *Dad's Army* comedy gold.

Initially, as producer and co-writer, David Croft had put forward the actor Jon Pertwee as the officer in the show, only to discover the actor was contracted to a project in America. Another actor (Thorley Walters) turned it down, and Perry then urged Croft to see a northern actor called Arthur Lowe, who happened to be appearing at the Theatre Royal, Windsor – in a role which, according to Croft, didn't do the talented Lowe any favours. Lowe was already famous for playing the character Arnold Swindley in the popular television soap *Coronation Street*.

Originally the BBC's Head of Comedy Michael Mills suggested John Le Mesurier should play the officer as he 'suffers so beautifully', and Croft logged the idea as he respected Mills' judgement as sound and decent, even though he believed Le Mesurier was often at his best playing languid, philosophical characters. Then came the idea that the actor John Laurie would be good to cast in the show as he was a Scotsman and perhaps in the character's civilian life he should run a fishing tackle shop. Then Croft considered the actor Jack Haig as Mr Jones who ran a butcher's shop, but Haig turned down the job because he had just been offered a role in a show called *Wacky Jackie*. (Haig went on to star in *'Allo, 'Allo* as Monsieur Roger Leclerc.) Croft said:

> If this all sounds like pure chaos, this is because it was. Casting is a very difficult craft, and each new character that is put in place affects the others enormously. Also, we were still very flexible about the team that we should assemble, the characters at this stage being very indefinite and woolly.
>
> I had known the actor Clive Dunn for many years and had written material for him in summer shows. He was now the fairly obvious choice for Jones. At the same time, he had been playing old men in several well-known shows. I thought on balance it would be best to avoid putting somebody in the part who was so well established in the mind of the public in a similar role . . .[20]

So before Dunn was offered the job, Croft had a look around and one day, following the recommendation of his wife Ann, he watched a young, dark-haired man on stage in a show. Croft thought at first he'd be worth auditioning. 'Oh, I'm just the electrician standing in for the actor who couldn't make it,' explained the young man, who wasn't interested at the time in being represented by Ann Croft's agency. Finally she signed him up, but after even more thinking it was decided he was too young to be turned into a 70-year-old man! 'The actor's name was David Jason,' added Croft. 'The role of Corporal Jones went to Clive Dunn, who then dithered about the idea of "playing another old man!" before finally accepting the role.'

While Croft was wrestling with the suggestion from the all-powerful Mills about casting Le Mesurier as the officer, Perry insisted and insisted vehemently that Arthur Lowe should play Captain Mainwaring. Some kind of miracle occurred when the debate was resolved. Lowe should be the 'pompous grammar school bank manager who had appointed himself the officer, while Le Mesurier should play the character of the ex-public school chief clerk of the bank, and sergeant. We can see here how Perry's own Home Guard and military experience of rank and flummery had begun to influence the casting.

***

Arthur Lowe, a well known gourmet and Second World War army veteran with solid theatrical experience of entertaining the troops, was invited to lunch by Croft and Perry. They were keen to chat to him, over mouthfuls of delicious courses and gulps of good wine, about the character of Captain Mainwaring. It took some effort and time, and reassurance about the show's potential as a winner, before Lowe agreed to take on Mainwaring.

The same couldn't be said at first for Le Mesurier, who wasn't keen on playing Sergeant Wilson until he spoke to his friend Clive Dunn over the telephone about it. 'Well, I suppose I wouldn't mind, as long as you're doing it . . . are you going to do it?' Le Mesurier wearily asked Dunn. Croft wrote: 'On dynamic exchanges like this, one's success hinges . . .'

The excellent actor James Beck, a naturally chirpy and cheeky man, was cast as the spiv Private Walker. Croft stepped in to secure the services of the excellent veteran actor and playwright Arnold Ridley to play Private Godfrey, the polite, retired gentlemen's tailor with a weak bladder who lived with his two sisters called Dolly and Cissie. The prospect of a bossy air raid warden called Hodges who attempted to usurp Captain Mainwaring at all costs went to the actor Bill Pertwee.

By the time 20-year-old Ian Lavender was cast as Private Pike – the character most like the young Jimmy Perry – the BBC's comedy chief Mills had decided he didn't like the title of the show and suggested it should be changed from *The Fighting Tigers* to *Dad's Army*.

Ironically enough, filming began on April Fool's Day 1968. The location manager and set designers discovered a suitable area with plenty of conifer woods at the Ministry of Defence's Stanford battle area near Thetford, Norfolk. The area was hired for a fiver a day.

To ensure *Dad's Army* was as lifelike as possible, the terrain at Stanford would prove ideal for all the explosions and wide-ranging adventures, involving various military antics and vehicles, which were written into each episode. There had been great progress and once Perry and Croft had written six episodes, and worked out a way of co-writing each one, they were thrilled. The show was all set to go – until disaster struck when the Controller of Programmes, Paul Fox, expressed 'grave concerns' about a comedy that mocked 'Britain's Finest Hour'.

Suddenly the series was in jeopardy as it was discussed intently at various high-level meetings by BBC men with furrowed brows and posh accents. There was a lot of hand-wringing until Bill Cotton, a key supporter of the show, suggested that each episode tapped into the government's latest campaign about 'buying British goods'. Fox, now beaten down by the arguments in favour of proceeding with *Dad's Army*, did a U-turn on condition that a prologue was included at the start of the show outlining Britain's triumph over adversity during the war, and encouraging the audience to 'Back Britain and Buy British'. Once this arrangement between the BBC and the show's creators was agreed, once again *Dad's Army* was ready to march forward. But were the cast on message?

Croft recalled:

> Jimmy and I were filled with a high level of excitement, but our enthusiasm didn't last long. Most of the actors were mumbling their lines as if they didn't want to commit themselves. Jimmy and I huddled in a corner at coffee time. 'I think we've got a right stroppy lot here,' said Jim. I tried to reassure him that my mother used to rehearse in this fashion so as not to reveal her performance to the rest of the cast until the actual first night, when she would produce the magic. Jim didn't believe me and neither did I . . .[21]

Flurries of snow and a drizzle of rain greeted the cast and crew who gathered together in Thetford on the first day of filming. Some of the actors didn't want to get out of Croft's ancient 1954 Rolls-Royce Silver Wraith. For almost an hour Lowe, Dunn, Le Mesurier, Beck and Croft huddled on the back seats, chatting inside the steamed-up windows. The tension of what the day might bring proved too much for the apprehensive Croft, who finally opened the door and got out of the car. He wanted to make a start. Insisting that the weather was brightening up, he called to his assistant Harold Snoad to start rigging up the lights.

Reluctantly the cast joined him and moaned about the snow. Croft mischievously observed in his memoir how over the years filming could not take place until Lowe 'had been' (as in, had emptied his bowels). Lowe enjoyed his food and while staying at the hotel he would eat a huge fried breakfast each morning and then Perry waited half an hour for him every morning while the actor was in the loo.

Perry acted as Lowe's chauffeur with a separate car, which followed the rest of the actors who had gone on ahead in a minibus. Lowe's lavatorial needs weren't the only dilemma Croft and Perry faced during the making of the show as he often forgot his lines or decided to change them 'because they might sound better'. This behaviour infuriated other members of the cast, particularly Le Mesurier, who pleaded with Croft to ensure Lowe knew his part and exactly what the character would say. Lowe was, according to Croft, quite unlike the other actors, who took their scripts home to prep up for the next day's filming. He said: 'Arthur would never take his script with him after rehearsals. He would place it in a drawer that he would close with great finality. Someone once asked him if he wasn't going to take it with him. "Oh no," he said. "I don't want that sort of thing – not in my own home!"' A possible solution, thought Croft, would be to send Lowe two copies with a note suggesting he keep one under his pillow so he might absorb his lines via the feathers, and the other to bring to rehearsals. The actor's reaction to this parcel came via Perry to Croft: 'All Arthur said about that was . . . "David seems to be very grotty these days."'[22]

When it came to punctuality among the cast, Le Mesurier took the gold star. He is remembered as being always ready in his uniform and always, always ahead of the game when it came to learning his lines. If he ever did forget, he would reveal proof of his photographic memory with a 'don't tell me, don't tell me . . . it's the second paragraph from the top of the page'. Le Mesurier was popular among the crew and always had time to chat to the props, electrical and carpentry staff. The make-up and wardrobe girls adored him and he was always quick with the compliments.

Croft wasn't so keen on the charming actor and described Le Mesurier as a 'behaviourist' – someone who was good at only one type of character and that was playing, er, John Le Mesurier. Was he envious of the languid Le Mesurier perhaps? He certainly wondered how the actor survived his days working in repertory theatre. Perhaps he had a lot of influential friends in the business and could afford to choose how he worked and when he worked? His laissez-faire attitude irritated Croft even more when it came to close of play each day. According to the *Dad's Army* co-creator, the louche Le Mesurier removed his webbing uniform belt, let it slide to the dirty floor and dropped the rifle, which potentially could have been damaged each time. It was always a nightmare for the properties crew who had to check that small stones had not gone down the barrel in case it was ever loaded with blanks to be fired for a scene.

Clive 'Permission to Speak Sir!' Dunn, however, got on famously with Croft and was described as 'genuinely creative' in rehearsal and brilliant at ad-libbing and amusing everyone with his own stories of his life in the real army.

The great Shakespearian and Scottish actor John Paton Laurie famously took the young Ian Lavender (Pike) under his wing and they often sat doing crossword puzzles together, with John chiding Lavender if he didn't know the answers by the end of coffee time. Laurie was always rather dismissive of Croft and Perry and once called them 'nearly damned illiterate'. He always had some comment to make about his contribution to the show, and when it was a just a few minutes in an episode he'd threaten to 'phone his appearance over'!

For the wonderful actor Arnold Ridley, who was well into his 70s at the time of casting, Croft had nothing but admiration and described him fondly as a 'dear old love':

> Arnold had a most distinguished career in the business and had written *Ghost Train* and many other plays. He'd also directed plays and films and worked in theatre and radio. My primary concern about him joining *Dad's Army* was all the running about he'd have to do.
>
> He said if I was game to give him the part, he was game to try. We got a lot of warm laughs when the others members of the platoon had to help him get aboard Jones's van.
>
> During filming he was often seen walking up and down flapping his arms like a penguin while muttering 'Tell them to get on with it!'

The 'spiv' in the show, Private Walker, gave the actor (Stanley) James Carroll Beck (1929–1973) a steady income. Professional through and through, even when he was drinking heavily, he never let anyone down. He was also never seen without a cigarette on the go. Beck is fondly remembered as a cultured man who was a good sculptor and artist with a gift for impersonations. Those actors he liked to emulate were Wilfred Hyde-White and Wilfred Lawson – two serious drinkers whose adventures were recounted often by the ebullient actor.

*Dad's Army's* resident 'spiv' was in reality born in North London and experienced a tough childhood, leaving home aged just 17. He was an art school graduate before he did his National Service, in which, ironically, he served as an army PE instructor. He had turned to the stage by 1960 and began a busy career appearing in *Dr Finlay's Casebook*, and as Shylock in *The Merchant of Venice* in 1963. Five years later he worked with Peter Cushing in the BBC's *Sherlock Holmes* and then along came *Dad's Army* – and his fame soared.

Croft knew Beck's love life was complicated and that he couldn't choose between his wife (Kay Bullus) and his mistress; it was to his regret that he didn't realise just how much alcohol Beck was imbibing. When the cast went to the pub Beck was often known to down a double before he collected the round of drinks to take to the table for his companions. Beck died sadly of pancreatitis in 1973 aged just 44.

But during the heady days of filming there was always banter and compromise arising from such a healthy gathering of diverse personalities. The communication between the actors Frank Williams (the vicar) and Edward 'Teddy' Sinclair (the verger) was also remarkably astute and their friendship off the set helped their scenes buzz with potential. Croft recalled:

> Teddy was the most worrying driver I ever travelled with. He would hold long conversations with me if I sat beside him, only rarely looking where he was going. I thought I would get over this problem by sitting in the back seat, whereupon Teddy insisted on turning right round to talk to me. But he was incomparable playing the verger and was singled out by the writer Alan Bennett for giving a memorable performance of the part.[23]

While Croft and Perry had enormous influence over the show and its ultimate design, there came an occasion when they were over-ruled about the back scenes of the end credits. Croft had won the day with his cast marching into battle as their names appeared beneath them but his initial goal to include black and white scenes of Nazi troops, rows of tanks, German guns and bombers and refugees was quashed by BBC boss Paul Fox. Croft wrote:

> I wanted all this to illustrate the enormity of the task the Home Guard were undertaking and the bravery of our little squad in preparing to meet the Nazi hordes. I was delighted with the result. But Paul had very strong objections to all this and thought it unwise to include the explosion of a tank and a stream of refugees in the sequence.

Croft went on to say that Fox was gracious enough to agree he had a point. Tom Sloan didn't want Fox to be unhappy so they shot the whole end credit sequence again, this time presenting a different, more gentle version. Meantime Michael Mills had stepped in to support the original idea, and the prospect of massaging departmental rivalries energised him to argue that 'Fox had misunderstood the show's message'. On 23 May 1968 his report, now in the BBC archives, said:

> The whole object of this comedy series is to contrast the pathetic, comic but valorous nature of the Home Guard, who believed at the time that this

[the Nazi hordes] was what they were up against. It seems to me to be not only right but essential that this fact is brought home to viewers – and it is, surely, our justification for doing a comedy programme on this subject.

While this argument may seem a little wayward of Perry and Croft's intention when it came to the idea of 'Nazi hordes', the episodes in which the platoon meet any Germans are very few. The best known is the episode called 'The Deadly Attachment', in which Mainwaring and his men are forced to guard a captured German submarine crew while they await an armed escort.

This is Captain Mainwaring at his best when he uses the opportunity to stress the difference between British troops and German 'automatons' and so comedy prevails over the rigidity of orders for fish and chips. Then we see the famous 'Don't tell him, Pike!' scene when the German commander (Philip Madoc) tells the platoon he will put their names on a list so they are taken in to account when the Nazis invade Britain. And the ensuing comic tension of the grenade down Jones's trousers is genius. What this episode with its triumphant ending does prove, in pure Croft and Perry style, is how the Home Guard had conquered the enemy more by luck than military management.

In the episode 'The Battle of Godfrey's Cottage' we witness another fine example of Captain Mainwaring at the ready, despite Sergeant Wilson's regular attempts to deflate his opinions. When Mainwaring is led to believe the invasion has started, he discovers that apart from himself, Frazer and Jones, the rest of the platoon are out at the cinema, and crossly comments: 'We've waited six months for this and now that Hitler's at our throats my platoon's at the pictures.'

We watch him, Jones and Frazer arrive at Godfrey's cottage and we are totally behind his valiant efforts to ensure everything turns out well when it comes to the British efforts on the war front:

> M: If we can hold out long enough there, it will give our regular troops time to regroup before they counter attack, y'see. Mind you, it will probably be the end of us. But we're ready for that, aren't we men!
> Men: 'Course (looking rather doubtful)
> M: Good show!

### *Dad's Army* on the stage
BY 1975 there had been calls by impresario Duncan Weldon for a stage production of *Dad's Army*. Both Croft and Perry were keen to write the script as they did not want a 're-hash' of the television episodes. Eventually they came up with the idea to write a series of sketches

and memories of the show in the form of a musical. It became *Dad's Army: A Nostalgic Music and Laughter Show of Britain's Finest Hour*. Josie Stewart, who had worked on *The Mikado* and *Iolanthe* for television, was chosen to work with Croft and Perry as musical associate.

Most of the cast agreed to be part of it all apart from John Laurie, who decided he wasn't fit enough to cope with a punishing schedule of eight shows a week in a theatre, so a substitute was found in the shape of actor Hamish Roughead. The actor John Bardon appeared as Private Walker, while Clive Dunn, who suffered stage fright, shared his role of Corporal Jones with the actor Jack Haig, who had actually been Croft's original first choice for the television series.

The premiere was at the Forum Theatre, Billingham, County Durham, and local critics praised the obvious affection between the cast and audience. A few revisions followed, then on 4 October it transferred to London's West End, where on stage at the Shaftesbury Theatre the audience enjoyed Arthur Lowe and Chesney Allen singing the Flanagan and Allen song, 'Home Town'.

This two-act show, produced by Roger Redfarn, went on tour across the UK after two bomb scares in London, and the final curtain came down on 4 September 1976. Since then, however, it has been revived as a musical and hit the stage again in 2004, 2005 and 2007.

Croft recalled:

> Rehearsals were a fascinating experience. The show opened like the television series with the song 'Who do you think you are kidding, Mr Hitler?' We had John Le Mesurier singing 'A nightingale sang in Berkeley Square'. He was reluctant to do this, but once we had settled him in a key that was very close to his speaking voice, he took to it as if he had been doing it all his life. In the event, his performance of the song was a notable experience. So too was Arnold Ridley's melodic performance of 'Lords of the Air', which was most moving, though for me the entertainment lay in watching Ed Coleman, the musical director, trying to keep pace with him.

It was disappointing when the no-nonsense impresario Bernard Delfont stepped in and removed some of the lines assigned to Corporal Jones (Clive Dunn), who had 'fallen apart through nerves'. The blue pencil was drawn through a scene where Dunn would sing about General Gordon being killed at Khartoum.

Dunn wasn't the only one to suffer ill-health during the show, as suddenly Croft had a heart attack. He attributed this life-threatening experience to the extreme difficulty he'd had in teaching Le Mesurier how to cross the stage on the same foot as the rest of the cast during

'Home Town'. He recuperated at the Royal Free Hospital. Everyone who knew Croft said it was often hard to tell if he was joking.

*Dad's Army* the musical was a huge success during the school holiday season and the decision was made to take the show on the road. Every two weeks consecutively from 10 April to 4 September 1976 it played to sell-out audiences in Manchester, Nottingham, Bradford, Birmingham, Bournemouth, Blackpool, Newcastle, Richmond-upon-Thames, Brighton and Bath.

When Croft died in 2011 he was described in one obituary as an extinct breed in British television: a comedy producer and writer who did not need a marketing survey to tell him what would make audiences laugh. He knew that if he found something was funny, it was a dead cert others would laugh too and he proved this often, along with Perry (and Jeremy Lloyd), with so many television hits including *It Ain't Half Hot Mum, Are You Being Served?, 'Allo 'Allo, Hi-de-Hi!* and *You Rang M'Lord!*

Croft was proud he had never had to 'do a hack' job on an existing series he had not created. This sort of work was alien to him. He once said: 'I write ordinary, non-controversial comedy which gives families a good laugh.'

# ARNOLD RIDLEY OBE

*To recount events, I would have to relive them, I am too afraid.*

WHILE both Croft and Perry wrote lively and famous observational anecdotes about their wartime experiences, the *Dad's Army* star who remained mostly silent about his own memories right up until his death in 1984 was hero, poet, actor and playwright Arnold Ridley. He served in both world wars, and it is clear from his son Nicolas's early memories of his father that the First World War was rarely, if ever, mentioned in the family home. But recollections of Ridley's time as a major in the army during the Second World War are even scarcer. As a boy, Nicolas learned not to disturb his father when he was sleeping as there was always the chance the veteran soldier, unconsciously suffering another nightmare of the trenches, would wake and grasp his young son by the throat.

And yet, from just a few rare conversations recalled by Nicolas in his book *Godfrey's Ghost*, published in 2007, we can begin to realise just why the *Dad's Army* star was determined to consign his trauma to the past and its complicit darkness. Ridley had undoubtedly suffered complete and enduring horror in his youth. He would suffer with post-traumatic stress disorder for the rest of his long life. In a fuller picture, provided in 2010 by the military historian Richard van Emden, who worked with Nicolas during his research into Ridley's war, there is dramatic proof of why the star had a dread, a terror even, of what lurked in his memory. Detailed examination of official military records of the time has proved vital as Arnold Ridley's own unpublished memoir, known in the family as 'The Book', did not include official reports of the experiences that would haunt him until his death aged 88.

The Book, recalls Nicolas, was penned only when his father's hand, still feeble from an ancient and horrific war wound, could stop shaking. And Ridley's rare utterances about a 'sickening hell' were only prompted after great care was taken by his son not to ask too much at once. This cautious reaction to the subject of discussing the wars with his father was understandable. The sensitive Nicolas realised quickly how the First World War had left Lance Corporal Ridley of the Somerset Light Infantry with nightmares full of screaming men, brutal medical examinations, a terrible fear of imminent death and the unholy chanting of an aggressive sergeant major. The trauma would only ease off when he woke to face each new day.

Back in 1915 Ridley was trained to kill by a vicious sergeant major, whose particular rhymes remained stuck in the heads of young recruits like a loud and debilitating ear-worm:

> One-two-three-four
> Step-on-his-jaw
> Just-to-make-sure.
> Next![1]

On and on went the words until the soldiers were brainwashed with them. The images conjured up by this gruesome chant were firmly planted in Ridley's subconscious.

William Arnold Ridley was born in Bath, Somerset, in 1896. He was the son of William Robert Ridley, a sports-mad gym instructor who also ran a boot and shoe shop. His mother Rosa (née Morrish) encouraged her son's academic and sporting enthusiasms (cricket and rugby were his favourites) and the bright young Ridley left Bath City Secondary School and after some deliberation by his parents about his future career they decided their son should become a school teacher. Ironically at the age of seventeen Ridley who 'did not shine academically' was offered a post as a student teacher at Bath's East Twerton School. It was here and in spite of his lack of interest in scholarship he obviously made an impression as the headmaster supported an application to the local Board of Education for Ridley to obtain a free tuition in the Education Department at the prestigious University of Bristol.

It was during this time Ridley fell in love with the theatre. Records reveal he appeared as Shakespeare's Prince of Denmark in a university drama production of *Hamlet*, which shows not only that he had a remarkable memory, which enabled him to deliver lengthy speeches, but also the talent to carry such a legendary play. His first steps on a professional stage were taken at the Theatre Royal, Bristol, in a production of *Prunella* just before the outbreak of the First World War in 1914. He recalled playing a 'tiny part in Laurence Housman and Harley Granville Barker's play *Prunella* using the name of "John Robinson" to disguise my non-scholastic and teacher training activities from university authorities'.

Ridley's unpublished 'Book' includes mention, too, of his triumph as Hamlet of the tortured soul. He wrote:

> In one scene I had to fall down a flight of stairs backwards clothed in a suit of armour – a procedure far more difficult and bruising than appeared in the script! But presumably this brought me to close notice, to such an extent that I was asked if I would care to accept a part-time professional engagement at a pound a week when cast. I accepted and in consequence of this made my first professional stage appearance.

The lively Ridley then collaborated on his first play with a good friend, a Welsh poet named Idris Jenkins. 'I had always shown a marked individuality in my school essays which had earned me nothing but censure. But Idris opened up a new and exciting world for me . . . The most important lesson I learned from him was that the arts were well within the reach of ordinary people,' recalled Ridley. By the time the play had a date for production the university arts calendar had been cancelled, as it was 1915 and the war was about to write off and thwart many fledgling theatrical careers.[2]

However, as a young man Ridley's personality was far from that of the mild-mannered and bumbling Private Charles Godfrey he went on to play in *Dad's Army*. Indeed it was an act of aggression that propelled him to leave behind his civilian life and join the British Army. He revealed:

> In July 1914 while on teaching practice at a Bristol elementary school, I succeeded in imperilling my scholastic career. A particularly irritating headmaster so aroused my hot temper by doubting my word of honour and wagging a finger under my nose that I seized him by the scruff of his neck and the seat of his trousers and pitched him out of the open window into his own playground which fortunately was heavily grassed. Although I reported myself immediately to my university tutor, who was sympathetic as to the provocation, I hate to think what might have resulted had not the declaration of war thrown life in general into the melting pot.[3]

Decades later, as a father he often made it clear to his son Nicolas how his word was 'never to be doubted', as to question it was to risk 'defenestration'!

***

When the clock struck midnight on 4 August 1914 18-year-old Ridley joined the 'cheering young men of Bath' who poured onto the streets to welcome the declaration that Britain was at war with Germany. Poignantly and succinctly, in his acute and learned way, he wrote: 'Youth regarded war as a glorious adventure and I don't suppose many of them realised that they were heralding their own deaths. The streets were full of people. Any man in service uniform was borne shoulder high. Everybody had gone mad, myself included.'[4]

When the sun came up the following morning, he joined six friends and ran to the recruiting office. He planned to join the Royal Marines and then move to the 4th Battalion, Somerset Light Infantry, which was a territorial battalion. All of his friends passed the medical that day but Ridley was rejected on medical grounds for a broken toe which had been 'badly set' after an injury during a rugby match. Irony seeped into his tone when he explained: 'My friends were all sent on garrison duty to relieve regular troops in India with the 4th Battalion and remained there until 1919 without ever hearing a shot fired in battle. By the autumn of 1916, I – as the 1914 reject – had been over the top twice in six months and wounded three times.' He went on:

> By the summer of 1915 everyone – myself included – was not so enthusiastic about the war. Also the physical perfection required of would-be infantrymen was very much a thing of the past. On offering myself again for enlistment on 8 December 1915 I was received into the Somerset Light Infantry (13th Foot), number 20481, and a few days later despatched to Taunton to be fitted out.
>
> This was the first time I had been away from home but I soon got used to the new life and it seemed good news indeed when my name appeared among those to be drafted to the regiment's reserve battalion stationed at Crownhill village on the outskirts of Plymouth.[5]

It is easy to picture Ridley as one of the 'merry party' weighed down with kit bags and other military paraphernalia arriving near Crownhill in the teeming rain so familiar to the residents of South Devon. At the station they received orders to march the 3 miles to their destination along a damp road that stretched before them. Crownhill itself was no stranger to troops. The village had an ancient link with military endeavours, and its original name was ironically 'Knackersknowle'. One of the series of forts that were the brainchild of Prime Minister Lord Palmerston had been constructed there in 1860 upon a hill, its purpose to provide a dominant lookout position across a large expanse of countryside. Lord Palmerston believed the dockyard at Devonport would need to be defended against any invasion by French agitators. As the years passed and the threat of foreign invasion evaporated, the Crownhill fort became known as a Palmerston folly. Today it is a popular tourist attraction.

However, when an exhausted Ridley and his fellow raw recruits of the Somerset Light Infantry reserve arrived there in January 1916 it was easy to recognise the place as a garrison. The sight of the Plumer Barracks nearby (now demolished) and soldiers training hard were unmistakable. All recruits at Crownhill were told to learn every military skill they could so that when they got to France they could simply do their duty and 'kill the Boche' for King and Country! A strident attitude of 'the reason not the need' was very much favoured by the British Army at the time.

After their long march, the new recruits took the heavy kit bags from their aching shoulders and lined up in the driving rain facing the battalion headquarters. They waited half an hour for the regimental sergeant major to give them their orders. When they saw his figure appear on an upper balcony, shielded comfortably from the downpour, Ridley felt that this man enjoyed a sense of power standing there above them all as he gave them a vile 'welcome' to the 3rd Battalion.

Years later, Ridley recalled with a shudder:

That day we were cursed at length by this man both collectively and individually. He ended on a cheering note which I still remember clearly after sixty years. 'Don't none of you think you're going to see your homes and mothers and dads no more 'cause you 'aint. We sent out a draft to our 1st Battalion at Wipers [Ypres] three weeks ago and where are they now? I'll tell yer – they're all bleeding well dead! And that's where you buggers will be in a couple of months time – all bleeding well dead!

As a first class warrant officer, he must have been a few years older than me so I presume Regimental Sergeant Major Chambers is now himself dead. If not, and he reads this, I'd like him to know that I wish him every possible evil!

Back then I thought I was doing my duty for my country. I didn't know I was going to be treated like a convict. Did it make better soldiers of the callow youths we were then? I doubt it.[6]

A gentler and much simpler moment was once relayed in Ridley's later life and stood in contrast to the violent memory of the sadistic RSM Chambers. Nicolas wrote: 'One evening and feeling wretchedly homesick, my father climbed to a high point above the village of Crownhill and stood there looking in what he knew must be the direction of Bath. He waited while the light faded and stayed there most of the night. A true vigil. An attempt to anchor himself to the reality of his family and home in preparation for the horrors that would soon be tearing away at everything he had ever known. It was, he told me, the saddest point in his life.'[7]

The young Arnold Ridley's dark prophecy of what was to come was at least lit by a tiny chink of light, and he was among the many who embraced comforting memories of their lives in peacetime as a survival tactic. Many memoirs and existing letters sent home by front-line soldiers show evidence of this emotional tactic.

Within days of his contemplative vigil on the hill, orders arrived for Ridley (now promoted to Lance Corporal) that declared 'it was now his chance to have a crack at the Boche'. He arrived in Arras in March 1916, having removed a badge awarded to him for excellent marksmanship because he did not want to be made a sniper. He explained: 'I didn't go to France to murder people.' (A statement that would have made his *Dad's Army* character Private Godfrey, a non-gun carrying Red Cross stretcher-bearer, most proud).

Just a couple of weeks later, facing the hell of the trenches, he suffered a shrapnel wound to his back and was carried off to a hospital in Étaples for treatment. It wasn't long before the enemy got him again – this time he was wounded in the thigh and was sent back to England to recuperate.

As the end of May approached, Ridley was passed 'fit' for duty and he rejoined his regiment at Devonport, near Plymouth. A few days later he was depressed to discover so many sad people there, trying to cope with the death toll, fears and heartache brought on by war. He'd been out for a walk in the town when he learned of the 6,094 men of the Royal Navy who had been killed during the battle of Jutland in the treacherous seas close to Denmark on 31 May/1 June that year. Many of the ships sunk in the battle had been commissioned and built at Devonport. In total, 151 British ships went into action against 99 German navy vessels, including deadly submarines. The British casualties also included 674 men wounded and 177 captured. British navy ships totalling 113,300 tons were destroyed. The German navy suffered 2,551 men killed and 507 injured. More than 62,000 tons of German shipping sank to the bottom of the sea.

Ridley wrote: 'That day on my walk I noticed the street was full of women – some hysterical, some crying quietly and others grey faced with staring unseeing eyes and leading small children by the hand. They had no illusions, these women – they knew only too well that, when large ships were sunk in battle in the North Sea, there could be but few survivors.'[8]

With his flesh wound now healed, Ridley found himself seconded as batman to the Cambridge-educated Lieutenant Edward Crozier MacBryan of the Somerset Light Infantry, who was awaiting orders to be sent back to France. A keen footballer, MacBryan had been sent home to recover from a serious wound he suffered at Ypres in May 1915. Tragically, the 21-year-old MacBryan, from the pretty village of Box, near Bath, was killed on 1 July, the first day of the battle of the Somme. Ridley had been due to join him a week later. Instead, MacBryan's death resulted in Ridley being sent to the trenches near Arras, where he spent the rest of July.

On 18 August the nervous men of the 14th (Light) Division, together with the 6th Battalion Somerset Light Infantry, were preparing to go over the top in a bid to capture Delville Wood. Lance Corporal Ridley was among them. By this time most troops attempting to take the area they had nicknamed 'Devil's Wood' knew they were stuck in a psychological no man's land – surviving an attack wasn't much to be jubilant about as it was regarded as only a brief delay to the actual day, hour, minute and second that their own deaths came calling. Ridley described this feeling of limbo as a 'great black cloud on top of one the whole time', and explained how there seemed to be no future:

> One lost one's sensitivity. You lived like a worm and your horizon was very limited to 'shall I get back in time for the parcel to come? Shall I ever get back to eat that cake that I know mother has sent me?' You certainly lived one day at a time, I didn't dare think of tomorrow . . . it was general abject misery. Your imagination became dulled. In the end you just became a thing.[9]

Within a few weeks he was on the move again. This time he would be 40 miles further down the line at the Somme. Not long after the sun rose on the morning of 16 September 1916 Ridley and the 6th Battalion Somerset Light Infantry were ready and waiting in trenches east of the village of Flers. With their bayonets fixed, and fear-fuelled adrenalin at a peculiar peak, their mission was to take a German stronghold just 200 yards distant. Ridley was among the men making their first attack in the battle of the Somme – a horror that had already been raging for two-and-a-half months.

Military historian Richard van Emden writes: 'The men had gone over the top the previous month at Delville Wood, Devil's Wood to the rank and file, such was its infamous reputation. There, they suffered nearly 50 per cent casualties, leaving only a lucky rump of the original battalion. Lance Corporal Ridley was not one of those 'originals' but he had gone into the action and was one of those fortunate enough to have come out unscathed.[10]

However, after four weeks Ridley and his battalion were back in a trench just a couple of yards from where they had sat and waited to go over the top before. This time it would be different, as 15 September marked a new phase of the battle, with the Somersets acting as key back-up to the 14th (Light) Division as it fought to break the dominant German defensive line just in front of Flers village.

It was an historic moment, as for the first time ever tanks would be let loose on the enemy. While they were still unreliable and hard to handle, their sturdy and domineering arrival stunned the Germans and helped the Allies win back Flers.

Van Emden wrote: 'Flers, a small, insignificant village, had fallen and it became a household name to every Briton, for one tank was reported being seen to drive right up the main street with cheering soldiers close behind. The newspapers loved it and praised the tank and Tommy who had so successfully given the Germans a bloody nose.'[11]

Ridley recalled the day: 'We in the ranks had never heard of tanks. We were told that there was some sort of secret weapon and then we saw this thing go up the right hand corner of Delville Wood. I saw this strange and cumbersome machine emerge from the shattered shrubbery and proceed slowly down the slope towards Flers.'[12]

But there was little time to celebrate as on the evening of 15 September the 6th Battalion, Somerset Light Infantry, marched towards the east of Flers and just south of the village of Gueudecourt. By 4am the men, sick from exhaustion and hunger, finally arrived on the front line. Immediately Lance Corporal Ridley was chosen to be a sentry, tasked with looking out for any stray enemy. He once said:

> If you've ever tried to keep awake when you haven't had any sleep for days, it's not a question of allowing yourself to go to sleep. I can remember lying in a sunken road behind Gueudecourt. The trenches were full of water and I can remember getting out of the trench and lying on the parapet with the bullets flying around because sleep was such a necessity and death only meant sleep.[13]

Hunger among all soldiers of the First World War was rife. Fresh water too was scarce. British, German, Canadian, French and American soldiers starved most of the time, despite the fact that scientists had determined the number of calories needed each day to keep a soldier healthy during a long campaign. What British men were entitled to according to the *Field Service Pocket Book* seldom applied and instead of the regulation 4,500 calories a day diet to help fuel intense physical work, they often received less than two-thirds of this amount. So the men grew thinner and weaker every day, huddled in lice-ridden holes surrounded by rats that ironically were grown fat from the gore of rotting corpses. Only if these troops were lucky would a swig of rum come their way, or a drop of wine, or a tiny square of cheese to help stave off the hunger pangs. Spirits were beyond being lifted.

So much then for Napoleon's famous remark: 'C'est la soupe qui fait le soldat' – loosely translated as 'An army marches on its stomach'. Most men in the First World War had little opportunity to partake in anything resembling a mealtime with one another. There was nothing so humane on offer to calm souls shattered so horrifically by the daily barrage of misery. Men went without and yet soldiered on in a coma of malnourishment. In a bid to keep up morale, a swig of rum was offered to the British by the captain and bad coffee was at times available. The French were given a quarter of a litre of wine every day.

Salty bully beef and biscuits made men thirsty and yet they couldn't drink water anywhere near the front line as it was contaminated by rotting corpses. Such horrors, of course, resulted in serious health issues, such as chronic heartburn, diarrhoea, swollen lymph glands and trench teeth, which resulted in grey, dying gums that made eating painful. Many men suffered from nervous exhaustion, which resulted in fatigue, headaches and emotional disturbance. Some endured poor kidney function, also known as nephritis, owing to the appalling diet, but still battled on. If they were lucky, and the problem was diagnosed in time, they were sent back to England for treatment, but more often than not their vital organs had been irreparably damaged.

For Ridley and his battalion there was often only iron rations to nibble on and there was little water available to them. As the hunger pangs gnawed away at any sense of morale, they waited with dread for their commanding officer, Lieutenant Colonel Thomas Ritchie, to order them 'over the top' into no man's land, straight into the German guns.

On 16 September 1916, at 4.30am, Lieutenant Colonel Ritchie received orders to send his men running towards the German support trenches at 9.25am – in full daylight. It would be a blind challenge as the usual procedure of checking of the terrain ahead had not been carried out. There had been no time to learn the ground and plan the best way forward. It was, according to historian van Emden, 'a costly mistake' as the Somersets, setting off in two waves, were left to stumble and scatter during the attack across a lumpy swamp littered with corpses. They certainly didn't know about an unfinished enemy trench in front of them, as it did not feature on Ritchie's map. His plan instructed the men to capture a German trench and then, while a few of the Somersets waited inside it as 'bombers' and 'bayoneters', the rest of the company were to run ahead to storm any support dug-out inhabited by Germans. The job of the 'bomber' was to throw grenades into trenches and dug-outs and the 'bayoneters' would be sure to kill any of the enemy who came out at them. The whole process would be then assisted by a six-strong back-up group.

As the artillery opened a barrage to provide cover, Lance Corporal Ridley and the battalion began their advance. Ridley recalled:

> We were told that there was a pocket of resistance left over and that two advances had left this pocket and we were told that we would attack. We would get a five minute barrage, which we got, but Jerry and the German machine guns were firing, saying 'We know you are coming over, come on, where are you?' Although the plans had gone wrong, the whistles blew and we went over the top just the same. I was a bomber and we got down in the first trench.

But this 'first trench' was not the target trench but the newly discovered unfinished one, and it was occupied by defensive Germans who let the bullets fly at the Somerset Light Infantrymen.

In a supremely rare moment of looking back at his war, the *Dad's Army* star recalled:

> I went round one of traverses, as far as I remember, and somebody hit me on the head with a rifle butt. I was wearing a tin hat, fortunately, but it didn't do me much good. A chap came at me with a bayonet, aiming for a very critical part naturally and I managed to push it away, so I got a bayonet wound in the groin.
>
> After that I was still very dizzy, from this blow on the head presumably. I remember wrestling with another German and the next thing I saw, it appeared to me that my left hand had gone. After, that I was unconscious.[14]

The blade which went into Ridley's hand had sliced through the tendons in his fingers. The damage was so great that his fingers were rendered fairly useless for the rest of his life. The sight of so much blood sent him into shock.

During the attack on this trench six German soldiers were taken prisoner and a hundred were reported to have scarpered. Confusion reigned, however, as the Somersets, believing they were in the correct trench, dug themselves in and didn't realise they were meant to have advanced even further.

Other companies were sent forward to help but were knocked back by machine-gun fire coming from Gueudecourt and 'Gird Trench'. The situation was atrocious and ill-conceived, and yet Lieutenant

Colonel Ritchie received orders that the men were to attack again at 6.55pm – this time, though, with the assistance of two companies of the 6th Battalion, King's Own Yorkshire Light Infantry, who were intended to provide back-up and relief to the men stuck in the newly discovered captured trench.

There was little time to send runners to tell Ridley and the rest of the group and by 7.30pm the Yorkshiremen had reached them, only to discover there was no space left in the trench. As they lay prostrate on the flat ground behind the embedded Somersets, they were slaughtered by enemy machine-gun fire. This almost inconceivable waste of life took place just yards from the injured, drowsy and suffering Lance Corporal Ridley. When he finally recovered from his bouts of unconsciousness, the 20-year-old Ridley noticed his appalling hand injury and thought 'that's it, I'm all right now, I'm out of it' and so began a long wait for help.

Van Emden writes:

> Every officer in the battalion who had taken part in that attack was killed or wounded, a casualty rate that made Lieutenant Colonel Ritchie comment that they had perhaps been singled out for special attention by snipers and machine gunners. There was no option for him but to withdraw any surviving men still lying in shell holes and hold the ground until early the following morning, when they could be relieved. His losses numbered seventeen officers and 383 other ranks, not far short of two-thirds of those who took part in the fighting that day.[15]

Decades later, Ridley showed signs of his enormous capacity for logic when he pointed out that a soldier couldn't expect to be lucky every time as that didn't make sense. The only 'glimmer of hope' at all was to be hit with a 'blighty one' – meaning a wound that needed medical treatment back in Britain. The young soldier noted it was the main reason why any war correspondents meeting the injured men always described them as 'merry and full of optimism'.

After that horrific day on the Somme, Ridley could claim several 'blighty ones', in his left arm, hand, groin and head. As his body coped with the dreadful wounds, he fainted on and off and was fed water and scraps of food by comrades during his brief seconds of consciousness. He waited quietly in agony for some hours before relief arrived in the form of the 13th Battalion, Northumberland Fusiliers, and then made his way slowly back to a medical aid point behind Delville Wood. 'I am all very hazy about this time because I didn't realise that I had a fractured skull, and that doesn't improve your memory,' he said. It would be two years before his damaged skull was diagnosed and for the rest of his life he suffered with headaches.

The battle of the Somme lasted from 1 July to 18 November 1916. The list of casualties topped one million and more than 300,000 men died.

After receiving first aid assistance at Le Tréport field hospital, the wounded Lance Corporal Ridley was sent to a Canadian medical base where his injured hand, which had turned septic, was operated on more than once. Speaking to his son Nicolas years later, he recalled:

> I was quite certain my hand would be amputated and I must confess that the next morning I felt a strong measure of disappointment when I found that it was still there. The loss of a hand would, at the worst, reduce me to the Home Service and save my life. I was twenty years old and rather young to welcome a prospect of being maimed for life![16]

But at the time, before his maturity installed any sense of reasoning, Ridley admitted he often wept tears of rage, fear and frustration. Nicolas explained: 'The fact the surgeons had saved my father's hand left him inconsolable. He told me after he'd been taken to Le Tréport he woke in darkness with a terrible weight pressing down on his chest. Someone was kneeling on him, sewing him into a sheet. He had been sleeping so deeply it was assumed he had died in the night.'

The memories which Ridley spent decades trying to ignore are so horrific they appear beyond any scope of psychological exercises recommended by today's specialists working with those suffering post-traumatic stress disorder. All we can do is try to imagine the hell he lived through in order to understand ever so slightly the appalling sounds of tortured screaming which kept him awake night after night.

The memory of no man's land and lying amidst the 'terrible shreds of a man who had been torn apart by shrapnel', lay at the heart of Ridley's terror. Fifteen of the men in his group had been killed or seriously injured soon after leaving the trenches when the preliminary barrage fell on them instead of on the German machine-gun posts. Nicolas believes the 'screaming man' recalled so often by his father during nightmares must have carried him, unconscious, to safety: 'My father it seems had been sheltered from the later burst.'

At this point there was a question which Nicolas found too terrible to ask his long-suffering father. Was the screaming man who had saved Ridley's life a pal? During his sobs, had he asked Ridley to spare him further agony? What was Ridley's decision at such a terrible moment? Either way, Ridley lived with the consequences of any merciful action and Nicolas rightfully understood it wasn't appropriate to press his father to draw out the worst of the demons from his memory.[17]

Back in no man's land in 1916, Lance Corporal Ridley bravely got together a group of men who had been left stranded with him at the mercy of the German guns. Heroically, he managed to take charge and lead them through Delville Wood to the British front line. Each man who was part of this remarkable escape was recommended for a Military Medal, while Ridley, who already had one stripe on his arm, was put forward by an officer for the Distinguished Conduct Medal. He was lucky to survive: at Delville Wood his battalion suffered nearly 50 per cent casualties.

During the First World War some 115,000 Military Medals were awarded to other ranks and yet Ridley, who had been nominated for a Distinguished Conduct Medal because he was a lance corporal, was unfairly turned down for the award and received nothing – a fact which he was rightfully hurt about. He had wanted a Military Medal like the rest of the men who survived that day, that's all, according to Nicolas.

Ridley was tremendously pleased, however, to learn that his *Dad's Army* character, Private Godfrey, had been awarded a Military Medal for being a medical orderly and stretcher-bearer during the First World War. In the show a photograph of a young Charles Godfrey in his British Army uniform being presented with his medal is seen above his bed at his home, Cherry Tree Cottage, Walmington-on-Sea. It seemed as if fate had cast its mystic wiles over Ridley and decreed he should have been presented with his own Military Medal in 1916, but instead it went to his character Private Godfrey, who would bring him a bigger reward in the future.

True enough, a little more than a decade later, in 1982 the television comedy star who played Private Godfrey – a conscientious objector during the First World War and a medical orderly at the Somme – was presented with a real OBE (Officer of the Order of the British Empire) by HM the Queen. Ridley, soldier, poet, playwright, actor and war hero was happy to forgive past oversights and was delighted with his royal honour, although Nicolas believes it was a poor and overdue salute to his father's service to his country during two world wars.[18]

Nicolas's opinion is quite correct. When we stop and consider the courage of Ridley himself, and all those called up to serve their country during the First World War, we acknowledge a piece of history which in today's terms is incomprehensible in its insanity – it was essentially a mad killing spree that lasted four years. Britain's longest surviving First World War soldier, Harry Patch (1898–2009), always described the conflict as 'legalised murder' which politicians should have sorted out among themselves. Certainly surviving diaries and letters from the men on the front line often record extraordinary psychological experiences at times of great danger. And while we don't know much about the content of young Ridley's correspondence to his parents, we can learn more generally about his situation from other men fighting in the war. In Richard van Emden's book *The Quick and the Dead*, for example, we read of Private Robert Renwich, who was taking part in an assault on Delville Wood. As he swerved and ran from shell-hole to tree stump, he suddenly saw himself back at school. He wrote home: 'Our schoolmaster was coming down his garden path to the wicket to call us in and line us up.' The image from his recent boyhood was shockingly vivid to the young man facing death.

Another soldier, Thomas Kehoe, had a similar experience after he had been shot in the thigh as he ran over the top. After a while, as he lay still and petrified on the ground, he heard some Germans prowling around. Terror gripped the young Tommy and just as he thought the fear would cause him to faint, he suddenly felt he was back home sitting up in bed and reading *Treasure Island*. Kehoe wrote: 'I was hurrying over the pages in my book for fear my mother would come stealing into my bedroom and take the candle away. The room dropped away from the dark, and I was Jim Hawkins himself, sitting on the cross-trees of the good ship *Hispaniola*, with Israel Hands below me coming up the mizzen-shrouds holding a dirk in his teeth.'[19]

When men were dying, they often cried out to those around them, thinking only of their family at home. Second Lieutenant George Atkins of the Royal Engineers remembered a man called Cox, who had been badly wounded during an attack in 1918. Atkins said the man was sobbing like a child: 'My wife, my kiddie, oh God! Sir, what's going to happen to them?' And then at once the life drained from his body and he was taken down the line on a stretcher to join the long row of the fallen.[20]

Whatever the men did to help themselves get through another minute, another hour and another day in hell, there was always the grim thought that by embracing fear it would give one the strength to never take leave from the Front, and in this way there would be no emotional struggle to hide the truth of the horror from the family. Many knew that once they had returned home for two weeks' leave, there was a risk they would find it impossible to return to the horror. The penalty for desertion was death. The situation was bleak and the anguish was as rife as the lice and diseases on their malnourished young bodies.

The deep and cutting contrasts between life at the front and life at home were enough to provoke surreal thoughts among the men, and when the moon was full any danger was exacerbated, as Lieutenant Geoffrey Fildes, serving on the Ypres Salient front, revealed in his memoir. Fildes recalled how he was on his way with a fatigue party to collect supplies from a Royal Engineers dump. On their way they found themselves 'struggling through a glutinous communications trench. Very lights lit up the night sky; rifle shots, and the splutter of machine-gun fire continued without a moment's rest.' He wrote:

> At this moment, I wondered whether people at home were giving any real thought to what was passing in this dark and sinister wilderness. Away in London people were filling the theatres; the plays would be in full progress, perhaps the second act had just opened; and here were we, glued half way up to our knees in a slough of graveyard fluid, listening to a running fire of rifle shots – and the same moon was up there looking down on us all alike.[21]

Lance Corporal Ridley of the Somerset Light Infantry would have no doubt appreciated this officer's thoughts, as when he did decide to break his own rule in later life and explain any details about his own war it was always about 'the mental suffering'.

While Ridley was robbed of receiving a medal for his heroic actions, one soldier of the Somerset Light Infantry who did receive a Military Medal was a lad named George Taylor who, like the young Ridley, had joined the regiment in 1915 and witnessed the initial short sharp shock of army life at Crownhill. Like Ridley, Taylor too had seized the opportunity to join up to avoid the possibility of criminal proceedings being started against him. While the hot-tempered 19-year-old Ridley had thrown a headmaster out of a window and might have faced gaol for it, George had been involved in an accident in which a woman was seriously hurt. He and a friend were riding home one night on their bicycles when a group of soldiers ahead of them refused to part to let them through. Angrily George's pal rode his bike at the group and there was a collision which left a woman who had been walking with the group badly injured. A policeman arrived and, after taking notes, said to George and his friend, 'We'll see you again . . .'

Not wanting to face charges, George lied about his age and, along with his friend, quickly volunteered to join the Army. They went to the local recruiting officer, who gave them the King's Shilling and told them to report to the barracks at Taunton. So, on 6 May 1915, aged 16 years and 9 months, but claiming to be three years older, the tall and strapping George Taylor was enlisted.

In Taunton the new recruits, just like Ridley, were given broom handles with which to practise marching and arms drill, and after a few weeks they received their uniforms and rifles and were sent to Crownhill in Plymouth. George joined the 6th Battalion, Somerset Light Infantry, which was attached to the 43rd Brigade, 14th Light Division, and served on the Western Front throughout the war.

Soon, George was chosen to be a lance corporal. He recounted how part of the selection process involved him and another potential NCO standing at opposite ends of the quarter-mile-long parade ground, and each of them having to be able to shout orders loudly enough for the other to hear.

On one occasion he was drilling his platoon of twenty-eight men; in the absence of anyone of a senior rank, he was giving them an easy time. Then, noticing the sergeant major's door beginning to open, George ordered: 'Attention. Slope arms. Left turn.' One man turned right. This was witnessed by the sergeant major, who yelled at the soldier 'Don't you know your left from your right?' Picking up some daisies from the grass, the sergeant major stuck them on the unfortunate soldier's left arm with the instruction 'Next time you hear "left turn", look at the daisies.' The soldier, whom George described as a quite ordinary and pleasant chap, looked the sergeant major in the eye and said 'Yes, you put some daisies on my arm. But I'll bloody cover you with daisies the first chance I get.' The soldier, whom George always referred to as 'Daisy Boy', was sentenced to twenty-eight days' detention at Devonport.

After about three months at Plymouth, they received orders to go to Belgium. As George was assembling his men, a van arrived carrying the soldier who had been sent to Devonport; he was pleased to be back. They marched to Plymouth railway station and from there they travelled to Dover, and sailed across the channel to Boulogne, disembarking on 2 September 1915. They marched to the camp on the hills above Boulogne, and the following morning they joined their battalion at Ypres.

Like Ridley, George was involved in the action at Delville Wood, where he witnessed the death of a man from his home town. He recalled:

All we were ever doing on the Somme was going over the top somewhere or other. Every month it was somewhere different. And then we had the big one – when we took Delville Wood. We got a good hiding there, but we took the area. Fifty-three were killed and 227 were wounded or missing in less than a day and a half. One of them was a chap called Perce

Shearn, who used to come around Midsomer Norton every Saturday night selling oranges, apples, bananas, and things. Well, I'd just taken four or five men into the front line and there was Perce Shearn standing by a German dug-out, so I went over to speak to him. I hadn't got to within half-a-dozen yards when two Germans came out of the dug-out, and went straight through him with a bayonet. I fired at those two, and put them out of their misery. Then I chucked a bomb down in case any more Germans were down there.

Today Perce Shearn is remembered on the Midsomer Norton war memorial.

The tragic story of the Jefferies brothers, from autumn 1916, was also clear in George's memory.

I had two brothers from Bristol in my platoon. They stuck together whatever they were doing, and would never go anywhere without one another. One day we were going up the front, when Jerry put a shell over and knocked one of the brothers clean out – you had a job to find anything of him. Of course the other brother was shook up. We went on up the line. A month or two later I was surprised to see them bringing up this other brother, who had run away. He'd got as far as Boulogne and tried to get on one of the boats. As he came past I told him how sorry I was for him. He had to go in front of a court martial, and he had to be shot next morning. And it was the Cornwalls that did it, not the Somersets, but men from our own Brigade.

Private Arthur Jefferies was killed in action on 16 September 1916. Just a few weeks later Private Alfred Jefferies was shot at dawn on 1 November 1916.

Because they had sustained such heavy losses in the battle of the Scarpe early in April 1917, the 6th Battalion, Somerset Light Infantry, had been in a composite battalion with the Duke of Cornwall's Light Infantry. Now, reinforcements, including many older men, had come out from England. They included the bullying sergeant major from Plymouth. In early May they were moving up to the front line prior to going over the top, and were being subjected to heavy shelling. George recounts: 'A shell came over and landed two hundred yards from where we were. And I heard a rifle go, quite clearly, just one crack; but I took no notice. Going up by, there was the sergeant major laid out flat, shot dead, he was the first one to go.'

When George was checking for casualties after the action, he was approached by 'Daisy Boy', who asked 'Did you see the sergeant major?' 'Yes, I saw him', said George. And neither of them ever said another word about it.

Another death he recalled was that of Joe Evans, a local Somerset man whom he had first met on Midsomer Norton railway station while they were on their way to Taunton to join up. George came across Joe at Inverness Copse in August 1917, and while speaking with him, he saw a German come along and stand up behind a tree. He mentioned this to Joe and warned him to stay low, and began to crawl away. He had gone only a few yards when the German fired. George turned around and saw Joe lying dead.

The heroic George was one of the very few members of his battalion who avoided capture during the German advance south of St Quentin in March 1918. Early in the morning of 21 March the whole of the front held by the Third and Fifth Armies was bombarded with mustard gas and high explosive shells. All the telephone lines were cut. By 10am the German infantry assault was in progress all along the front. His Somerset accent loaded with emotion, George took up the story:

> By now Jerry had come over and taken the whole of the Somersets. In fact he came straight through and took the best part of Gough's army. We were round in a horseshoe. He came through the ends and cut us off.
>
> I got back to Battalion HQ, and I went to the Adjutant, Captain Frampton, and said 'The Jerries are coming in each side . . . Let's get back.' We burned anything that was any good. Some troops stayed, but I thought to myself 'you can do what you like, but I'm off' and I got away. When I looked back I saw the Jerries going down in there, searching for anything useful, I suppose. I crawled on my hands and knees for a mile or so. When I thought it was safe I walked on until I got to the river Jussy, where the German advance had stopped. They were patrolling the bank; they walked about sixty yards along then turned and came back. I couldn't swim. So I said to Frampton 'We got to get over there.' When midnight struck we waited until the patrol had passed then got into the water. The Germans must have heard something, because they came and looked; but they didn't see us. Then Frampton got hold of me and we sort-of-waded across; it was about fifty yards.

On the other side of the river there were Indian troops and members of the RAMC. The officer in command was a doctor. George explained what had happened and was given a drink and made welcome, and he found somewhere to sleep.

In the morning the Germans started to cross the river. All the soldiers who were there decided to leave, and so did George. After a few miles he came across a fully stocked but deserted officers' mess. George said:

' I went in there and got a bottle of whisky, and supplied myself well with fags, and came out.' He saw a machine gun in perfect working order, with a supply of ammunition. 'Well, I could see these Germans coming over, so I stuck a pan on the gun and fired; and I know I got some. I then smashed the pan on the gun and ran off.'

This act of bravery was witnessed by a French officer, as a result of which George was awarded the Military Medal. The award was announced in Army Orders dated 20 May 1918 and in the *London Gazette Supplement* dated 6 August 1918. He also featured in his local Somerset newspaper, the *Bath Herald* – the same publication which published a story about fellow local hero and Somerset Light Infantryman Arnold Ridley in 1919.

George says that on the day of the action he ran until about nine o'clock, and reached a wood where there were French soldiers. He recalled:

> I had never seen so many guns in my life. They were wheel-to-wheel. I reckon there were about 250 in that bit of wood. The Frenchmen went crazy, caught hold of us, took us down, got us some grub. We stayed there the night with them. In the morning the Germans came again. Everything, guns were rapid fire, you know the big ones. Well, that stopped them. They started going back.

Eventually, George was sent to Étaples and was posted to the 8th Battalion, Somerset Light Infantry, the 6th Battalion having effectively ceased to exist.

George was wounded three times during the war. His military service was ended by the third wound, inflicted at the battle of Albert in August 1918, when his knee was badly damaged by shrapnel from a German shell. He was sent back to England, arriving in London on a hospital train. Seeing a GWR train at the station, he expected to be shipped back to his home. But no, he was told, instead he was destined for the London & North train, to be sent to hospital in Liverpool. After three or four months there he was sent to a hospital in Birmingham.

Eventually returning to Midsomer Norton on a week's holiday, George was visited by the manager of the Norton Hill coal mine. 'I'm glad to see you,' he told the young soldier. 'I'll get you out of the army. I could do with you at Norton Hill.' 'Well, you'll be lucky. But I shall be glad anyway,' thought George. But within a few weeks he received his discharge, returned home and started work back at the mine.[22]

\*\*\*

Lance Corporal Arnold Ridley had made it out of the trenches two years earlier than his regimental comrade Lance Corporal George Taylor. In 1916 Ridley with his lifeless arm and hand was sent to Woodcote Park military hospital in Epsom, where he would be judged for fitness. Surely his disablement exonerated him from being sent back to the trenches?

He was disappointed to learn he wasn't able to pack up his kitbag and head for home just yet. Instead he was ordered to face a humiliating examination by a group of travelling army medical officers. After removing his clothes and waiting naked in a room chilled with the temperatures of a mid-January morning, he faced more torture. Suddenly a surgeon-general arrived and demanded to know what was wrong with the shivering soldier, who was still in pain and clearly suffering from shell-shock. Ridley showed his shattered hand to the sadistic medic, who twisted it violently and sneered, 'How did you do this? Jack-knife?' The sarcasm was too much for Ridley, who responded with equal hostility: 'Yes, sir! My battalion is famous for self-inflicted wounds. And just to make sure, I cracked my skull with a rifle butt as well, and ran a bayonet through my groin.'

The medic went puce with rage, twisted Ridley's injured hand again and barked out loud: 'Treatment at Command Depot.'

Once again the lance corporal had to face the prospect of more misery at the hands of the military medical boards as he made his way to No.3 Command Depot, County Cork. He told Nicolas that it was a terrible place, freezing cold, and embedded deep was an epidemic of scabies and impetigo. There was even a strong suggestion that men were sent there to die in order to save the government from paying out disability pensions. Now fully determined to get away from the place, Ridley reported sick every day and so began a battle of attrition with the medical officer.

'I had read the King's Rules and Regulations and from this I knew it was impossible to accuse me of malingering but, if so charged I could demand a court martial. I persisted and eventually the senior medical officer was the one to crack and I was returned to my Taunton depot with a note I was "unsuitable" for further medical treatment,' explained Ridley.[23]

So at last in April 1917 he heard he was to escape the hideous conditions at Cork and was ordered to return to England. His luck went even further, as he learned he would receive official confirmation of a pension of 13 shillings 9 pence a week. And with this knowledge, he picked up his kitbag and boarded a ship that rolled and tumbled in some frightful spring gales. The vessel was also full of drunken

Irishmen. Ridley knew he would need to avoid them, as following the recent and violent Easter Risings, these hearty big labourers wouldn't take kindly to the sight of an English soldier.

As he tried to take shelter and sleep on deck, he was whisked away by an austere stewardess who steered him into an empty first class cabin, where he stayed until the ship docked at the Welsh port of Fishguard. Ridley explained: 'I can't say I had a peaceful night. There were times when I thought I'd survived Arras, the Somme and the command depot only to be drowned on my way home. But in the morning the woman brought me an excellent breakfast. Appearances can be deceptive. Without that grim woman's kindness, I doubt if I should have reached Taunton at all!'

By 10 May an official decision was finally made that Lance Corporal Ridley been through enough for King and Country, and he was discharged from duty on 27 August 1917. His parents William and Rosa, at home above their shop in Bath, welcomed their wounded son through the door and nursed his half-starved, battered body back to some semblance of good health, although his injured hand and arm still caused him great pain and his confidence was at an all-time low.

According to Nicolas, there was a day when his father was in Taunton just after his discharge in 1917 and suddenly a bold young woman presented him with a white feather in an attempt to expose him as a coward. Ridley told Nicolas years later that he accepted the feather that day and placed it in his pocket. It was his own fault, he said, as at the time he wasn't wearing his special badge which informed the world he had been seriously wounded and could no longer be of use in battle. The astute Nicolas wrote: 'My father felt, I believe, the aching guilt of those who survived; the wretched knowledge that they, too, should have died.'[24]

In the final year of the war, Ridley, like so many troubled young men, attempted to rebuild his life and with help from his sporting father he managed to reawaken his love of rugby and cricket. But in his memoir, 'The Book', he described how crucifying and difficult it was to beat back the waves of depression and the overwhelming sense that everything was meaningless. He explained how his friends were either all dead or still in the services, and he refused to make new ones. 'I wandered alone through the streets and gardens of Bath in a state of Stygian gloom,' he recalled.

Thankfully a wake-up call came from out of the blue as a sense of self-preservation kicked in. Ridley added: 'I realised that unless I made a supreme effort to pull myself together, I stood a fair chance of being put quietly away in some convenient mental hospital. I had to do something about it and quickly too.'

This important decision got him thinking again, and finally he couldn't resist the idea of being a professional actor. His happy and productive pre-war involvement with the Bristol University Dramatic Society had introduced him to the famous theatrical impresario Sir Frank Benson, who in 1917 encouraged the war hero to get back on the stage. In August 1918 the young actor, who claimed his general health had been 'somewhat restored', received an invitation to join Barry Jackson and John Drinkwater's highly esteemed Birmingham Repertory Company.

Jackson, who created the company in 1913, had a good eye for young talent and employed many actors who became the stars we know and love today, including Sir Laurence Olivier, Dame Peggy Ashcroft, Dame Edith Evans, Stewart Granger and Sir Ralph Richardson. After the Second World War the company transferred to Stratford and heralded the success of more young greats of film and theatre, including Derek Jacobi, Albert Finney, Paul Scofield and Peter Brook. The energetic Jackson (1879–1961) was also director of the Royal Opera House in London, and in 1929 he created the now famous Malvern Festival with playwright George Bernard Shaw.

Young Ridley's early appearances on the stage were recorded at home and noted in the *Bath Chronicle*. A cutting from the newspaper printed in 1919 describes the 'only son of Mr and Mrs W.R. Ridley of Manvers Street, Bath as a clever young actor who artistically camouflages his war wounds from the Somme'.

But Arnold's hopes of playing Hamlet again, this time on the professional stage, were crushed by a director named Esme Filmer. Originally cast as a young lord in a play called *Milestones*, Ridley was immediately disliked by Filmer, who then quickly demoted him and asked him to 'double up' in lesser roles. Exactly why the actor was bullied by Filmer remains a mystery, but yet more evidence of Ridley's observational skills are recorded in 'The Book'. In it he describes the man whom Nicolas says 'blighted' his father's career, as an 'odd character' – which seems rather complimentary considering the misery he attempted to inflict upon the quiet, talented war hero.

Always fair-minded, Ridley attempted to understand Filmer's behaviour towards him:

> Filmer was small, dark and saturnine with a vitriolic tongue. He once asked me (and before the whole company too!) if I could oblige him by walking across the stage looking more like a man and less like a constipated rat. Another pleasantry consisted in asking me to do something my physical disabilities rendered impossible. He would

then apologise profusely, murmuring something about having to make allowances for 'our brave fighting men'.

I shall never know if Filmer had deliberately set out to break me as an actor. If he did, he very nearly succeeded. He destroyed my confidence in myself to such an extent that, even after sixty years it hasn't completely returned. To this day whenever I see my director in whispered conference with the author or manager, I always feel they are planning the best way to get rid of me.[25]

Confirmation of Filmer's behaviour is confirmed, albeit vaguely, by the famous critic J.C. Trewin, who described in his book about the repertory theatre of the day how Filmer was an earnest perfectionist (irritating hair-splitter) 'with centrally-parted dark hair, intense gaze, dangling monocle and slender figure who preferred to direct Spanish plays above all others'. This description sits next to a sketch of Filmer drawn in 1920 by an unknown artist. The image is held in storage at the Victoria & Albert Museum collection, though Filmer's name is long forgotten.

Some years later it would have been fair surely for Ridley to have stuck two fingers up at the loathsome Filmer, especially so as Ridley's fame soared first as a playwright and then, of course, as a star of *Dad's Army* and a royal favourite. His name is now legendary. Who was Filmer? All we do know for sure is that he was involved in bringing the set and costume designer Paul Shelving into Birmingham Rep. Shelving's artistic creations in a robust production of the *Beggar's Opera*, produced by Jackson, became the talk of London. Research into the history of Birmingham Rep offers just one more mention of the uppity Filmer, this time in the 1920s when he was an 'assistant director' (which meant his job was to see the actors through their rehearsals) in a production of *The Marvellous History of Saint Bernard*.[26]

Nicolas is keen to point out that his father was not a vengeful man but he did have the last laugh against Filmer a few years later in 1926 when Ridley was by then a famous playwright and the toast of the West End. The buoyant young Ridley was in Oxford around this time to oversee the production of his new play *The God of Mud*. He had been invited to see *The Seagull* by Anton Chekhov and then spotted, to his amusement, the name of the director on a poster: A.E. Filmer. How he must have laughed to himself.

Writing in 'The Book', Ridley said it was going to 'be fun' meeting Filmer again as he, Arnold Ridley, was no longer a 'small-part actor' but a successful West End author and far better known than the odious Filmer. 'But I hadn't bargained on his skill in dealing with the situation,' recalled Ridley. 'When I entered the theatre, Filmer was there waiting for me. Before a word could be spoken he had bowed to me deeply and graciously and, with his hand on his heart, said, "Ah! The great Arnold Ridley. How perfectly splendid!" There was nothing I could say.' Nicolas explained that his father had no cruelty or malice in his own make-up, and therefore he had always found it difficult to believe or understand such behaviour in others. There's little doubt Filmer's attitude in the early days of Ridley's career had been a damaging experience.

In 1918 the Spanish 'flu began to wage its indiscriminate war, killing victims in their millions, many of them men already weakened from the ravages of the First World War. Ridley himself records how he 'went down badly and thoroughly' with the Spanish influenza. This excerpt from prize-winning novelist Louis de Bernières' 2015 novel *The Dust That Fall From Dreams* says so much.

The novel tells the story of a young hero, Sergeant 'Hutch' Hutchinson of the Honourable Artillery Company, who after miraculously surviving four years on the Western Front returns to visit the grieving fiancée (Rosie) of his best friend (Ashbridge), who was killed in action. 'Hutch' is notable for being among a tiny minority of men who saw out the war in the same regiment, and comforts Rosie with tales about Ashbridge's bravery at the front. He then finds romance himself with the maid, Millicent. Sadly, within weeks of the Armistice Day celebrations in London he collapses – his body, fatigued by the ravages of the war, is unable to beat off the deadly 'flu virus. Despite being nursed for weeks and feeling 'as if his lungs were full of talcum powder', he stops breathing.

Rosie, who had nursing experience, had spent the nights trying to soothe his fever but alas she couldn't save his life. When the second wave of this pandemic resurfaced in February 1919 Rosie herself contracts the disease but fortunately is able to fight and win the battle to survive.

De Bernières writes:

Hutch was exhausted when he collapsed with a terrible headache. He was running an extremely high temperature, he was coughing drily in his stupor, and his tongue was coated in a thick grey fur. His eyes and nose were running, and when he awoke it was almost impossible for him to talk, so sore was his throat.

Rosie knew it was unreasonable to expect him to eat anything, so she gave him honey from a spoon for his throat, tea and weak vegetable soups, planning to add milk and eggs when she thought he might recover.

Throughout the vigil the nurse forbade anyone to come near Hutch, including his fiancée Millicent. Firstly, she didn't want anyone else to catch the virus and secondly she didn't care about risking her own life as Hutch was the last link to her late beloved Ashbridge. Despite all her efforts, Hutch died.[27]

The poignant excerpt from this beautiful novel illustrates the horrific symptoms experienced by Ridley, who had himself collapsed by the side of the stage shortly after the premiere of *Abraham Lincoln*, a new play by John Drinkwater. The production by Birmingham Rep opened on 18 October 1918 and within days the curtain came down as the virus swept across the country wreaking destruction.

Ridley's memory of the Spanish 'flu is clear. He recalled how he was put in a cab after he fainted and returned directly to his digs. On his arrival his landlady was terrified and wouldn't go anywhere near him. He lived in an unheated room and his only sustenance was the glass of milk left for him at the end of the corridor. This gesture was all the anxious landlady could offer. Despite her efforts, within weeks she had perished from the disease. Just before her death, Ridley was visited by an exhausted doctor, who advised him to return home to Bath – a tall order when most public transport had ground to a halt. He wrote: 'But somehow I managed to leave my digs in Birmingham and get back home to recover. But my convalescence was cut short by a telegram from John Drinkwater. If I was fit enough, would I come back as things at the theatre were desperate. Despite my mother's protests and foreboding, I did so.'[28]

Once back at the theatre the young actor, who had survived yet another battle as deadly as the horrors of the Somme two years previously, discovered the stage doorkeeper and a member of the company had gone the same way as millions of others and died of the epidemic sweeping the country. Other members of Birmingham Rep were too ill to work. Ridley recalled:

The wholesale undertaker was working overtime and unvarnished coffins were piled high in Hinckley Street. The cast of *Abraham Lincoln* is a very long one with practically every member of the company playing two parts at least. The epidemic had played such havoc that many of us were obliged to appear in far more than that.

One night I played as many as seven characters, donning and whipping off uniforms, beards and moustaches in the wings. There were moments when I felt that, as I rushed on for the next part, I might meet myself hurrying off from the last!

Ever the hero, Ridley played a major role in saving the fortunes of the Birmingham Rep, only to be treated appallingly shabbily by the management about eighteen months later. In June 1920 he had an 'unpleasant shock' from a note informing him he might well be made redundant as the former serviceman who had been with the company before the war would be accepted back. 'The company is becoming too big,' said the poisonous little note, so Ridley decided to see the co-founder Barry Jackson.

That day in Jackson's office, Ridley told him he had been offered another professional opportunity elsewhere anyway. Jackson replied with 'Sorry to see you go and good luck' and the proud actor walked out, dignity intact. Years later Ridley admitted: 'I still wonder what would have been the result if my vanity hadn't prevented me from speaking the truth.'[29] His decision at the time, though, was justified and he probably protected his mental health in more ways than he could have imagined, as to escape from the dreaded Filmer and his malicious bullying and nit-picking ways was a good move forward and there would be a chance for the actor to regain his confidence too.

The next chapter of his life was a time of limbo for his theatrical career. Despite attempts to network via letters and visits to theatre managers, he found it 'depressing' as the 'no thanks' became an all-too-regular response. It was a very different world now that all the actors who had survived the war were back out there hunting for jobs.

In December 1920 his luck changed slightly and he was invited to join the Plymouth Repertory Company. He arrived eager to be back at work and was told he had just two days to learn the lines of a script. The actor he was replacing had been fired by the manager George S. King for drunkenness. Ever keen to impress and do his job well, Ridley said he was given just a few lines from the pages of a script but had little idea about what kind of character was saying them. When he expressed his concern about the minimal information offered him, he was met with blank stares. It's little wonder he 'stammered his way' through his part on opening night. The hostility from the rest of the cast left him nervous and unhappy, until he discovered the man he had replaced had been a popular friend to them all and they believed he had been unfairly sacked.

Although it was 'nothing personal', Ridley sat in his dreary bedsit in Plymouth on Christmas Day to eat his dinner alone. It wasn't long before the curtain came down on the Plymouth theatre season and the noble and courageous actor returned home to Bath. What followed was an unfortunate alliance with a local playwright, who can only be described as a 'serial optimist'. His peculiar name was Lechmere

Worrall, and in 1914 he was the co-author of a well known wartime play, *The Man Who Stayed at Home*.

Ridley, obviously impressed that Worrall lived so close, decided to approach him about a job. The two got on well and Worrall offered Ridley the post of general manager of the 'new theatre company' he hoped to set up in Bath. At the start there was another playwright named Charles McEvoy involved, but he parted company with Worrall not long after Ridley joined – and later on the reasons would be made all too clear as to why this man had fled the coop. Worrall was still raising finance for his project and asked Ridley if he wouldn't mind waiting before taking his salary of £ 10 per week. If only alarm bells had gone off at this point, much grief would have been spared all around.

Years later Ridley's son Nicolas sat down with his father over a bottle of wine to hear the full sorry story of Mr Worrall. As it unfolded, it revealed very much how the road to his father's fame as a playwright and then, of course, as a star of *Dad's Army* had been a tremendously rocky one. Mr Worrall, it seemed, was something of a Mr Micawber. He let his debts pile up and pile up, and yet remained cheerfully, insanely, positively convinced his theatrical projects would take off and money would flood in. Even after being turned away from producers' offices one after another his attitude was always alarmingly bright and yet in hindsight he was obviously deluded. Ridley realised all too late that he was in a terrible position, as he had borrowed money from friends for the Bath entertainment plans and when Worrall suddenly disappeared he felt it only fair that he should pay those friends back out of his own pocket.

Nicolas said his father was left penniless thanks to Worrall, and to complicate matters even further he had just got engaged. But it wouldn't be fair to blame him for wanting Worrall's theatre plans to work. Times were tremendously tough and the opportunity to work with such a charming colleague in a project so dear to Ridley offered hope and encouragement. Remember that until he met fellow local Mr Worrall, he had been treated very shabbily in theatre-land and he understandably believed that surely this run of bad luck was now about to stop?

The police finally caught up with the absconding Worrall, but the courts found it hard to prove he was a confidence trickster and so the amiable buffoon was imprisoned briefly for minor fraud and was later sent by doctors to live in a home for the wayward. It's no surprise that at this point Ridley decided he'd been kicked enough by the theatre and decided to take a break from it. He didn't have long to wonder about what to do as his father William stepped in and offered his son the chance to run a new branch of his boot and shoe shop in the High Street. He commented:

> I was far from happy and loathed every minute of it, particularly the tiresome elderly female customers of which Bath seemed to have a super-abundance. Some of them could be particularly irritating. An 'old trout' – a name I bestowed on most of them – would say she took size 4. Then, after one had succeeded in getting her foot into a size 6 she would say: 'Of course I always take size 4 in good shoes.'

This job lasted for four years. During any free time Ridley used his imagination and observations to inspire him to begin writing for the theatre. He liked the sense of control this gave him and after squirrelling himself into a small unfurnished room with a cracked window above the shop he set to work. And work he did, creating more than thirty plays upon a desk made from a large old packing case. His lighting and heating were supplied by an oil lamp and stove. Around him he often heard crumbling plaster falling from the walls.

The idea for the comedy-thriller *The Ghost Train*, which he wrote in just one week in 1923, came from his real-life experience of being stuck out one night at Mangotsfield railway station on the main line to the Midlands. The station was deserted, and during his long wait for the next train Ridley noted the loud and eerie rattle of the non-stop Bath to Gloucester Express which shot along on a nearby diversionary line, bypassing old Mangotsfield station. The atmosphere of the whole experience had lodged in the young man's mind and he soon realised the illusion of a train approaching and suddenly disappearing was perfect as a successful theatrical device which would influence each character. *The Ghost Train* is set in a haunted railway station in Cornwall. When the passengers learn their train has been cancelled and they face a night together, strange occurrences begin to frighten them. One of the characters is actually a secret agent of the British government, who is trying to find Bolsheviks.

During his free time from the boot shop the busy playwright also managed to bombard various London agents with his scripts until finally luck smiled on him when an influential contact, Bernard Merivale, read *The Ghost Train*.

It's not widely known but no fewer than thirty plays were written by the prolific Ridley, including *The Keepers of Youth* (1929), *The Flying Fool* (1929) and *Recipe for Murder* (1932). Many of them involved a mystery death or two, which shows he was tapping into the zeitgeist of the day, which had revealed a public thirst for murder stories. But it was *The Ghost Train* that wrote his name in the annals of theatrical greatness.

The actor and theatre manager Arthur Bourchier loved it and wanted to draw up a contract with Ridley immediately to produce it, providing the terms and conditions were agreeable to both parties. Initially, Ridley was asked to change one or two of the characters, and Bourchier was keen for his wife, the famous actress Violet Vanbrugh, to be in the cast to star alongside him. There was also an important alteration to be made to the idea that the 'ghost' train was being used to help smuggle cheap cars across the continent into Britain. In reality, Britain had just had an election and the new Labour/Liberal coalition changed the law, resulting in the axing of import duty on foreign vehicles. Quickly Ridley thought of a solution to save the credibility of his story – smuggled cars would be replaced by weapons and ammunition.[30]

On 20 June 1925 the curtain finally went up for the first time on *The Ghost Train*. The venue for this momentous premiere took place at Brighton's Theatre Royal. Ridley recalled the press reviews were 'beastly' and empty seats were often seen during the play's tour, which included Golders Green, Glasgow, Birmingham, and Brixton. 'It was always the same story. Those who came liked it tremendously but there were so few of them,' recalled Ridley during a conversation years later with his son Nicolas.

The miniscule ticket sales failed to deter the management's enthusiasm for the play and it went on another tour, but once again it failed to draw the crowds and the sad decision was made to cancel the rest of the bookings. The disappointed playwright returned home to Bath and wondered again about his future. Had the theatre pushed him out again after so cruelly allowing him a little hope?

Then one night, when Ridley was taking part in an Armistice Night Ball in the Bath Pump Room, he received a telegram asking him to return to London as a theatrical manager named Harry Cohen wanted to put on *The Ghost Train* at the St Martin's Theatre. Cohen was desperate to fill the theatre as the original play he had staged there had been a massive flop. When the curtain went up on *The Ghost Train* the ticket sales began ticking over again and it wasn't long before a small profit had pushed Ridley's bank balance back into the black.

There are twelve characters in this successful comedy-thriller and on many occasions over the years Ridley himself played old Saul Hodgkin, the station master. *The Ghost Train* proved to be tremendously popular, boasting sell-out audiences from 1925 to 1927. During its runaway success in London, Ridley often starred as Saul both at the St

Martin's Theatre and then later at the Garrick. The play was praised for its dramatic special effects and creative use of thunder-sheets, garden-rollers on wooden lathes, and all manner of backstage cacophonies of sound to fill the auditorium with the sense that a train was about to hurtle through.

Its financial success was in part owed to Cohen's brilliant publicity strategies – an art form Ridley paid tribute to. He said Cohen had worked out a way to get people queuing all along Charing Cross Road to get in to see the production – certainly offering cheaper seats helped. One clever promotion involved a tobacconist, who complained that the queues along the front of his shop were ruining his business. Cohen persuaded the man to go to court and he duly won the case. A cheery Cohen happily paid the tobacconist compensation as the story appeared on the front pages of every London newspaper! The audience figures continued to climb, and what with four tours of Britain on the go and productions in Australia, the United States and Germany, Ridley suddenly realised he was rich.

In 1926 Ridley had married his first wife, and this union lasted until 1939. Still childless, he married again but once again divorce loomed. However, Ridley remained friends with both former Mrs Ridleys, according to his only child Nicholas, born to his third wife, the actress Althea Parker. Ridley married Miss Parker in 1945 and remained her with for the rest of his life.

In the 1930s, still working hard on various projects, Ridley began to notice his money was running low. The curtain came down on one new play, *The Lord of the Manor*, in which he had a monetary interest, after just a month. Sadly he didn't heed his earlier decision, made after the Worrall scandal, to never invest in the theatre. It was a great disappointment, too, when he was forced to close his own film company when the distributor went broke, owing several hundred thousand pounds. This meant the famous playwright with the big heart and talent was forced to stop work in the middle of a production.

Nicolas said his father's attitude to money wasn't irresponsible and in fact he worried about it incessantly. However, his expenditure on wonderful holidays and taxi cab journeys had begun to exceed his income, even though Ridley wasn't a man who wanted 'things'. By 1939 the playwright was admirably fighting off advice to go bankrupt. With typical determination, he set about paying back his financiers. As Nicolas points out 'only the Inland Revenue – relentless, insatiable, implacable – remained'.

By the early autumn of 1939 productions of *The Ghost Train* were stopped in their tracks. Ridley was still mourning the death of his friend and literary manager Bernard Merivale, and he decided to sell his rights to *The Ghost Train*. Messrs Samuel French (publishers) had offered Ridley £ 200 for the amateur rights to *The Ghost Train* and he agreed and took the money. It was a decision that meant he lost out on 'thousands of pounds' of future income. Ridley commented:

> Numerous people have tried to stir me into a sense of grievance over this but I positively refuse to have one. It was a perfectly straightforward proposition. The play had failed recently in the provinces and the chances of it going in to the West End were nil – and I badly needed the money. In fact, I was lucky. Had Samuel French offered me £ 500 for the entire world rights, I should have accepted joyfully.

Nicolas remarked how his father's comment about 'thousands of pounds' would in later years have meant hundreds of thousands of pounds – money that would have kept his parents in comfort for the rest of their lives. In spite of this knowledge, Ridley remained 'steadfastly philosophical' about why he sold the rights. At the time, he said, he hadn't known that amateur theatres all over the land would present his play over and over and over again. And even today they still do. Ridley concluded: 'I refuse to regret my decision.'

On 3 September 1939 the 43-year-old actor and playwright, who by then was pondering his future, heard Prime Minister Neville Chamberlain declare that Britain was now at war with Germany. Ridley prepared himself to put on a uniform again, and within a couple of weeks he found himself on the way to France as part of the British Expeditionary Force. He had been commissioned to the General List (an army specialist group of men, usually reserves) on 7 October with the rank of Second Lieutenant and his service number was 103663.

In those strange and eerie early days of autumn that year, Ridley's main task was working as an intelligence officer and organising journalists covering the action on the front line in the north. For seven months he was engaged in helping France, which had declared war on Germany following the Nazi invasion of neighbouring Austria and Poland. Hitler had his sights on France and plans were quickly drawn up by the British and French to create a naval blockade and other military operations to prevent a German advance. A mission was also undertaken to invade Norway and its Atlantic ports in a bid to drive out the Germans and thus prevent the export of Swedish iron ore to Germany.

Now promoted to Captain Ridley, the hero of the First World War found himself party to insider knowledge – through his link with the press – that the powerful German army, equipped with tanks and guns, and supported by the deadly Luftwaffe, was on its relentless, ruthless march towards northern France. His civilian life in the theatre by now had become a distant dream.

Meantime his parents back home in Bath had started putting up the blackout curtains and adjusting their lives to a big change on the home front. In 1939 their brave son was one of 897,000 men who made up the British Army. When during the 'phoney war' of 1939/early 1940 Chamberlain was unable to form a coalition government, he stepped aside and Winston Churchill became Prime Minister on 10 May 1940.

By 21 May that year Boulogne, just across the Channel, was at the centre of a fierce battle as British, Belgians and French fought hard to defend the town from the German advance. The 20th Guards Brigade had just arrived to bolster troop numbers. The German army was led by the ambitious General der Panzertruppe Heinz Guderian. His men were briefly driven back by French troops at Samer and met more resistance from the defiant men of the Irish and Welsh Guards. But the Allied triumph didn't last long as the determined Guderian continued to push forward with the vast might of his artillery.

By 22 May Ridley was suffering ill-health, his symptoms no doubt triggered by his undiagnosed post-traumatic stress disorder from his horrific experiences on the Somme in 1916. He was given permission to return to Britain. The following day, 23 May, he was among the wounded able to board HMS *Vimiera*, an escort destroyer which had arrived in battered Boulogne to rescue stranded troops.

Just a few hours before HMS *Vimiera* had sailed through the narrow channel between the two long stone piers jutting out from the sizeable town harbour to help rescue her next cargo of war-torn passengers, there were scenes of chaos. Captain Ridley would have probably been aware of the panic among the men as he waited his turn to get home. A witness standing near the quayside described the hubbub of civilians, refugees and soldiers of the Irish Guards as a 'rabble' – all of them desperate at that stage to board the waiting destroyers HMS *Keith* or HMS *Whitshed*.[31] The whole area was under siege and facing a bombardment from naval guns captured that morning by the Germans at Fort de la Crèche, north of Boulogne.

Buildings all around the harbour were blown to pieces. Commander Edward Reigner Conder DSC, DSO, MBE was the officer in charge of HMS *Whitshed*. He recalled how the Germans firing the guns from the fort must have hit a nearby ammunition dump because there was a massive explosion. He then saw a shot fired at a column of tanks edging towards the quay. He said: 'One huge tank disintegrated completely from a direct hit.'

The frenzy to evacuate Boulogne was intense but before HMS *Whitshed* and HMS *Keith* sailed for home, Brigadier William Fox-Pitt CVO, DSO, MC, a veteran of the First World War, received orders to ensure that the 20th Brigade 'fought to the last man'. After gaining support opposing this order from HMS *Whitshed*, Commander Conder and Commander David Simson of HMS *Keith* composed a reply pointing out the impossibility of such a request, which was hurriedly jotted down by Fox-Pitt as he sheltered from the Luftwaffe beneath a railway train. He informed the politicians that without sufficient aircraft cover and artillery, Boulogne could not be held. Permission to evacuate Boulogne was promptly agreed by a British government very much in the dark about the horrors facing hundreds of thousands of troops and civilians just across the Channel.

Still the onslaught from the air continued as another British destroyer, HMS *Vimy*, sailed in to assist in the evacuation. As the Luftwaffe continued to strafe each ship, the sound of bullets cracked the atmosphere. Commander Simson, the hero on the bridge of HMS *Keith*, was killed outright. Lieutenant Graham Lumsden recalled the moments before his Commander's death:

> Finally the Captain decided that, as we could do nothing useful, he and I would leave the bridge of the ship. I stood back to allow him down the bridge ladder to the wheelhouse, as courtesy and seniority demanded, but he signed me to precede him. No Captain liked to leave his bridge when under attack. I had taken one or two steps down when, alas, he fell down on top of me, shot in the chest by a German sniper's bullet. . . . We laid him on the settee in the tiny chart house . . . then the doctor arrived and pronounced him dead.

Several crew members were also killed.[32] Imagine the horror and panic as the German snipers holed up in a beachside hotel began firing directly at HMS *Vimy*, now moored alongside HMS *Keith*. The captain of HMS *Vimy*, Lieutenant Commander Colin Donald, was using his binoculars to try to locate the gunmen when suddenly he fell backwards. Crew member Don Harris recalled that he had been shot in the forehead, nose and eyes. His whispered last words before he was carried dying below deck were to Harris: 'Get the First Lieutenant on to the bridge urgently.' As Harris got up to carry out his order, another man, a sub-lieutenant, was hit and fell directly in front of him. Harris saw four bullet holes across his chest: 'He must have been dead before he hit the deck,' he added. Lieutenant Commander Donald made it back to Dover, but he died in hospital within hours of his terrible injuries.

While the air raids and snipers' bullets cracked the atmosphere over and around the harbour of Boulogne, fear was at an all-time high. There was relief for the waiting ships, however, when the RAF flew in twelve aircraft to drive back the deadly German Stukas. The sailors operating the guns of HMS *Whitshed*, moored just outside the main harbour, fired at the enemy aircraft and Commander Conder ensured his ship controlled the harbour at Boulogne. The destroyers HMS *Vimy* sailed out stern first, followed by HMS *Keith*. Both were heading home to Dover, with HMS *Keith* stopping only briefly to bury her dead. A little over a week later this gallant ship was itself destroyed in a German air attack on Dunkirk.

Boulogne now became a gruesome battleground, with the Germans relentlessly driving the Welsh and Irish Guards through the town towards the sea. The Pioneer Corps was unable to hold off the German assault. Witnesses accused the Pioneers of being drunk as their bullets often struck the Guards in error.

Lieutenant Commander Conder then signalled Admiral Ramsay at Dover to explain that more air support was required if another destroyer was to make it to the harbour to rescue more men. At 7.20pm RAF planes flew over and HMS *Whitshed* was joined by HMS *Vimiera*. Aboard HMS *Whitshed* the crew cheered as the ship's 4.7-inch guns blasted the German tanks in their sights. By 8.25pm records show that HMS *Whitshed* and HMS *Vimiera* had set sail for Dover. On board each ship were more than 550 men. Their escape had been under serious threat. The Germans had tried hard to sink another destroyer, HMS *Venetia*, hoping that she would sink and block the harbour exit. But confusion reigned in the German ranks and they failed to sink *Venetia*.

In the dark early hours of 24 May HMS *Vimiera* returned to the shell-blasted harbour of Boulogne to rescue more troops, many of them Welsh Guards, desperate to escape the carnage. Lieutenant Commander Roger Hicks was in command of HMS *Vimiera*, the last British destroyer to sail into Boulogne. He recalled: 'The silence was eerie. The only noise came from a burning lorry on the quay, the flames of which and a full moon gave plenty of light.' There was no sign of life until Lieutenant Commander Hicks called out. When a voice answered him, he learned there were still more than a thousand soldiers waiting to be evacuated. Sadly, Hicks had to leave behind several hundred disappointed men. His ship did, however, manage to rescue 1,400 troops and return them safely to Dover. In total, 4,368 men, women and children were evacuated from Boulogne by the Royal Navy, and the heroic Captain Arnold Ridley, future star of *Dad's Army*, was grateful to be among them.

As HMS *Vimiera* docked in Dover that morning, the Germans across the Channel were about to sit back for a few days now they had reached Dunkirk. Some historians believe this wait followed a disagreement between Hitler and his generals. The Führer made it clear he was the supreme commander and no campaign should go ahead without his permission. Whilst he had achieved a political victory, his vanity had scuppered any immediate military progress at Dunkirk.

There's another argument which suggests Hitler did not want hundreds of thousands of prisoners on his hands so he halted the attack in order to let them get back to England. Or was he really still wanting a peaceful settlement between Britain and Germany and therefore made a gesture of pseudo-reconciliation?

On 24 May Churchill's *Operation Dynamo* began. It would last until 4 June. The Royal Navy and the vast flotilla of little ships enabled 338,226 men to be rescued from the beaches of Dunkirk. Many men, though, didn't make it on to the ships, 122 of which were destroyed by the Luftwaffe's Stukas.

Private Harry Cole of the Suffolk Regiment was killed during the retreat to Dunkirk. In a letter only recently discovered by his family he wrote: 'Well mother, dad and boys, I guess I must close once again, hoping you all keep well, roll on when this do is over so we can get back to rest peace and quietness once again. Don't worry if you have to wait a long while for a letter or card sometimes Mother, as we can't always write for days at a time, also there is delay in getting it away.' For many soldiers like Private Cole his only instruction had been to 'get to the beaches and wait', as it was every man for himself. But all there was at the time was hope.

During Captain Ridley's time with the BEF he would have heard stories from so many men, including those of men like Harry Leigh-Dugmore. Harry was a lance corporal in May 1940 and recalled:

> We spent the first eight months in France digging holes in the ground to extend the Maginot Line to the Channel coast. Then when the Germans poured into Belgium, instead of sitting in those holes and going bang, bang when the Germans got there, we drove on through Belgium to meet them – to the welcome and temporary delight of the Belgians. But we could not hold them and started falling back.
>
> We then followed on behind the truck in front. After that none of us had any idea where we were supposed to be going. With no maps and no knowledge of the terrain we could often only take our direction from the refugees. They too were moving away from the Germans but sadly and forlornly, there was nothing we could do to help them.

> We found our battalion eventually but most of them didn't know who I was, where I'd come from, or why I was there. We queued for the best part of two days for boats coming to the mole [the long stretch of harbour wall running out to sea, where troops waited for ships to pull in to rescue them]. When German aircraft came over bombing and machine gunning we spread out as far as possible but sportingly returned as nearly as we could to our position in the queue.[33]

Harry and hundreds of others boarded the old peacetime cross-Channel paddle-steamer *The Maid of Orleans*. Once aboard, Harry helped a bombardier on the ship load a Lewis gun and shoot down a Luftwaffe Me109. The ship arrived in Dover three hours after leaving the war-torn beaches of Dunkirk.

Perhaps this story, and memories of the terrifying evacuation from Boulogne, gives us just a hint of what *Dad's Army* star Ridley may have witnessed and endured at the time. Nicolas explained that his father's experiences in the Second World War were as dreadful as those he suffered in the First, or even worse: 'We have no inkling of what happened because it was too appalling for words; there was nothing he could hint at. He shouldn't have been there; he had volunteered even though over age. However, his second marriage had broken up and he was in a bad way and I think it was just an escape.'

When Nicolas read through Ridley's diary, he noted again his father's eternal reluctance to speak about the First World War. Mainly, he said, it was because he firmly believed that 'others had already described it all'. Ridley wrote this, despite the fact he was often tortured by his recurring memories of the Somme. But whether talking about it would have helped him is difficult to know, as he came from a generation when men didn't talk about their feelings. Strong and silent was the ultimate motto back then.

Of the Second World War he explained:

> I shall write even less about my days with the BEF in France in the early months of the Second World War but I have a very different reason: fear. Within hours of setting foot on the quay at Cherbourg in September 1939, I was suffering from acute shell shock again. It is quite possible that outwardly I showed little if any, of it. It took the form of mental suffering that at best could be described as an inverted nightmare.

It's hardly surprising. For while the early weeks of the 'phoney war' in northern France were a haven of tranquillity, any soldier believing it would last was living in a fool's paradise. The noise and hell of war would be upon them by the early spring of 1940. For Ridley it acted as a trigger to his subconscious, forcing him to relive the nightmares of the Somme and destroying any sense of peace or mental stability. Captain Ridley's medical condition was worsening, despite his courageous efforts to fight it off since that first day at Cherbourg. When he boarded HMS *Vimiera* in Boulogne around 23 May, his relief was no doubt soured by fears of being labelled a 'coward' once he arrived back in England. However, for the hundreds of thousands of British, French and Belgians who were evacuated in what the Press described as a 'disaster turned into triumph', there was nothing but a hearty surprise welcome befitting the returning heroes.

Within days Ridley was demobilised from the Army. His son Nicolas reports that by this time his father had achieved the rank of major. Instead, he briefly became a member of the Local Defence Volunteers, just before the organisation morphed into the Home Guard. When the militarisation of his life got too much for him again, this great war hero was discharged and went back to his life as a writer and director. Life in uniform wouldn't arise again until twenty-eight years later – only this time it would make him famous as television's legendary Private Godfrey.

There's little doubt the internal trauma he endured through his wartime experiences shaped his work in film, television and theatre. As a bright young playwright hailed as a star in the 1920s for his masterpiece, his experience of the brutalities of war had taught him the value of time. He had learned through fear how to make use of a moment – to seize it and focus on the idea of less being more. After all, intensity in an actor can also bring gravitas to any character.

Let's not forget either how the success of *The Ghost Train* enabled him to bask in a kind of popularity which draped its thin veil of strange forgetfulness about the First World War over so many. There was among the new generation of champagne drinkers and partygoers a comforting feeling of 'never again' when memories of the recent conflict threatened to destroy their new-found optimism.

In 1941 a young actor named Derek van den Bogaerde, later better known as Dirk Bogarde, was awaiting his call-up papers. He would go on to serve as a British intelligence officer during the war. Derek appeared in *The Ghost Train* as one of an ENSA ensemble and remembered Ridley very well. When the episode of the popular television show *This is Your Life* about Ridley was aired in 1976, there was an appearance by Bogarde himself, by now an international film star and writer, via a big screen in the studio. The dapper Bogarde filmed his tribute to Ridley at his home in the south of France. He recalled:

It was thirty-five years ago in January 1941 and I joined the ENSA production of *The Ghost Train*. Everyone had been called up at that time and I was just waiting for my turn and I was the only thing left. I remember you very well on our tour of all those army camps and a very beautiful voluptuous lady in a red dress who you later married, Althea Parker, who I send on a big kiss to. So we got on with all those shows at all those army camps and when the show got to Amesbury in Salisbury I got called up. It was seven years before I took to the stage again.

Well, you've been in two world wars now and you are still in *Dad's Army* so no sign of demob yet! [Smiles and laughter from Ridley's family and friends.] Anyway I bet this has been a huge surprise to you. I hope it hasn't thrown you. Much love . . .

However, long before this televisual look back on his life, Ridley and the world had learned that time is perpetually changing and mankind's never-ending appetite for death and destruction marches on. He admitted that the years after the war were not always full of good times. 'I would wake up drenched in sweat, sometimes I was afraid I would black out when I was on stage,' he recalled.

In 1944 he was to suffer further injury when a doodlebug hit his home in Caterham, Surrey. Some hours after the event he opened his eyes and despite bruised ribs appeared to be in one piece and feeling fine. It wasn't long, though, before the shock set in for good and the real reaction began to blight his life. He described it in 'The Book':

One morning in June I woke at about 6am and got up to make a cup of tea. It was dull, misty and a slight drizzle was falling. I was just pouring boiling water into the teapot when I heard a rather unfamiliar noise and went out into the garden to investigate. There was a very off-shaped aircraft hovering overhead which suddenly dived over the roof of my cottage as if it had been shot down.

If I had stayed where I was I would have been perfectly all right. I didn't. I ran around the thick protecting walls to see what was happening. The next thing I knew I was waking up at the base of an apple tree into which I had been blasted. I got up and went back to the house – in which not even a window had been broken – and found that my tea was stone cold. I must have been 'out' for some time.[34]

Then there were the fainting fits and episodes in which he was paralysed to the spot. After so many setbacks in recent years, it's no surprise Ridley began suffering from psychological problems. The army camp and airfields tour of *The Ghost Train* with ENSA had proved exhausting and provided small comfort.

Soon after surviving the doodlebug blast, he began to really suffer. By now he was in London, where he was due to appear in an Old Vic production of Ibsen's *Peer Gynt* with Fleet Air Arm pilot and renowned actor Ralph Richardson. Ridley explained what happened next:

> I was just starting a short speech when to my amazement I couldn't speak. The director, Tyrone Guthrie, asked what was the matter but I could only reply in inarticulate sounds and was trembling violently all over. The strange thing was that there were no bombs falling at the time and in any case we were in a place of comparative safety (the basement of the National Gallery). Guthrie was most kind and suggested I should stop rehearsing for the day. Actually there wasn't much point in doing otherwise.

A doctor was called in some time after he'd left the rehearsal and Ridley learned his spinal column was concussed and he was suffering severely from delayed shock. He was disappointed when he was urged to take a break for several weeks and had to pull out of the play. In order to recuperate, he organised a trip to 'the Potteries' to stay with friends, and within weeks he was back on stage at the historic Harrogate Theatre, where he played more than fifty leading roles. During the run he drew himself a strict timetable to keep up a routine and all was going well until he swallowed a small bone one lunchtime that got caught in his throat. After an agonising session in which a throat specialist removed the obstruction, Ridley was ordered to keep quiet and 'not speak a single word' while his throat healed. Still he went back to work and all seemed fine until someone at the back of the audience asked him to 'speak up!' He revealed how his voice always had a particular rasp to it after this attempt to shout, and he went on to suffer often from laryngitis.

But by 1945 his life had begun to look brighter. That year he married the actress Althea Parker, whom he met during his ENSA tour with his most famous play. She was 35 when they married and Ridley was nearing 50. Their son Nicolas was born in 1947. Althea provided her husband with emotional support during the dark times of his blackouts and nightmares, and always stood by him during the financial difficulties of the 1950s when opportunities for his plays had diminished and the bright new era of television began to fascinate the world.

Nicolas recalls how he was often terrified for his father whenever he was appearing on stage. He was anxious about him fainting, or what if he misses an entrance or fluffs his words? 'I would have been powerless to help. I know he often plays a part every night without me watching but it makes no difference and I really didn't want to be there.'

In 1956, some twelve years before *Dad's Army* was created, Ridley landed a role in radio playing the character of a baker called 'Doughy' Hood in *The Archers*, the hit BBC radio show about a farming family and the village community of Ambridge. The show, created in 1951, was a popular nightly event and by the time Ridley joined the cast, it already had millions of listeners devotedly tuning in to hear every episode. He played 'Doughy' for more than ten years.

Then as televisions began appearing in homes all over the land in the 1960s, Ridley took to the small screen. In 1964 he appeared as the vicar in the drama series *Crossroads*, as Alderman Pratt in *Carry On Girls* and as a gardener in *Z-Cars*, and even had a brief role as an elderly gent in *The Avengers*. Around this time he snapped up any work he could get, fighting off the fear there might come a time when the opportunities would run dry and financially he'd be in the doldrums more than ever. Nicolas described his father's life at this time as 'all very seat of the pants'. However, he adds, if 'The Book' had ever been published, ardent fans of *Dad's Army* might have been disappointed. Fewer than three pages of the 206-page typescript relate to the legendary television series. 'There are no odd anecdotes or indiscreet revelations. There is nothing to fascinate or shock. There is simple gratitude,' explains Nicolas.

But there was obviously some excitement when Ridley received an invitation to visit BBC producer David Croft to drop by for a chat about a new television sitcom about the Home Guard. Croft had already met Ridley in recent months during the making of the series *Hugh and I*, after scriptwriter John Chapman had recommended him for a role similar to that of Private Godfrey. During the casting for *Dad's Army*, the canny Croft wrote:

> I was keen to have Arnold Ridley for Private Godfrey, who was a very polite retired gentleman's tailor with a weak bladder. He'd had a most distinguished career in the business and had written *The Ghost Train* and many other plays.
>
> He'd directed plays and films, and he was well known for the parts he'd played on radio and in television.
>
> He was in his early seventies and I was concerned that he wouldn't be physically up to playing the part of Godfrey as there was bound to be a certain amount of running about that I couldn't avoid requiring of him, but he said that if I was game to give him the part, he was game to try.
>
> During filming he was mostly to be seen walking up and down, flapping his arms like a penguin while muttering, 'Tell them to get on with it, tell them to get on with it.' I found him to be a dear old love and remarkably like his television character.

I have many happy memories of Arnold floundering around. There was enormous comedy to be had from the way he had to be lifted onto the back of the van and things like that. All his disabilities were an enormous advantage from the point of view of comedy. And the wonderful look of bewilderment in his face.

*Dad's Army* writer Jimmy Perry said the part of Godfrey, a devout conscientious objector who had joined the Royal Army Medical Corps in the First World War, was Croft's brilliant idea. Perry described Ridley as 'delightful', adding: 'His gentleness made such a wonderful contrast to the aggression of the angry Private Frazer.'

In the brief observations made by the actor in 'The Book', we learn that Ridley informed Croft at their initial *Dad's Army* meeting that he was 'very fit' and had 'survived two wars'. He wrote:

> Looking back, I am surprised how little I concerned myself over the matter and it is just as well that I didn't realise how much was at stake and how much becoming a member of the cast of *Dad's Army* would change my status as an actor. Hearing from my agent that David [Croft] had booked me for six episodes was good news. I received a batch of six scripts in due course and read them with great interest before coming to a conclusion which was as definite as I now know it to have been completely wrong.
>
> I was quite certain that Jimmy and David had written six quite excellent scripts which would delight the 'oldies' but wouldn't contain a shred of either humour or interest for the younger generation. How wrong I was, and how glad I am of it!

Nicolas reveals how it was his father's new agent Bill McLean who pushed and pushed for Ridley to get the role, although Croft had been nervous because of the actor's age. Bluntly, there were fears he might not last the series and that goes some way in explaining the difference in salaries in the early episodes. Now, of course, such discrimination based on age alone would not be permitted, but back in the late 1960s the pay-roll looked like this: John Le Mesurier (Sergeant Wilson) received £ 261.10s per episode, both Arthur Lowe (Captain Mainwaring) and Clive Dunn (Corporal Jones) £ 210, John Laurie £ 105, James Beck £ 78 and Ridley – the most experienced in all forms of life including the theatre – £ 63.

Ridley was 72 years old when filming began, which made him a target for comments by the rest of the cast, who deemed them humorous at the time. The actor James Beck (Private Walker) was with Ridley one day during a scene in a graveyard in Thetford when he turned to him and said 'Hardly worth your leaving, is it Arnold?' This amusing aside, however, was somewhat inaccurate as the 44-year-old Beck died in 1973, eleven years before his elderly co-star. However, it is heartening to know Ridley enjoyed his time in the show and, of course, he must have been delighted that Perry and Croft provided so much information about the character of Godfrey to help motivate his performance into the realms of greatness.

On the subject of conscientious objectors, the actor particularly expressed his admiration for the First World War soldier and poet Siegfried Sassoon, who had spoken out against four years of conflict and saluted those who decided out of moral duty not to carry a weapon into battle. 'I knew one man who was very badly treated as a Conscientious Objector because he wouldn't submit to a medical examination. Had he submitted, he would have been grade 99 and they would never had had him. He was half-blind and weedy but he just wouldn't on principle,' recalled Ridley.

Pertinently, his son Nicolas himself goes on to describe the 'post-war generation' and noted how his own awareness of military conflict had been a literary one, learned through watching Sir Laurence Olivier in *Henry V*. As a boy, he saw the film with his mother, who was helping him find a speech for an event at school. 'I felt, as with many of my own generation, defined by what I missed, the hardship, the heroism, the sacrifice, the victory.' He then points out that to his father 'the war', although rarely mentioned, was always the 1914–1918 conflict – 'the war to end all wars' – except that it didn't.

At first, when Nicolas attempted to ask his father about his service, all he heard in reply was: 'So much has been written that I don't think it necessary to give a fully detailed account of my war experiences.' And he more or less stuck to this decision whenever Nicolas asked him to open up a little more about it, especially as his father had been in the ranks and therefore had a different view of the conflict from the more famous poets, writers and artists who had mostly been subalterns.

But still Ridley wouldn't heed his eager young son's call to write down the unique 'material' and it was only later on in his own life that Nicolas twigged why his father's response was always the same gently worded reply: 'Oh, I don't think so, old boy. No, no. There are plenty of people with more to say than me.' Nicolas said: 'When I was older I began to understand that my father had to justify his survival and that the only way to do this was to forget. In order to survive he had to train himself to forget. Or to remember less vividly, less unremittingly. His nightmares he couldn't command.'

Ridley himself had explained how the psychological torture was far worse than any physical pain. In a BBC interview in 1971 he said: 'The vital question wasn't if I get killed but when I get killed, because a battalion went over 800 strong, you lost 300 or 400, half the number, perhaps more. Now it wasn't a question of saying, "I am one of the survivors, hurrah, hurrah", because you didn't go home . . . Out came another draft of 400 and you went over the top again.'

He talked of a war that was not a succession of different battles but one long, continuous one with varying intensity: 'Battalions were wiped out, not once but time after time. What happened to survivors? Did they go home in glory? Not a bit of it. The best they could expect was that they might get a week or so out of the line, while the battalion was being brought up to strength again with drafts of fresh troops, before going back to yet another "over the top".'

When Ridley appeared on the BBC radio show *Desert Island Discs* in 1971 he talked about memory being a strange thing. 'After a lapse of time, even the most miserable set of circumstances, roses seem to grow round them a little bit,' he said. But there was nothing floral to sweeten the psychological stench of his memories when it came to the Second World War. While on rare occasions he could talk about his service in the First, the 'mental suffering' he experienced meant he would not speak of his time in the Second. He said: 'To recount events, I would have to relive them. I am too afraid.'

And while we will always remember Ridley as Godfrey, a sweet, gentle old man who never set out to hurt a living soul, it's important not to forget that the man who played him was very different. He was not afraid to take life by the scruff of its neck and move on with courage. Remember, he once threw a man out of a window!

In *Godfrey's Ghost* we read of the day Nicolas went to meet his father's agent Bill McLean, who talked about attending a first night performance of a 1976 revival of *The Ghost Train* at the Old Vic with Ridley and his wife Althea:

We sat down in the stalls, the curtain went up and Arnold promptly disappeared from the seat next to me. I didn't see him again for the rest of the production. Come the end of the performance, the producer stands up on stage and starts to say they are very honoured to have the author in the audience and would he like to stand up and take a bow. Upon which a spotlight starts to sweep over the auditorium towards what is still an empty seat beside me.

Althea doesn't bat an eyelid – maybe she's been through this before – but I am sitting there wondering what to do when the spotlight arrives at the empty seat. Can I stand up and pretend to be Arnold? I'm not required to say anything. I only have to wave. But just as the spotlight hits the seat, so does Arnold – I've never seen such good timing – and he stands up as if he's been there throughout the whole performance. Later on, in the bar, having a drink, the director came up to him and asked him what he thought? It was always a mistake to ask Arnold this unless you were sure what the answer was going to be. 'Well,' he replied, 'perhaps one day *you'll* write a play and I can bugger *that* up!' This is a gentle old man?!

McLean added quickly that he never knew Ridley to be nasty about anyone. Questioned by Nicolas about the actor John Laurie's alleged rows with Ridley, he replied:

I don't think there was anything serious. I always understood it was because they could never decide who was oldest. Arnold used to celebrate his birthdays at least one year early in case he didn't make it to the next one. I was certainly confused about how old he was and I strongly suspect he was confused, too!

Towards the end of his life Ridley lived at Denville Hall in Hillingdon, London, a residence for retired actors. He died in hospital aged 84, following a fall. Today visitors to Bath Abbey in Somerset can visit his parents' grave, where his ashes are buried.

*** 

IN concluding this tribute to Arnold Ridley OBE I was delighted in the summer of 2020 when his son Nicolas kindly agreed to write about his father exclusively for this book. He wrote:

People remember things differently. There were those who, in later years, said they'd always known that *Dad's Army* would be a winner; and there were those who said that at the start they had had their doubts. When my father received the first batch of scripts in the post, he thought they were wonderful. He was certain the show would appeal to those who remembered the Second World War, but he didn't think it would be of much interest to a younger audience. How wrong he was, and how thoroughly pleased he was to be wrong!

*Dad's Army* wasn't an instant success. Its popularity built steadily from series to series. By the end, its viewing figures were extraordinary, but no one could have predicted that the show – more than fifty years after it was first aired – would have continued to attract audiences old and new, and to have woven itself into the very fabric of popular culture.

What, then, was – and is – the unique appeal of the show? The description 'unique' is a much overused term but in this case I feel it's justified because – really – there's nothing to compare with *Dad's Army*. Admirers of the show will offer a variety of explanations, and mine are probably much the same as many other people's.

First, there was the wonderful cast – excellent actors from very different backgrounds bringing with them a mix of comic skills and experience. They were actors who became their characters and later, as the writers and the actors learnt more about each other, the characters became the actors, displaying behaviour and frailties which the audience could readily recognise, associate with and enjoy.

Then there were the beautifully crafted scripts, which succeeded in putting on display an extraordinary range of comedy from visual gags, through satisfying plots and character-driven stories to, in some cases, tragicomedy. But whether we were being entertained through slapstick or pathos, there was an underlying gentleness and innocence that touches all but the hardest heart.

Next there was the authenticity. Huge care was taken to ensure that period details were absolutely correct. Most of the audience would have either forgotten or never have known such details but I believe 'getting it right' somehow cemented the show's belief in itself. *Dad's Army* created an unshakeable world that the passing of time hasn't undermined.

There are other elements, too, not least David Croft's magnificent man management and his ability to build a team. Actors aren't always easy to work with. There are vanities and insecurities that can surface easily. The lines and laughs in a script are counted and can be the subject of jealousy and debate. But David Croft forged a friendship between cast members through his care and concern, and their camaraderie seldom if ever wavered.

My father loved playing the part of Private Godfrey. It came very late in a long theatrical career and followed an arid period when he had struggled to find acting parts of any kind. Godfrey's gentleness, innocence and loyalty were genuine and drew on my father's own reserves of courage, steadfastness and stoicism.

He was the only member of the cast to have fought in both world wars and had the dubious distinction of being invalided out of the British Army on two separate occasions. Not content with this, after being evacuated from France in 1940 he joined the Local Defence Volunteers, who became the Home Guard, and saw active service as the Battle of Britain raged over Biggin Hill.

As with all those who served on the Western Front, the First World War affected him both physically and psychologically for the rest of his life. His wounds from the battle of the Somme remained with him, and his nightmares never entirely ceased. He was a man of great moral strength, who coped with the perils of success and wretched episodes of misfortune with extraordinary fortitude. Did his war experience feed into his acting and writing? I'd argue that in a strange way it helped him through his sense of survivor's guilt. But like many men who saw active service he always felt he owed a duty to his fallen comrades to live life with gratitude and without complaint.[35]

What the iconic Ridley shared in common with Private Godfrey, his famous television character, was the memory of serving with great bravery in the First World War. They also shared a love of sport. Godfrey had worked for more than three decades in the sports department of the Army & Navy Stores, and, like the actor who played him, was keen on amateur dramatics. Godfrey, a bachelor, liked peace and quiet in his later years, and so did Ridley.

Indeed, if anyone truly understood the character of Private Charles Godfrey it was of course the great actor and war hero Arnold Ridley OBE, whose creative talents combined with his personal strength to overcome harrowing experiences of war-driven trauma, made Godfrey a genuine legend in the realm of British television comedy.

# JOHN LAURIE

There's a four letter word which describes the Somme. I can't describe it, I haven't got the heart.

EVERYONE knows someone with the characteristics of Private James Frazer – grumpy, pessimistic, a stoic coper shuffling around carrying a triple dose of reality draped upon their shoulders . . . and yet beneath the soul of iron there's the odd twinkle of refreshing sanity glinting into a soapy yet crafty smile. Doom-monger and cynic, the Scots character of Frazer made the perfect undertaker – he was a kind of dark-eyed Aristotle of the *Dad's Army* platoon and the Walmington-on-Sea community. His role in life was to focus on humanity's end first and then later philosophise about its beginnings and shortfalls.

So who better than seasoned Shakespearian actor the lugubrious and gaunt-faced John Laurie to play the role of the dour and cantankerous Frazer, a character who was written into the show by the artful Jimmy Perry – a creative man who relished a good cliché and discovered actors able to embody and manifest the comedic power of a character in a script.

How funny that when the 71-year-old Laurie was originally offered the script, which required Frazer to be 'a Scotsman', he took one look and shrugged off the show as 'doomed' but approached it with his sardonic devil-may-care attitude. Laurie had a reputation for never turning down an offer of work, although he reckoned no one would be interested in a series about the Home Guard as it was all 'so mundane'. He was speaking from real-life experience there, having served among its doughty ranks during the Second World War. So how else could he approach the role of Frazer in *Dad's Army* than with the cynicism that became the character's badge of honour?

Jimmy Perry created the character of Private James Frazer as a chief petty officer and cook in the Royal Navy in the First World War, who had seen action at the Battle of Jutland in 1916. In the episode where the platoon go on parade wearing their medals (except

Captain Mainwaring, who embarrassingly didn't have any to show), Frazer is seen wearing among his First World War medals one of the rarest: the white-ribboned Polar Medal. This suggested he had been among the crew of *Nimrod*, the ship that ferried the great explorer Ernest Shackleton and his men to the Antarctic in 1909. This adds yet another fascinating element to Frazer's remarkable life experiences.

John Laurie, with his uncanny staring eyes, made Frazer the watchful sage of the *Dad's Army* outfit. He was always ready with a melancholic Celtic anecdote to steer a scene out of the realms of stagnancy. Frazer's ghostly tale of the 'auld empty barn' . . . er, which was just 'an auld empty barn', revealed to audiences that the undertaker enjoyed using his professional association with death to wind up the men around him. The episode where the wind is howling around a farm building as he lounges on a bed of straw next to a spooked Captain Mainwaring during a military exercise is comedy legend. Frazer's propensity to build up the psychological drama before imparting a dark ghost story which comes to nothing is profoundly funny.

Writing this chapter led me to a series of lively anecdotes about Laurie which had mostly been included in the memoirs of his fellow cast members. As far as I know, Laurie did not write his autobiography and therefore it is from these stories that I was able to derive a character description of the wily Scotsman whose theatrical talent brought Private 'We're all doomed' James Frazer into the public consciousness. It was telling in many ways that Laurie decided to steer clear of any eager publisher wanting him to write the story of his life. He must have had offers, and generous ones at that. Indeed most of his co-stars had taken this road.

His *Dad's Army* co-star Bill Pertwee (Chief Warden Hodges) wrote: 'It took me a long time to find out anything about John. It wasn't that he couldn't be bothered to talk about all the marvellous things he had done, he just thought it was all in the past and people didn't want to listen to, as he would say, "the ramblings of an old man".' He went on:

> Occasionally, I did find a way to draw him out. I would tell him how much I admired all the great classical actors and that I certainly hadn't got the talent or even the inclination to tangle with that side of the 'game'. John would then be happy to tell me all about the actors he had worked with and in doing so he naturally talked about his involvement with them and the productions he had been in. However, it took me the best part of nine years to find all this out.'[1]

One fact which was always certain was that Laurie hated speaking at length about his experiences as a soldier in the trenches of the Western Front during the First World War. Like his co-star Arnold

Ridley, he saw active service at the battle of the Somme in 1916. Occasionally he was known to sit quietly with Ridley near the set when not filming, and if Laurie was of a mind to get on with his fellow septuagenarian Ridley, they would share stories about their war in the trenches.

Writer Jimmy Perry recalled in his own memoir:

> The shadow of the First World War hung heavily over everything when I was young. Most people were connected with it in some way or another. I remember John Laurie, who had served, saying, 'You know, laddie, I still have nightmares about that time. Even after all these years.' In the 1970s I did a television series called *The Old Boy Network* (terrible title but who am I to talk – I once wrote a television series called *Lollipop Loves Mr Mole!*) I featured John Laurie in one of the episodes and we told the story of his life. In the section about the First World War I threw up a huge picture of the battle of the Somme behind him. A single tear trickled down his granite face and he whispered, 'Take it off, I just can't bear to look.'
>
> How it must have brutalised those young men. Oh, that terrible war, the flower of British manhood butchered, a million dead and another million crippled, not to mention the French and the Germans. Everywhere after the war, men with an arm or leg missing, suffering from shell shock or the effects of poison gas. I don't think our dear old country ever recovered from it.[2]

This illustrates how the doughty Laurie suffered dark memories of the battlefields, which threatened to cloud his heart and soul. It's inconceivable to think he did not suffer the effects of post-traumatic stress disorder – and just as Arnold Ridley fought hard to bury all memories of the war, Laurie too was keen to avoid anything that might trigger another night made sleepless by unbearably bad and torturous dreams.

John Paton Laurie's war began on a chilly day in March 1916, around the time of his 19th birthday. The grammar-school boy from Dumfries, Scotland, described as a 'bantamweight', had volunteered for the oldest regiment in the British Army, the Honourable Artillery Company, which was formed by King Henry VIII by royal charter in 1537. In order to serve his country, Laurie's studies and ambitions to become an architect were put on hold and instead he was given his number 7244 as a private in the famous HAC. The teenage son of a Dumfries mill worker named William Laurie and his wife Jessie, John was sent immediately for training in Richmond Park. In one of his rare statements about that time he said: 'It was a great war . . . for the first seven months.' However, that positive opinion ended dramatically in November 1916 when he was sent to fight on the Somme with the 1st Battalion: 'There's a four letter word which describes the Somme . . . I can't describe it, I haven't got the heart,' he recalled bleakly.

The history of the HAC's valiant participation in the First World War is spectacular. In September 1914 the 1st Battalion HAC was in France, taking part in the first battle of Ypres, and the battles of Ancre and Arras. Soon afterwards, it focused on officer training. The 2nd Battalion HAC was formed in August 1914 and had arrived in France by October 1916. On 25 February 1917 it took part in battles at Bucquoy and then Arras. It also saw action at the battle of Ypres in October 1917. By November 1917 the 2nd Battalion had moved to the Italian front. In the battle of Vittorio Veneto in October 1918, the HAC men led a force of Italians, Americans and British which defeated the garrison of the strategic island of Papadopoli. For this remarkable feat the HAC was awarded two Distinguished Service Orders, five Military Crosses, three Distinguished Conduct Medals and 29 Military Medals.

Both A and B Batteries of the Honourable Artillery Company went to Suez in April 1915. In July B Battery fought in the recapture of Sheikh Othman. In 1917 both batteries took part in the Palestine Campaign and were in action at the first and second battles of Gaza. In the German counterattack during the second action at Es Salt on 1 May 1918 A Battery was forced to withdraw under heavy fire, which resulted in the loss of all its guns. Both A and B Batteries took part in the battle of Megiddo in September. A third battery, the 309th (HAC) Siege Battery, went to France in April 1917 and saw action at the battles of Messines and Amiens. During the First World War the HAC suffered a total loss of 1,650 men, with two Victoria Crosses awarded for action in 1917 at Gavrelle.

Whilst the fighting on the Somme was winding down by the time Private Laurie arrived in November 1916, nevertheless the gruesome sights and sounds and the ultimate horrors of death he encountered there remained planted in his mind for ever. The spectacular immensity of human destruction embedded in the murderous trenches and no man's land beyond left Laurie, as with so many other veterans, utterly speechless. It was as if no words had the power to counter the enormity of despair: 'I only remember the misery, the futile running across open ground, the price paid to gain a few yards of useless land and, in no time at all, the running back again. I don't think many of us expected to come out of that alive. It wasn't a question of *will* I die? Only of *when*?' he said.

Laurie also fought at Passchendaele but within weeks he had caught tuberculosis and trench nephritis and was shipped back to Netley Military Hospital, Southampton. Medical historians reveal how the latter disease first appeared among the troops in the spring of 1915. They suffered from breathlessness, swelling of the face or legs, headache, sore throat, and the presence of albumin and renal casts in the urine. This debilitating condition was a serious problem for the Allies during the First World War, leading to 35,000 casualties in the British forces and 2,000 in the Americans. There were also hundreds of deaths. The medical response to trench nephritis was largely ineffective, with commentators recognizing that there had been a lack of medical progress. Poor diet and the scarcity of nutritious food also led men to suffer weakened kidney function and other diseases including trench foot, gum and dental rot.[3]

Decades later, *Dad's Army* star Bill Pertwee recalled how Laurie, then in his 70s, often suffered from asthma and bouts of coughing during filming, and occasionally he would make sarcastic remarks to the aged Arnold Ridley. Clive Dunn (Corporal Jones) went on to remark on Laurie's resilient attitude and stoicism:

John was by far the most energetic, bright-brained, outrageously outspoken septuagenarian in the profession. This energy sometimes encouraged David Croft the show producer to treat him as if he were a young athlete instead of an ageing actor. John was determined not to allow his age or his chronic chest complaint to prevent him from joining in, or even leading the dashes across the Norfolk countryside carrying a heavy gun wearing full equipment. The sight of Arnold Ridley being given a special chair to sit on often enraged John, who was often too out of breath to deliver his caustic criticism. I used to egg him on to say naughty things about actors or producers or politicians; he loved a bit of scandal or excitement.

Sometimes the highly temperamental John would fluff his lines in the studio. Then he would run to the audience with his lean arms outspread and say in broad Scots, 'Y'see, ladies and gentlemen, why ah'm given a small part. Ah cannie even remember the simplest thing, ahm such a silly auld sod!' The audience would cheer him on, and in a now heavily charged atmosphere John would have another go and get it right. John was quite well to do and had no need to work but he was attracted by the convenience of television.[4]

***

IN the National Archive John Paton Laurie's official medical report of 1917 reveals him as a 20-year-old man who had experienced 'one year of service'. He spent nine months with 'Field Force'. His 'Ailment' is listed as Albuminuria (a serious symptom of trench nephritis). He was first admitted to hospital at Le Havre on 17 August 1917 and a week later transferred to 'Sick Convoy', sailing back to Southampton aboard a Glaswegian-built hospital ship named *Warilda* (which was sadly torpedoed and sunk by German submarines almost year later, on 3 August 1918, despite its Red Cross insignia. Of 801 passengers, 123 died in the tragedy.) On Laurie's official medical report his religion is listed as Presbyterian, and his regiment is given as 1st Battalion, HAC. Other information for Laurie is recorded as 'PU' – Permanently Unfit.

Towards the end of 1917, when he was recovering well, he rejoined his regiment on light duties. He was appointed Sergeant of Musketeers at the Tower of London, which meant learning how to warn the city against Zeppelin raids. It was in 1918, during this time of his activities at the Tower, that Laurie, now 21 years old, discovered his older brother William had been killed in battle. Eventually discharged from his duties in January 1919, he recalled: 'Well, I stuck it . . . the First World War . . . and was not killed, though I died many times. It was a horrible war.'

The idea of continuing his architecture studies had evaporated, the idealistic young man now very much changed by the brutalities of war. It is not known how or when he decided to become an actor, but in 1919 he marched into the hallowed rehearsal rooms of Elsie Fogerty's Royal Central School of Speech and Drama in London, based at the Royal Albert Hall. It would be just a matter of months before Laurie appeared in his first professional stage production in 1921. This time he was back home in Dumfries, Scotland, appearing at the local Lyceum Theatre in *What Every Woman Knows*, written by J.M. Barrie of *Peter Pan* fame. But his real passion was anything by the great Shakespeare.

Still enjoying the resounding buzz of thunderous applause for his performances, and rewarded with notably high grades for his prowess in acting classes, Laurie joined the Old Vic company. Here in 1925 he met the actress Florence May Saunders, who became his first wife. Tragically, Florence died in 1926 after contracting meningitis. For two years Laurie dealt with his grief by focusing on his work in the theatre, and went on to find happiness again when he married Oonah Veronica Todd-Naylor. During his time with the Old Vic he was offered a place at the Shakespeare Memorial Theatre in Stratford-upon-Avon, the home of the great Bard.

Although he had left drama school expecting to play various character roles as a Scotsman, his tremendous talent for Shakespeare

Jimmy Perry, Second World War.

Jimmy Perry and pals in the Watford Home Guard, 1940. Perry had removed his helmet here to look 'heroic'!

Jimmy Perry's glamorous neighbour June Duprez, starring in a film with Louis Hayward.

ATS women who served alongside the men of the Royal Artillery. ATS girl Brenda Usherwood (née Soughton) is second from the right, standing in the top row.

David Croft (*middle row, far right*), and pals of the 4th Independent Infantry Brigade in Singapore, 1945.

The show's creators Jimmy Perry OBE and David Croft OBE. (*PA Images/Alamy*)

The Royal Artillery Bofors gun which both Perry and Croft learned to operate at the start of their military careers.

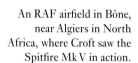

An RAF airfield in Bône, near Algiers in North Africa, where Croft saw the Spitfire Mk V in action.

Arnold Ridley, First World War.

Arnold Ridley in 1921.

Nicolas Ridley and his biography of
his actor/playwright father, Arnold.
(*Andrew Ruff/Alamy*)

Arnold Ridley in his role as Private Charles
Godfrey. (*Trinity Mirror – Mirrorpix/Alamy*)

A few heroes of the Somerset Light Infantry during the First World War.

HMS *Vimiera*, the ship that carried Captain Ridley to safety from Boulogne.

Major Arnold Ridley, Second World War.

George Taylor served with the Somerset Light Infantry in the First World War.

In a scene from the show, Captain Mainwaring is shocked to discover Private Charles Godfrey won the Military Medal for heroism as a stretcher-bearer in the First World War.

Arthur Lowe served with the Corps of Royal Electrical and Mechanical Engineers (REME) in the Middle East during the Second World War.

Arthur Lowe addresses the cast during rehearsals of a play in Alexandria, Egypt, in 1944.

The cast in all their glory in a scene from the show. From left: Ian Lavender as Private Frank Pike, Bill Pertwee as ARP Warden William Hodges, Arthur Lowe as Captain George Mainwaring, James Beck as Private Joe Walker, Clive Dunn as Corporal Jack Jones, John Le Mesurier as Sergeant Arthur Wilson. Standing behind them are John Laurie as Private James Frazer and Arnold Ridley as Private Charles Godfrey. (*Allstar Picture Library Ltd / Alamy*)

A smiling Bombardier Arthur Lowe in 1940 (*back row, second from the left*), with army pals at Pembroke Dock in South Wales.

*Amazon* – the yacht loved and owned by Arthur Lowe. (*Picture by courtesy of Jack Lowe*)

Jack Lowe's picture of the *Dad's Army* cast received a note of recognition from the RNLI at the 1977 International Boat Show. (*Picture by courtesy of Jack Lowe*)

Arthur and Joan Lowe at the Twickenham & District RNLI 13th Annual Ball in 1973. (*Picture by courtesy of Jack Lowe*)

Classic! Make way for the Walmington–on–Sea Home Guard action men! (*PA Images/Alamy*)

John Le Mesurier served with the
Royal Tank Regiment.

John Le Mesurier in the film *Private's
Progress*, made in 1956.

Arthur Lowe as Captain
Mainwaring and John Le
Mesurier photographed
during filming in 1971.
(*Everett Collection Inc. /
Alamy*)

John Laurie served with the 1st Battalion, Honourable Artillery Company in the First World War.

John Laurie saw action in the Battle of the Somme in November 1916 and at Passchendaele in 1917.

Michael Powell directed John Laurie in the epic drama *The Edge of the World* in 1936.

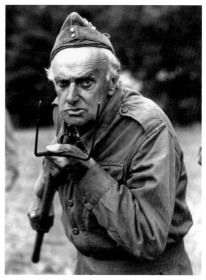

John Laurie, known to so many as the doughty, dour and dry-witted Private James Frazer. (*Allstar Picture Library Ltd/ Alamy*)

Clive Dunn and his fellow prisoners of war in Austria, 'smiling for the family' back home. Dunn is in the middle row at far left, showing off his centre-parting hair.

Clive Dunn was captured by the Germans in Greece.

Clive Dunn as Corporal Jones is ready for action. (*Allstar Picture Library Ltd/ Alamy*)

Germans occupying
Greece during the
Second World War.

Charles Read in the Home Guard in East
Kent during the Second World War. Charles
is the grandfather of the author of this book.

Easy does it! From the back it's Frazer, Walker, Godfrey, Pike and Jones making light of the load in a scene from the hit show. (*Trinity Mirror – Mirrorpix/Alamy*)

Ian Lavender, who played the affable young Private Pike in the show, went on to star as Brigadier Pritchard in the 2016 film of *Dad's Army*. Ian is pictured here in a recent parade. Series producer David Croft is seated behind him. (*Keith Mindham/Alamy*)

was evident as he went on to star successfully as Richard III, Othello and Macbeth. He was only in his second season at Stratford, and still only in his 20s, when he played Hamlet, one of the ultimate challenges for any actor's career, in a performance which is still regarded as a magnificent achievement for one so young and inexperienced. In an interview he once claimed his character portrayal of Shakespeare's troubled Danish prince was the definitive version. He told *Dad's Army* co-star Bill Pertwee, and anyone else who asked: 'That's the way to play Hamlet, don't wait too long like some of the boys are doing today.'

As well as appearing at Stratford and making a name for himself as Britain's brightest young classical theatre star, Laurie caught the attention of film director Alfred Hitchcock. It turned out the young Scotsman was adored by the camera, and Hitchcock, making his first ever talking picture, offered Laurie a role in the 1930 tragicomedy film *Juno and the Paycock*. Subsequently Hitchcock cast Laurie as John the crofter in his famous 1935 production of *The 39 Steps*.

Within two years the actor found himself working with the great Michael Powell, who became one of Britain's leading directors of surreal and authentic wartime propaganda films. Laurie was top billing starring as a character called Peter Manson in Powell's epic drama *The Edge of the World*. This black and white classic, filmed in 1936 and released the following year, was inspired by the true story of the 1931 evacuation of the tiny population of the isolated Scottish island of St Kilda at a time, Laurie describes, 'when the Shetlands meant wool and fish and ponies and the best deep sea fishermen in the world'.

As the younger generation decide to relocate to the mainland for reliable work, the remaining families left behind on St Kilda found it impossible to sustain a living and survive the rugged conditions. Powell, his actors and crew, however, were forbidden to film on the island, and instead shot each scene in Foula, one of the Shetland Islands. Laurie, a proud Scotsman through and through, was in his element and enjoying the opportunity to enrich the role of Peter with the resonance of his true Celtic heritage. Powell created a compelling drama driven by a cast of quality performers.

Forty-two years later, in 1978, when the Shetland Islands were renowned for their North Sea oil, Powell made a heart-warming documentary called *Return to The Edge of the World* about how his early film came to be made. Then, along with Laurie, Sydney Streeter, Grant Sutherland and others involved at the time he flies to the island of Foula, to be reunited with some of the islanders who were there in 1936. Powell recalls: 'It was important to us to see the places and people we knew on Foula when we were all very much younger.'

As the documentary proceeds, and we note the impressive rawness of the cliffs, Powell is revealed as a tiny and distant figure walking among the rocks and hills as waves crash beneath him, and then comes one of the rarest appearances ever seen – that of Laurie as himself. The footage is vital if we are to get an indication of the personality of the First World War veteran warrior who went on to create the legendary Private Frazer.

In Powell's documentary, Laurie introduces us to Foula, on the western coast of Scotland. His voice, so recognisable and beautifully poetic with its Gaelic lilt, narrates the following:

> Latitude 60 degrees, as far north as the southern tip of Greenland. Eight hundred miles north of Piccadilly Circus. Nothing between us and the north American continent but the Atlantic Ocean. The edge of the world. This is the Kame – the highest sea cliff in Great Britain. 1,220 feet from sky to sea. This is where a young film director called Michael Powell brought us in 1936 to make a film about the death of an island. It started out as a film but became an experience that changed all of our lives.
>
> Shetland Islanders are proud of their descent from the old Viking rovers. 'We're not Scottish, we're Norse!' they'll tell you. The name Foula is Norse: the island of birds.

Superb footage of the island's famous puffins can be seen, and we catch a rare sight of 'bonxie' in glorious flight – the great Skua, which Laurie gently informs us got its nickname from the islanders because it likes to swoop down upon its human neighbours and headbutt them during the Skua mating season! 'So watch out!', warns Laurie as if to start yet another eerie and cautionary tale to the Dad's Army platoon.

When the actor arrives on the island and gets out of the aircraft, we see him as a jovial 81 year old wrapped in a tweed coat and braced against the cold winds, but full of warm greetings for the small group of people he first met back in 1936. Powell refers to the star as the 'one and only John Laurie'. The relatives of those long-gone islanders are there too. Laurie reels off their names and shakes their hands and hugs them all vigorously. His response to their smiles, stories and memories is genuine. He meets a woman who played a girl in the original film and says 'Ah, you were a bonny girl and now you're a bonny woman.' The rugged-looking actor is welcomed by a sea of faces – Jimmy, Robbie, Hamish, the Ibister family father and son, and another elderly woman with what Laurie calls 'a real Foula face'. Laurie then chuckles about all the politeness and 'behaving like an Englishman!' He turns to the camera and says waspishly, with a roll of his famous intensely dark eyes, 'Ah Foula again. Oh! Oh, by the way I'm John Laurie. You may have seen me around, after all I've been acting for 57 of my 81 years. *Hamlet* at Stratford-upon-Avon, a crofter in *The 39 Steps*, and Private Frazer in *Dad's Army* and, of course, Peter Manson in Michael Powell's *The Edge of the World*.'

In person Laurie is as engaging as any character he played on stage or on screen. We watch him take the arm of one of the islanders and talk about *The Edge of the World* – how in order to win the role of Peter he had to 'age up a wee bit' and when Powell saw him at the audition he asked 'been in a snowstorm have ye, John?' Laurie then chuckled and remarked that at age 81 he'd not have to worry about adding on the years to play an older man.

For the rest of the documentary we see Powell and Laurie together walking about the island and recalling each scene, each shot they made in 1936 with poetic resonance. Laurie is then seen sitting on the ground with Powell and the Foula islanders, talking about the golden days of film. With hints of Private Frazer's theatrical melancholy he recites: 'It was Spring here down north! The time of the white nights and the long days and the flowers. Forty-two years since the yacht with Michael and his wife Frankie (Powell) and Niall Guinness on board dropped anchor down there in the wee harbour and we started our film.'

The documentary shows Laurie as still an imposing figure, despite his age, 'although the mind's gone a bit', he says, recalling his memories of Foula, and paying tribute to the noble people who appeared alongside him in the film. 'Ah, a Scotsman never retires,' explains Laurie with a roll of his eyes. 'In the Shetlands, though, the age of miracles is always here.'

\*\*\*

AFTER *The Edge of the World* in 1936 Laurie's work with the enigmatic Powell continued and his contribution to the powerful canon of wartime propaganda films which were essential to the Allies' military campaign against Hitler should not be forgotten. In total he worked on four films with the director, including the controversial *The Life and Death of Colonel Blimp* (1943), in which he appeared as a character called Murdoch, the ever trustworthy manservant/batman to Clive Wynne-Candy (Blimp).

This romantic war film begins with Major General Wynne-Candy as a senior commander in the Home Guard during the Second World War. Before a training exercise, he is 'taken prisoner' in a Turkish bath by troops led by Lieutenant 'Spud' Wilson, who has struck pre-emptively. He dismisses Candy's indignation and protests that 'war starts at midnight!' There's an ungainly scuffle in the bathing pool. An extended flashback ensues and the film takes us through the ageing Wynne-Candy's extraordinary life as a soldier. It starts with the Boer War, where he won the Victoria Cross for bravery, then moves on to the First World War, where we see Laurie as the devoted Murdoch on hand to keep Wynne-Candy functioning on and off the battlefield, and then to the Second World War where we see Candy at the head of a Home Guard unit. Powell had also cleverly woven into the script a German officer, Theo, played by Anton Walbrook, who remains friends with Candy during the Second World War. The glamorous star Deborah Kerr was cast as the women characters in Candy's life, revealing how Powell and his scriptwriter Emeric Pressburger had a genius grasp of dreamlike surrealism to mix with representations of shades of time.

In his memoir, *A Life in Movies*, Michael Powell recalled: 'When working in Dumfries I'd drop in for tea with John Laurie's two sisters, who kept a clothier's and haberdashery shop on the Square. They were delighted with his performance as Murdoch in *Colonel Blimp*, but of course, being his sisters, they couldn't understand why he hadn't been offered the leading role! I would usually return home with a haggis or a black pudding tucked away somewhere in my rucksack.'[5]

\*\*\*

IT was while appearing as a newspaper editor in the 1939 wartime propaganda film *Q Planes* that Laurie got to work with his friend Laurence Olivier, who had ambitions to join the RAF and become a fighter pilot. In fact, Olivier was too old to realise this dream, so instead settled for flying briefly with the Royal Navy's Fleet Air Arm. For Laurie, his small role in *Q Planes* led him on to appear in Olivier's all-important Churchill-backed 1944 production of *Henry V*, a morale-boosting epic in full colour intended to raise public awareness of the Allied conflict against their enemy. He played a character called Jamy, and years later told his *Dad's Army* co-stars that when he watched the battle scenes in *Henry V* it 'made his hair stand on end', and he described the film as 'a masterpiece of photography and atmosphere'. Laurie later appeared in Olivier's 1948 film of *Hamlet*.

Coincidentally, both Olivier and Laurie played the same historical character in two very different films. Both portrayed the Mahdi, scourge of General 'Chinese' Gordon: Laurie essayed the part in *The Four Feathers* (1939), while Olivier played the role in *Khartoum* (1965). No fan of the remarkable Laurie can forget his brilliant performance in

Zoltan Korda's *The Four Feathers*. This famous adventure epic was set in Sudan during the Mahdist War of 1895 and went on to inspire the special *Dad's Army* episode titled 'Two and a Half Feathers'. It wasn't the first time the lively actor had revealed his expertise as a horseman. His *Dad's Army* co-star Bill Pertwee recalled:

> On one occasion when we were filming an episode, John and I were playing a couple of desert Bedouins in a flashback sequence that involved Corporal Jones's experiences with General Gordon and the Mad Mahdi in Khartoum. This sequence was being filmed near King's Lynn in Norfolk in some huge sandpits to simulate the desert. John and I were on horseback and had to ride at a leisurely pace into an open space beyond some high dunes. Film sequences were being prepared on the other side of the dunes, so John and I took the chance to get used to the horses. I was, and still am, very raw in the saddle (no pun) but John was an experienced rider.
>
> However, even the most docile of animals can sometimes be disturbed and this is exactly what happened. Suddenly, a couple of practice rifle shots rang out from the other side of the dune and John's horse bolted. He managed after a time to bring it under control and pacify the animal but I knew he was shaken by the mishap.
>
> I asked him if he would like to go back to the caravans for a cup of tea, but he said, 'No, laddie. I'll be all right, and don't mention it to the others, I don't want any fuss.' And that just about summed John up. I think he believed he might break down and not be able to carry on at all if anyone had started showing concern or sympathising with him – which of course would have been the case because we were such a caring company.'[6]

There is evidence that Laurie felt he could relax with his co-stars, when at a farewell dinner event after the final episode of the show much wine was consumed and, according to producer David Croft, Laurie became amusingly abusive!

***

IN July 1940 the veteran hero of the trenches Laurie, now aged 43, decided to join the 5th (St Marylebone) Battalion, County of London Home Guard, apparently mostly keeping an eye on gasometers in Paddington. He soon became bored, however, with his new role for the war effort, declaring: 'The area was full of professional soldiers and I must say I felt very silly drilling with a make-believe rifle. I found it totally un-comical and an excess of dullness – as Frazer would say "A lot of useless blather".' Laurie left the Home Guard unit after just a few months' strutting about with a broom handle and decided to get back full-time to the film set. Little wonder he used the experience to help create the character of Frazer almost thirty years later.

His highly valued participation in war-themed films continued and he appeared in *Convoy* (1940), *Ships With Wings* (1941), *Dangerous Moonlight* (1941), *The Gentle Sex* (1943), *The Demi-Paradise* (with Olivier in 1943), *The New Lot* (1943), *Fanny By Gaslight* (1944), *The Way Ahead* (directed by the great Carol Reed, 1944) and *Medal for the General* (1944). During the 1950s and 1960s his screen work continued, and included television, too. His efforts revealed him to be one of the most enduring actors of his time. He also worked with some of the greats, including director David Lean (*Hobson's Choice* in 1954), Second World War hero and film icon Dirk Bogarde in *Campbell's Kingdom* (1957), and the Australian actor Peter Finch, another outstanding veteran of the Second World War, in *Kidnapped* in 1960.

In 1967, as David Croft and Jimmy Perry began thinking about casting *Dad's Army*, the BBC's new Head of Comedy Michael Mills suggested casting Laurie because there should be a 'Scotsman' in the platoon.

It was the wry and observant Croft who noted in his memoir:

> John Laurie formed a close relationship with Ian Lavender. They would sit together poring over *The Times* crossword puzzle. John would usually have finished it by coffee time. "What's the matter with your brain, boy? Use your brain." John as a great Shakespeare scholar didn't have much regard for Jimmy Perry and me. 'The trouble with you two is you're damned nearly illiterate,' he once said. On the occasions when we wrote him a small part he would threaten to phone in his performance. In the latter days of the series he was rather resentful that he was being remembered for the weird Scottish undertaker rather than for all the important parts he had played throughout his career. But he had a rare and canny ability to spot any comedy possibilities in his part and milk them to the full.[7]

Croft also recalled a time in 1977 when they were filming the last episodes of the series and because the aged Arnold Ridley had badly injured his leg, he arrived at the location in a limousine. 'By the time I went to greet him he had slid to the floor, and as I opened the door he smiled bravely at me from the prone position. I shook him warmly by the hand. John Laurie saw us from the steps of the make-up caravan. "Look," he said. "Look – look – they're pumping him up."'

Arthur Lowe's (Captain Mainwaring) memoir was written by his son Stephen. In it he describes Laurie as a 'gruff, abrasive man who spoke his mind. He knew *Dad's Army* to be well beneath him. . . .'[8]

Jimmy Perry writes with great candour in tribute to Laurie:

The part of the aggressive Frazer was first thought up as a wonderful contrast to Private Godfrey's gentleness. Michael Mills suggested the character of Frazer should be a Scotsman. Now, every southern English town has several Scots living in it, who are usually doctors, lawyers or chemists, and they form themselves into Caledonian Societies and do very well. What was it Dr Johnson said? 'The best sight a Scotsman ever sees is the English Border as he crosses it.' Well, when I discovered John Laurie had been chosen for the role I couldn't believe it! I remembered those wonderful characters he'd played in British films ever since I was a kid – the eagle face, with the mad, rolling eyes. Writing for him was a joy. I can still hear his voice saying, 'Can you no hear the wind? It's the moans of sailors drowned at sea. Don't forget to lock your door tonight, and ignore any strange noises you may hear,' followed by, 'Doomed! Doomed!'[9]

Over the nine years of *Dad's Army* it's fair to say the hearty Laurie played the part of Frazer with energy and aplomb. However, he remained sceptical about the worth of the series, reminding people of his dramatically brilliant Shakespearian roots. His famous phrase 'We're all doomed' was almost created by him, after the writers of the show David Perry and Jimmy Croft heard him complaining about some facet of the show being doomed to failure!

However, he did admit *Dad's Army* and his new career in television was a bonus at his time of life as he was not stretched too far, and most of the time rehearsals were 'fairly leisurely', apart from the filming in Norfolk and recording days in the studio. In his later life he travelled in to work on the show from Chalfont St Peter, Buckinghamshire, where he lived contentedly with his wife Oonah and daughter Veronica.

Bill Pertwee said:

I shall always remember John Laurie as a larger-than-life character with a natural personality for making even the most ordinary dialogue sound extraordinary. With his eyes flashing he would say, 'We're doomed, I tell you. I remember the time on the lonely Isle of Barra, the wind whistling around the headland; there in the silence of the mist, it appeared. Bloodshot eyes, a huge body and a long tail, creeping nearer and nearer . . .' And then just as everyone was in a state of paralysed fear he would scream out, 'We're doomed, I tell you, doomed, doomed.' Of course there would always be a perfectly simple explanation for the monster or phantom he had suggested to us . . .'

Ian Lavender added: 'I don't think John meant it when he said the show was rubbish. I was there when he said it; he was a wicked and impish man and he didn't really think it was terrible at all – 'I've played every part in Shakespeare, I was considered to be the finest Hamlet of the twenties and I had retired, and now I'm famous for doing this crap.' But how many thousands of people saw him as Hamlet and how many millions saw him as Frazer?'

On 23 June 1980 John Laurie, veteran hero of the First World War, and legend of the stage and screen, died at the age of 83 from emphysema which had complicated a long-standing lung ailment. His spirit, however, lives on whenever we happen to catch *Dad's Army* being shown on a screen near us.

# ARTHUR LOWE

As everyone began to get sand happy during the war when I was in the Middle East I resurrected my old love of the theatre and here we are today really after many vicissitudes along the path!

WHILE researching the life and military times of Arthur Lowe, I couldn't help but be reminded of the lyrics sung by the actor Walter Cartlett, who played the strutting, charismatic fox Honest John Worthington Foulfellow in the 1940 Disney film of the puppet boy *Pinocchio*:

> Hi diddle-dee-dee
> An actor's life for me
> A high silk hat and a silver cane
> A watch of gold and a diamond chain
> Hi diddle-dee-dee
> An actor's life for me
> A wax moustache and a beaver coat
> A pony cart and a billy goat . . .
> An actor's life is fun . . .

The rest of this song, written by Ned Washington and composed by Leigh Harline, serenades the mystical joys of a theatrical life. Its particular interpretation of happy-go-lucky days as a chance-taking stage artiste certainly illuminates a Lowe-ish element or two . . . that's providing, of course, that we park to one side the fox known as 'Honest John' and his various dodgy antics which keep the film rolling along.

For beyond the high jinks and seat-of-the-pants experiences that often surrounded ropey stage productions in the early part of his career, Arthur Lowe went on to become a seriously committed and dedicated actor, with an authentic aptitude for comedy. By the late 1960s he was such a professional, with a long, varied experience in show business, that he felt comfortable enough to ditch his *Dad's Army* scripts and allow his natural instinct for humour to carry the show.

119

Unconventional at times, yes; perceived as having an infuriating attitude to his co-stars, including John Le Mesurier (Sergeant Wilson), who liked to be fed word-perfect lines, then yes; but was Lowe ever unsure of his own talent? No. Indeed, the avuncular embodiment of *Dad's Army*'s pompous Captain George Mainwaring reveals a man who had no qualms about showing an audience how buffoonery came naturally to him, and yet once he had accepted anyone as a friend he proved to them a kind and caring individual.

This soft side of Lowe, which was beyond any Mainwaring-esque bluster, has often been confirmed by his co-star Ian Lavender (Private Pike). Indeed, it was Lavender who in 2011 unveiled a blue plaque at the door of a terraced house in Kinder Road, Hayfield, Derbyshire, where his *Dad's Army* friend and mentor Arthur Lowe was born in 1915. 'Arthur was always very generous towards me when I was so new to television and show business in general. He often told me to stand beside him and get into the shot and was always a great encouragement,' said Lavender in his BBC radio documentary series, *Do Tell 'Em, Pike*.

Many actors who worked with Lowe confirmed that he used elements of his real personality, which had evolved during his own wartime service, to create Mainwaring as a symbol of a certain type of British character in full flourish during wartime – stoic and overtly ambassadorial of the morality which existed at the time. Not quite Colonel Blimp, the character created by the indomitable powerhouse of wartime film icons Michael Powell and Emeric Pressburger (*The Life and Death of Colonel Blimp*, 1943), but more of an indignant character with a uniform and rank which supported his bid to forget his lower-middle class self.

Indeed, the theatrical tour-de-force who played the undaunted Captain Mainwaring is perhaps more comparable to Charles Dickens' creation in the novel *David Copperfield* of the optimistic Wilkins Micawber, who always believes and tells himself and others around him to 'never mind, something will turn up' during times of adversity. Lowe, acknowledging the similarity between Mainwaring and Micawber, did in fact star as the Dickensian optimist in the 1974 television adaptation of Dickens' famous story.

In discussing Lowe's portrayal of Mainwaring, the British cultural historian Professor Jeffrey Richards writes:

Touching and truthful was the episode about the chaste *Brief Encounter* love affair of the unhappily married Captain Mainwaring – whose wife Elizabeth is never seen in the series but remains a formidable presence at the other end of a telephone line. These three-dimensional characters in the show quickly turned into our old friends.

Like the great comic creations of Shakespeare and Dickens, the *Dad's Army* characters took on a life of their own. J.B. Priestley writing in his perceptive volume *English Humour* (1930) argued that the dominant strain in the best English comic writing was the comedy of character, 'the richest and wisest kind of humour, sweetening and mellowing life for us'. He goes on to describe this observation of characteristic English individuality as 'tender mockery' and how we laugh at those we love ... because we have come to know them so well, that certain traits or habits as familiar to us as their faces, seem peculiarly absurd.[1]

But just how the ginger-haired and freckle-faced 'Little Arthur' Lowe from Hayfield, Derbyshire, rose to become one of television comedy's greatest stars, and often discussed by one of the world's leading cultural academics, takes us on a long road. Much of this vocational expedition involved years of arduous work in provincial theatres and in weekly rep, as well as intense endeavours as a director and producer, too. When Lowe arrived at the signpost in that career route which said 'television', he strode on towards great fame but instead of buying 'a high silk hat and a silver cane', as 'Honest John the fox' sings in 'Hey Diddle-dee-dee', Lowe ploughed his money into his beloved houseboat, *Amazon*.

However, long before he lived his dream of sailing along on a calm sea, where *did* his life begin? Thanks to my contact with his son Stephen and grandson Jack, and the hearty reminiscences of him by his co-stars and biographer Graham Lord, I will endeavour to ensure the picture of his life is as complete as possible.

*** 

ARTHUR Lowe was born in a small terraced property in Kinder Road, Hayfield, Derbyshire on 22 September 1915, during the second year of the First World War. Life was hard for women at the time, as it was for his mother Nan (née Ford) when her husband 'Big Arthur' Lowe, then aged 41, was called up in 1914 to fight in the trenches of France and Belgium. Judging by military records, it seems likely 'Big Arthur' joined the Lancashire Regiment, a unit that endured great punishment early on in the conflict as they learned by trial and error how to tackle the rudiments of brutal and bloody warfare. They realised there was more to combat than their training had implied, and sticking a bayonet in an enemy soldier was a vast and desperate horror compared to an assertive prod of the bayonet into a faceless sack of straw. Men like 'Big Arthur' quickly discovered it was a deadly game of survival to be endured hour by hour in the most treacherous conditions.

In the early autumn of 1914, for instance, inexperienced men of the 1st East Lancashires were only just beginning to understand why 'shallow scrapes of trenches' would not protect them from the German bombardments in the fields of Solesmes, a tiny village in France famous for its ancient Benedictine Abbey. Photographs taken there in late 1914 show these courageous British troops lying on their stomachs, with rifles poised, in a gully just inches deep. These mini dug-outs provided them with no protection at all from enemy fire.

After two horrendous years on the front line, and having survived the battle of the Somme (10 July–18 November), 'Big Arthur' was permitted to return home for good. By then aged 43, he had not escaped unscathed, as he had inhaled mustard gas and endured serious attacks of bronchitis for the rest of his life. During the writing of this book, the mindful Stephen Lowe related to me how his father's ('Little Arthur') birth certainly had 'something to do with the First World War'. He recalled:

> Family myth and legend has always told it this way: 'Big Arthur' fought in France; he was gassed early on in the war in 1914, and was brought home to convalesce and that was seen as lucky because he got to live. Many young wives often relying only on a postcard for news of their husbands were inclined to forget to wear a douche at the time.
>
> The first mass use of gas shells was at the second battle of Ypres (22 April–15 May 1915). For 'Little Arthur' to be born in the September of 1915 that works out too late for my grandfather to have breathed in the deadly poison during that battle. However, gas shells were used in a limited way at the battle of La Bassée in northern France in October 1914 and that timeline fits with the family story.

Records reveal that from 12–29 October that year the 2nd Lancashires in La Bassée experienced severe fighting and suffered heavy casualties. Seven officers and more than two hundred men were killed on 21 October and yet, despite the regular bombardment from the aggressive German army, the battered British line of heroes never dispersed.

Stephen recalled:

> My grandfather always had a 'bit of a chest', but then that might have been the railway coal in the open grate and the cheroots he liked to smoke when he worked with steam trains. He never spoke of the 1914–1918 conflict but I recall he had some gruesome brass trophies converted to cigarette lighters and so on and balanced them on the red brick fireplace at the old cottage at Hayfield.

Every time he lit up I thought I could smell German blood. My grandfather was a tall man and must have been powerful in his day, a sturdy infantryman with a bayonet and muddied boots. The archetypal tough British Tommy.

'Big Arthur' then suffered from a serious chest condition probably because his lungs had been ravaged by gas and then there was the coal dust and the combination of both meant he was unable to carry heavy objects too far. My father ('Little Arthur') always complained he had to carry the heavy suitcases from the station whenever we went to stay with our grandparents. 'Who designed this suitcase?!' he'd grumble and stagger, truly weighed down, along the road to the cottage.[2]

Back in 1917, and many years before this memory cemented itself into Stephen's psyche, 'Big Arthur', the hero of the trenches, and his wife Nan had moved to Manchester. Between the wars they lived just off the Lonsdale Road in Levenshulme. No doubt they would have noticed how the ramshackle beginnings of a Local Defence League had begun to rattle around the cobbled streets of the city. This organisation was, of course, the forerunner to what would eventually become the Home Guard in 1940, and more latterly famous for inspiring *Dad's Army*. 'Little Arthur' was a pupil at the Chapel Street Elementary School and was encouraged by the female teaching staff to always do the best he could. Drama classes were a particular favourite lesson.

Years later Arthur's parents moved back to the village where their son was born. 'Big Arthur' died a popular man well in his 80s, and was saluted by pub regulars who knew him well at the historic Lamb Inn, Chinley, Hayfield, in the glorious Peak District. Nan died in her late 90s. Their grandson Stephen made a pilgrimage to Hayfield in 1995 and in his own memoir of his famous father writes how he was soon recognised by the local community as the 'son of "Little Arthur" from *Dad's Army*'.[3]

As a toddler in 1917, Arthur, future star of stage and screen, spent much of his early life living with his maternal grandmother Mary Ann Ford in the countryside around Hayfield. Much later in his life Lowe told his son Stephen that his own mother Nan had 'bullied' him and life with granny Mary 'had been much better'.

By 1927 Arthur had returned to Rusholme (2 miles from Levenshulme) in Manchester to be with his parents, where his life was always brightened by the prospect of visiting any one of Greater Manchester's 295 picture houses. In Rusholme was a busy and prosperous theatre which had first raised its curtain in 1903. It was here that an entertainer from Blackburn called Harry Leslie (real name Harry Makinson, born in 1871) was determined to make himself a success in show business.

As far back as 1893 he was appearing on theatre bills as a 'Humourist and Ventriloquist'. Popular summer shows were staged under Leslie's large marquee and the show bills of 1908 proclaimed it 'the only al-fresco' pavilion in Manchester.[4]

Leslie's Pavilion stood on the south side of Birch Villa, near the junction of Wilmslow Road and Dickenson Road. At the time it was very much hidden from the view of those walking nearby as it was shielded by enormous advertising boards along the adjacent Wilmslow Road. In 1914, by now established as an impresario, Harry Leslie managed 'The Nobodies' – a touring troupe of entertainers including Charles Wade, Lillian Errol, Vivien Stafford and Neville Delmar – who raised essential cash for war charities. That year there was also a group of theatricals known as 'The Grotesques', who went on to entertain the armed forces in France and Belgium.

By 1916, and after hosting a raft of popular entertainers including 'Leslie's Komedy Kadets', Cecilia Gold, Fred Field, Jack Waller and The Gay Lieutenants, the marquee and its rotting leaking canvas had been replaced by a solid wooden frame and roof. Complaints from audiences forced to sit under umbrellas during performances left the management little choice but to make these necessary changes. Even the sturdy folk of Manchester wanted comfort for their money and 'al-fresco' wasn't so grand in the winter months.

A few months before the end of the First World War a local press headline described the venue's entertainment as a 'Treat for Wounded Soldiers' and reported how in celebration of the French Flag Day Leslie's troupe 'The Nobodies' had delighted 'eight hundred wounded soldiers, Red Cross Nurses, and soldiers' wives at the Rusholme Pavilion'. After the show the Lord Mayor of Manchester Sir Alexander Porter addressed the audience from the stage and thanked the entertainers.

By the time the 12-year-old Arthur Lowe arrived to watch a show at Leslie's Pavilion, he would have been aware of the regular stars. One regular patron and local resident was Mrs Maria Hill, who recalled in 1980:

> My family and friends were regular patrons from about 1930 until Leslie's [the Pavilion] closed in the autumn of 1939 because of the air raids. But we'd spent many happy hours there, despite its sparse appearances, but some very good acts were seen, many of them far better than are seen on the television today. Billy Manders' Quaintesques were the most popular, as it was an all-male show, the girls came in their hundreds!

'Little Arthur', sitting near the stage at Leslie's Pavilion, may well have enjoyed 'The Curios', a theatrical collective of seven cheeky-looking performers described on the bill as 'Composed, Upholstered, Renovated, Invented, Offered and Staged' by Ernest Crampton. 'The Curios' performed their act dressed in blue and white to match the colours of a set painted in the famous style of Wedgwood pottery. The great impresario Leslie also represented the bizarrely named troupe known as 'The Squibs'. In 1930 young northerner Wendy Hiller, who later became the stage and screen star Dame Wendy Hiller, was learning her craft as assistant stage manager at the venue.

Two years later in 1932 the impressionable young Lowe may have seen Harry Leslie's daughter, the starlet Mabel Leslie, on stage in David Day's production of *Boy o' Mine*? Described on the playbill as 'the sweetest story ever written with power and comedy', the show ran at the Rusholme venue for six nights. Ticket prices ranged from sixpence up to one shilling and sixpence.

At the end of the 1930s Jack Parker (full name Albert Rostron Parker), the Pavilion's piano player, left to work in London and co-wrote the wartime hit 'There'll always be an England' – a musical number much loved by Dame Vera Lynn.

Among the many entertainers to have taken their early steps towards stardom from the Rusholme stage was former First World War Royal Flying Corps pilot Leslie Henson. Always a keen showman, Henson was released from active service by the British government in 1917 to put together a concert party to boost troop morale. Henson, of course, went on to form ENSA with Basil Dean during the Second World War.

The Rusholme Pavilion was managed by the redoubtable Harry Leslie from 1903 until 1941. In 1934 his services to social and charitable causes were recognised by a testimonial presented on stage in his honour, organised by a representational committee. The venue hosted BBC broadcasts between 1934 and 1939 and became the first home of the Northern radio shows. Harry Leslie, one of Arthur Lowe's first big heroes of entertainment, died aged 74 in 1944.

It's clear that Leslie made a lifelong impression on the *Dad's Army* star, and Lowe often admitted a great admiration for those who had been an influence on his career. 'He loved people who were larger than life,' explained Stephen Lowe. *Dad's Army* co-star Bill Pertwee (Warden Hodges) recalled how his co-star loved to reminisce about 1920s and 1930s comedians like Robb Wilson and Harry Tate. 'They had the sort of characters who said ridiculous things and pretended like Captain Mainwaring to be in control of everything but very much were not!' As a tribute to the men of 'Big Arthur's generation, Lowe was heard at one time praising *Dad's Army* co-star Arnold Ridley, who had served in the Somerset Light Infantry during the First World War. In the 1970s

Lowe told Stephen that Ridley had served with a 'fine body of men'. Perhaps Ridley put him in mind of 'Big Arthur' – another survivor of the 1914–1918 conflict.

According to Stephen, his father's awesome theatrical talent was seized upon by encouraging teachers at the Alma Park Central School in Levenshulme, Manchester, where in 1929 he appeared in two productions aged just 12 years old. One of them was a detective drama called *The Grand Cham's Diamond*. These productions would have taken place within two years of Lowe's first visit to Leslie's Pavilion in Rusholme, where he had been hugely influenced by the energy and theatrical prowess of the professional entertainers. Stage acting wasn't the only highlight of his school year, as records show the young Lowe had also proved to be 'a solid, light on his feet and aggressive little boxer in the sporting ring'.

There's every chance he inherited his famous deep voice from 'Big Arthur', who, after returning from the First World War, became a music-loving railway worker. His job involved the transportation of theatrical touring companies which travelled arduously to and fro between venues around Northern England and the Midlands. 'Big Arthur's booming vocals were a somewhat useful job requirement if he was to get his message over loud and clear above the deafening noise of steam trains.

Any fans of the 1983 film *The Dresser* can never forget the sight of its star Albert Finney playing 'Sir', the alpha-male head of a harried theatrical touring company during the Second World War. We see 'Sir' standing on the bridge at the railway station with his dejected company, just too late to catch the train as it pulls out. Suddenly, he raises his actor's 'silver cane' and pointing at the stationmaster, he yells above the hubbub in his loudest projected voice, undoubtedly akin to that of 'Big Arthur', 'Stop, that, traaaiiin!' The brakes screech and the company scramble to get on board. Oh, to have the vocal power and physical presence to stop a mighty steam locomotive with just the roar of a spirited theatrical voice!

\*\*\*

BY 1931 it was time for 15-year-old 'Little Arthur' to leave school. At first he was keen to join the Merchant Navy but his poor eyesight put an end to his dream of a life at sea. (He would remedy this later in life, when as a famous actor he had the wealth to buy his own former steamship, *Amazon*, in 1971.) Instead, and despite the fact the country was in the grip of the Great Depression, he got a job working in the stores of Brown's Bicycles in Manchester. His salary for 51 hours a week was £2, and colleagues remembered him as 'well spoken, slightly pompous with an attitude resembling that of Capt. Mainwaring'. The young slim Lowe was also dapperly dressed and it was noted how he often wore a snakeskin-coloured tie.

Five years later he landed a position at the Fairey Aircraft Factory as a 'progress chaser' – a role he explained later as a signing-off procedure to ensure a certain variety of jobs had been achieved by the workforce that day.[5] The company was founded by Charles Richard Fairey and its headquarters were in Hayes, Heaton Chapel, near Stockport. Many aircraft that went on to play a pivotal role in the Second World War were designed and built by Fairey, including Albacores, Barracudas, Beaufighters, Fireflies, Fulmars and Halifax bombers. The work took place in great hangars and close ties were made with the Royal Navy's Fleet Air Arm. It's worth noting, too, Fairey's famous 'Stringbag': the fabric-covered Swordfish and its aircrews were heroes of the Second World War and played their part in the sinking of the *Bismarck* in May 1941.

But in 1939 Lowe, during his brief time waving a clipboard around the floors of the Fairey Aircraft Factory and filling in forms, had been revelling in awe at the entertainment world of George Formby, Max Wall, Tommy Handley, Bud Flanagan, Chesney Allen, Sandy Powell and Tommy Trinder. It soon became clear the starstruck 24 year old was seriously bored by his day job and was drawn to a career beneath the spotlights. Another of Lowe's favourite entertainers during the Second World War was the Liverpudlian comedian Robb Wilton. It was the joker Wilton who arguably created the foundations for *Dad's Army* by mocking the Local Defence Volunteers. His wisecracks on stage rippled through the British population and the LDV soon became known to everyone as 'Look, Duck and Vanish'.

At the outbreak of war, and with fame still so far away, Lowe joined the Territorial Army. He was keen to learn to ride a horse and signed up as a cavalry trooper in the Duke of Lancaster's Own Yeomanry (The Dukes). On 3 September 1939 24-year-old Trooper 322499 Lowe of Whalley Road barracks, Manchester, heard Prime Minister Neville Chamberlain's famous BBC broadcast and expressed his sadness. Arthur was, said his friend Bill Bateman, unlike the other men of 'The Dukes' who cheered at the news that Britain was at war with Germany again. No doubt many of them knew of the regiment's awesome bravery during the First World War. 'The Dukes' were decorated with military honours after fourteen battles during that conflict, and twenty years later they carried their swords and rode their horses with pride.

But the regiment was now seriously outdated, and could even be laughingly compared to the seat-of-the-pants antics of the men in *Dad's Army*. Lowe and the rest of the Troopers had horses and ponies to ride, many of them donated to the regiment by farmers and their families. Lowe's pony Daisy arrived one day with a note pinned to her bridle along the lines of 'Please take care of our family pet.'

Regimental duties included the cleaning of brass harnesses, soaping saddles and polishing boots to a high shine. At this time 'The Dukes' were stationed at a rat-infested old cotton mill in Hawkshaw, a village situated between Bolton and Bury. During the seriously cold winter of 1939/1940 Lowe was sleeping on a concrete floor every night; along with the rest of the regiment's squadron, he was up at 5am to muck out the horses.[6]

At night when spirits were low Trooper Lowe liked to sing and attempt to bring comfort to men missing their homes and families. During the day he would try out his entertainment skills again, impersonating German and British officers. According to his friend Batemen, the balding Arthur was already turning into Captain Mainwaring as he used to call out in his rather important voice: 'Now gather round, men.' Indeed his aptitude for mimicry became a regular source of fun for the old cavalry unit, which had now been deemed too outdated to participate in modern warfare. In Graham Lord's 2002 biography, *Arthur Lowe*, there is a telling quote from Ernie Skidmore, another veteran of 'The Dukes' who served with the future television star:

> The Army took all the good stuff from us because we were cavalry and didn't fit in with all the new weaponry available. Then they found a lot of our blokes weren't fit to go out to Palestine, so they sent the Cheshire Yeomanry instead and took all of our best equipment, our super-lined cavalry greatcoats, even our rifles. We got some Canadian rifles instead. They needed the better stuff for the people who were doing the fighting, I suppose. We even had some 1914–1918 men with us, men over 40, so they were naturally *Dad's Army* weren't they?!

When the spring of 1940 arrived, and with the evacuation of Dunkirk just weeks away, the RAF realised that a tremendous fight was about to begin for the skies over Britain. During this tense time, still shrouded in the idea of the 'phoney war', Lowe and 'The Dukes' travelled by train to a new base – Llanion barracks at Pembroke Dock in South Wales. By this time the regiment had no horses, and Lowe's rank was now 'Gunner' and he belonged to A Troop, A Battery – which was subsequently renamed the 77th (DLOY) Medium Regiment Royal Artillery (TA). He was presented with an RA gun badge to wear on his cap and a rose of Lancaster badge for his collar.

Many years later, in an interview with Ed Doolan for Australian Television in 1976, Lowe shared his memories:

> During the war I was eventually in the Middle East with the REME [Corps of Royal Electrical and Mechanical Engineers] and as everyone began to get sand happy I decided to resurrect an old love and here we are today really after many vicissitudes along the path!
>
> As a serving soldier I didn't see the Home Guard differently to the way I'd see them now. Er . . . I don't know, no, I don't think so very much because you see in certain branches of the real army it was just as chaotic. I mean when we changed from being cavalry to being medium artillery, er, it was very, very different, let me assure you, because until they gave us the actual guns, and when they arrived they were iron, tired old howitzers from the First World War and before that we had to use the officers' trap as a gun you see and . . . you know, with the shafts down, and loading it with old sweeping brushes . . . it was ridiculous you see.[7]

In 1940 Lowe, now promoted to the rank of bombardier, was put in charge of organising motor transport. His role involved administering the drivers' work sheets and the place soon became a frenzy of training with a cacophony of haphazard activities resembling a scene from *Dad's Army*. One veteran bombardier, Harry Hartill, recalled: 'We had a six-inch Howitzer gun which had probably been used in the Boer War. It had a plaque on it which said "Property of Birmingham Parks".' He went on:

> We also had one flat-back lorry, also a fruiterer's lorry, with a huge board behind the driver's head which said 'Persil'. And just as *Dad's Army* had Jonesie's butcher's van, we also had use of a furniture vehicle with 'W. E. Evans' written on the side. This came to grief beneath a low bridge and the top came right off. We really were expecting the Germans to invade us, and when they reported that parachutists were landing, we used to jump into this furniture van, armed with sticks, and go off into the night to round them up. It was exactly the same as *Dad's Army*.

It was Hartill who taught Lowe how to use semaphore and Morse Code. He liked Lowe and described him as a quick learner who made him laugh with his funny voices and energetic humour.

By the early June of 1940, as the Battle of Britain began in the skies of south-east England, 'The Dukes' were still in Pembrokeshire waiting for their call to take an active part in the war. On tenterhooks, they spent days and nights avoiding the bombs that the Luftwaffe were dropping around the docks. One soldier was killed, and another time Bombardier Lowe narrowly escaped death when an explosion shattered the glass in his billet. When he looked out of the window he recalled seeing a massive 500lb unexploded bomb sticking out of the ground.

The only large defence weapon they had was a Lewis gun on a tripod. The Luftwaffe aircrews were safe from 'The Dukes' as the only damage the gun inflicted was when the British soldier who pulled its trigger shot holes in one of the RAF's finest Blenheim bombers! In response, the local RAF station commander promptly sent a stern letter of reproach to the commanding officer of 'The Dukes', Lieutenant Colonel Musgrave-Hoyle. Whether an apology was sent in reply is not known.[8]

Back home in Manchester, many residents were at the mercy of the new 'Home Guard' unit which was busily engaged in a political row over the supply and use of sandbags, first aid boxes and stirrup pumps. Supplies were never plentiful, and when the German bombing raids created more and more destruction through the streets and homes of the city, there was only so much a few drops of water from a lonely stirrup pump could achieve in the fight for survival. 'Big Arthur' and Nan Lowe would have witnessed how some 30 acres of properties were ruined during the Luftwaffe's Christmas blitz on 22–23 December 1940. This massive raid reduced five hundred buildings to piles of rubble, and horrendous damage was caused to more than a thousand others, many of them family homes. An extra four hundred fire engines and more than three thousand firefighters were called in from outside the city.

Many people on the streets watched the beloved Free Trade Hall fall victim to the German bombs, and parts of the city's magnificent cathedral, dating back to the fifteenth century, were completely destroyed. The Exchange and Victoria railway stations suffered similar serious damage. Doreen Herring was just 7 years old when she saw an enemy aircraft flying overhead as her family, from Pendleton, made their way to an air raid shelter. She recalled: 'We looked up and saw the pilot pause and then the plane sped ahead without dropping a bomb. I am convinced it was because he could see us.' Her father, George Pinder, refused to go to the air raid shelter, commenting: 'If a bomb wants to get me, it will get me.' On leaving the shelter, people dreaded finding their house had been destroyed. Doreen said: 'Next door to us had been bombed to bits. All you wanted or could do afterwards was to have a cup of tea.'[9]

The destruction led to great sadness as children's funerals became a regular occurrence, and the smell of rotten food only exacerbated the stench of death long after the bombing ended. When the Luftwaffe headed back towards France or Germany, the Mancunians took a deep breath and gathered themselves to fight on. Those families who found themselves homeless were able to cook food by using broken furniture to make fires in their gardens. If the water mains were damaged, they would drink water from hoses and bowsers.

Bombardier Lowe's parents 'Big Arthur' and 'Nan', then in their early 50s, escaped from the blitzed suburbs of Heaton and returned to the safety of the Hayfield countryside in Derbyshire. They moved to a small cottage and lived not far from Kinder Road, where their son had been born twenty-five years previously.

Meanwhile Bombardier Lowe spent October 1940 at camps in Sennybridge and Pontypridd in Wales, where he learned how to operate all sorts of weaponry. Today the British Army is still active in Sennybridge, where it operates its third largest training area, covering 37,000 acres to the north of the Brecon Beacons National Park. When Lowe's Medium Regiment (TA) of the Royal Artillery arrived ready to learn how to take aim, fire and hit the target (if possible), the camp was in its second year of operation.

In November 1940 the lively Bombardier Lowe received another promotion and was made office clerk at the battery at Gosford Castle in Northern Ireland. Years later his son Stephen heard his father describe one pompous officer who didn't like to see more than one pen sticking out of the top pocket of a tunic because he thought too many pens looked common! In a *Dad's Army* episode viewers laughed when Captain Mainwaring scolded Private Pike for having a row of pens peeking out from his top pocket – it seems likely that the scene was inspired by Lowe's memory of that fussy officer at Gosford Castle, although *Dad's Army* creator Jimmy Perry explained that he had written the scene after a similar experience during the war involving an officer obsessed with the etiquette of writing utensils and top pockets!

By the end of 1940 Royal Artillery Commander Lieutenant Colonel F.H.C. Rogers was the top man at Gosford Castle and the troops were being given gunnery training. Lowe was often on the firing range and learning wireless, driving and vehicle maintenance, too. But despite the Royal Artillery's passion for discipline during manoeuvres, there were always haphazard and comical events. At one point the men were asked to install an electric bell at the entrance of the Castle but it was doomed as it wouldn't stop ringing!

At around this time the call came for 'Fred Lowe', as he was then known, to show off his talent for mimicry during an audition to join a concert party. Sadly he was turned down as the troupe already had a comedian and impressionist. Lowe's weak eyesight also meant he wouldn't be overly involved in the theatre of war either and he was medically regraded. A wireless course in Coventry beckoned and he was trained in radar to work with the Royal Ordnance Corps on searchlight duty in Lincolnshire.

By the spring of 1942 he was bound for the hot sands of Egypt in North Africa, and along with thousands of other soldiers stood on the deck of the liner *Queen Mary* waving goodbye to England. They arrived after a long sea journey in June, when the heat was at its worst. One young soldier in the REME recalled how when he drank a glass of water it was sweated out in the next few seconds. Some crazy decisions were made at this time. The men were forced to train hard in the searingly hot sun while continuing their workshop duties, too. 'Morale dropped like a stone,' explained the soldier.

Wartime entertainer and 'Forces Sweetheart' Dame Vera Lynn recalled her brief visit to the Egyptian capital Cairo, writing: 'When I stopped off at the Khan al-Khalili bazaar, en route to Burma, I remember thinking I'd never forget the sights and smells: it was a magical maze of narrow streets bedecked with mirrors, spices, shoes, lanterns and jewels. The smells were of dried roses, spices and tobacco. I suddenly felt a long way from the London East End of my childhood.'

But while the British armies fought a desperate battle against the ever-advancing Field Marshal Erwin Rommel and his Afrika Korps at Tobruk in Libya, Bombardier Lowe and the Royal Ordnance Corps were lucky to have been sent on to the Suez Canal area. A further move away from the potential dangers at Cairo came some months later, when General Bernard Montgomery pushed the Germans back at the second battle of Alamein and Lowe was posted east to a large ordnance base at Rafah, not far from the shores of Palestine. Whilst he escaped battle, he didn't escape the scorching heat, bogs, flies, torrential rains and all that went with the summer season on the Gaza Strip. Indeed, surviving the exhausting conditions was a battle all of its own.

A thin little balding figure of an Englishman, who walked about wearing army spectacles, sporting a large black moustache and showing laughably knobbly knees in his khaki shorts, Lowe was promoted to acting sergeant major. Often described as 'stroppy' if things didn't go his way, he is remembered as a person 'no one took seriously' – an early sign, perhaps, of how his real character often found its way into his portrayal of Captain Mainwaring.

Lowe was based by this time on the northern edge of the Sinai Desert with the REME craftsmen of the 15th Radio Repair Workshop. This section of the REME was run by Captain Macmillan, an exceptionally eccentric professor from Aberdeen University. Lowe lived in a tent perched over a 3ft hole to protect him from the icy cold nights. He held the grade of Radio Mechanic Class 1 but according to a friend named Norman Littlechild, who knew the actor at Rafah, 'Arthur had no real experience and couldn't repair radios. He was third in command of the unit after the captain and the sergeant but he wasn't mechanical at all.' According to the honest Littlechild, there was an air of self-importance about Lowe and he was 'always busy doing paperwork'. Littlechild also commented on Captain Macmillan, who 'knew nothing about radios or anything military!' The word 'useless' was used to describe other senior figures in the ranks, and the men, all technical types, never saw any combat action at all. 'The only enemy I saw', revealed Littlechild, 'were PoWs. I even went on strike in the army three times and got away with it. We didn't even do guard duty; they got African soldiers to do it. This led to many trigger-happy incidences and more often than not the entrance to the workshops would be littered with dead Arabs.'

More often than not it was Lowe who organised the use of an American lend-lease truck or two equipped with various drills, lathes and tools to repair important military kit including searchlights, radar and radio. Following the great battle at El Alamein, various tanks were left outside the REME base and Lowe may well have seen 'all the blood and bits of flesh all over the place'.

When Lowe wasn't obsessing over orders and invoices and other bureaucratic activities, he lived in the sergeants' mess at another camp. His routine began at 7am each day when he would say 'Gather round, men' and they would shoulder their rifles and parade around the ground, then stride forcefully to the workshops which sat a mile along the road. When it came to lunchtime, usually at mid-day, he would march the men back to the cookhouse where 'the food was dreadful'. 'Camel sausages and bread with weevils in it. It was all you had and if you refused to eat it there was nothing else,' said Littlechild. Those who knew Lowe in those days said he could be 'very pompous' and 'took himself very seriously, just like Captain Mainwaring'. But despite the posturing to grandstand himself, Lowe was called 'Arthur' by the men under his wing. 'He was an ordinary bloke and we weren't that sort of strict military unit,' recalled Littlechild.

Meantime the recently promoted Acting Sergeant Major Lowe was allowed in the sergeant's mess for lunch, where the menu was the same and the class system did little to help the uniformed diners toiling in the Sinai Desert! It seems the hot sands and humid conditions proved a great equaliser in many ways.

The evenings were long and warm, and the beer no better than the food. The men entertained themselves playing darts or football, and sometimes they would walk half a mile across the desert to watch a film starring the great comedian W.C. Fields, but only when the projector was working efficiently. Lowe, of course, was a massive fan of the deep-voiced, bulbous-nosed, cynical old actor Fields. One of his favourite jokes was about why he never drank water? Fields replied with a loud grunt: 'Because fish fuck in it!'

At one point life became so boring that Lowe organised a dance but the women never showed up so yet another evening passed by in a drunken haze. One day, when the men discovered their radios had been stolen and there was no BBC to entertain them, Lowe decided to set up an amateur dramatic society.[10]

Whilst he was a great mimic and good at impersonating Churchill, everyone agreed it would be a hoot to get involved in some theatre and Lowe ordered from Cairo a handful of plays. In January 1943 he sat down to a formal meeting to declare the REME No. 1 Welfare Club Dramatic Society well and truly open for business! Among the group of eight enthusiasts was Lowe's pal Norman Littlechild. They agreed to stage a melodramatic old 1902 horror saga by W.W. Jacobs called The Monkey's Paw, and turned the end of the NAAFI hut into a stage.[11]

The drama focuses around an elderly couple, Mr and Mrs White, who bought a magical monkey's paw. It grants them three wishes, but with grim results and unintended consequences. As the final curtain comes down, the last scene includes a resurrected corpse of their dead son at the door, Mrs White fainting by the doorstep and her horrified husband on his knees praying for his life. It was a powerful theatrical offering for the audience seated in the stifling desert beneath a moon as big as the world, but they loved it. Playing Mr White, 28-year-old Lowe had begun to carve his destiny, and his talent for playing characters older than himself had taken root. Littlechild, as stage manager, remembered Lowe was 'the only actor who was any good!' Private Thomas was cast as Mrs White, and wore a wig made by a former barber in the ranks. A real monkey's paw was also used and an awesome poster advertising the show was placed about the camp. Finally, on 8 February 1943 Lowe tottered onto the stage in his first ever play, and showed all the signs of a professional actor by keeping the play on track. Forty men had bought tickets to witness the production and nobody walked out.

It's worth considering if this popular theatrical event, combined with Lowe's determined morale-boosting efforts, lay behind the British Army's decision to promote him to sergeant major. At this point he travelled 90 miles with the unit to Haifa, where the work of the entertainments unit would continue in full flourish. It was 16 May, some four days after the Germans had surrendered in North Africa.

Now good friends, Lowe and Littlechild decided to take a trip and visit the Church of the Holy Sepulchre, the Mount of Olives and the Garden of Gethsemane. Whilst the fussy Lowe was not overtly religious, he took great pleasure in visiting Jerusalem, Bethlehem and Jericho, but took issue with a waiter who served his tea in a cracked cup, remembered Littlechild.

What followed was a new posting to a far-flung spot in the desert where masquerade became reality as the unit was ordered to create a large 'mock' army camp complete with wooden guns and life-size model aircraft. Yet another *Dad's Army*-style experience evolved as the men lived in a hessian world, and washed their uniforms in petrol to save water and demolish any lice dwelling in the seams. Their efforts would pay off and indicated to the Germans looking down from the air that the British Army was thriving and ready for action. Soon enough it was time to move on again, this time to the far west of Cairo, not far from Tobruk, where a sprightly Sergeant Major Lowe and his men took up arms with a Royal Artillery unit.

Sure enough there was time to produce another play, and this time Lowe opted for Eugene O'Neill's one-act drama *Bound East for Cardiff*. The play was written in 1914 and tells the story of a sailor named Yank, who is injured and dying aboard a British steamer, the *Glencairn*. During his last days Yank talks to his friend about old adventures at sea and bemoans their poor life on the waves. As Yank breathes his last, he has a vision of a young attractive woman dressed in black.

It has been suggested that Lowe chose the drama because he himself was a big fan of the seaside, but with a cast of eleven, it gave more actors the chance to tread the boards. A room in a Derna hotel in Libya became the set for the show, and parts of old wrecked aircraft were dressed to create the steamship. However, the war brought the production to a halt as the men were called back to Rafah.

According to Stephen Lowe, his father knew by this time that he wanted a professional life on the stage and as soon as he was able, he produced another play, ironically a thriller named *Recall*, which was fully rehearsed and this time it went ahead.[12]

There followed a series of one-off variety entertainments for the troops. Not only was the versatile Sergeant Major Lowe proving to be a talented comic actor, but he could also turn on the drama when needed. Massively keen to concentrate on keeping the homesick allied armed forces in reasonable cheer, he joined a Field Entertainment Unit run by a well known man of the theatre, Captain Torin Thatcher. Many knew RADA-trained Thatcher from his performance in Laurence Olivier's stage production of *Hamlet* (1937) and the 1941 film *Major Barbara* co-starring Wendy Hiller. After the war, and his commendable service with the Royal Artillery, the deep-voiced Thatcher starred in several well known films, including *Mutiny on the Bounty* (1962) with Trevor Howard and Marlon Brando.

The energetic Lowe had found a good leader in Thatcher and while in Cairo he was set to work on a festival of plays by George Bernard Shaw and to take part in radio performances with the Forces Broadcasting Unit. The memories of the hot, arid sands of the desert and their accompanying malaise soon began to fade as he awoke each day to the vibrant, colourful, noisy bustle of civilisation in the Egyptian capital. Having impressed his commanding officer as a sergeant major, Lowe found himself a proud and fully signed up NCO with Thatcher's No. 2 Field Entertainment Unit. He was now tremendously busy helping out troops in and around Cairo to produce morale-boosting theatrical productions. One of those soldiers went on to become one of Britain's best loved comedians: Tommy Cooper wore a red fez and performed a series of bungled magic tricks to bring the house (tent) down. One of his tricks was to ask a member of the audience onto the stage to help him with some magic and then humiliate the naive participant by turning the joke on him. One solder who fell victim to Cooper's antics recalled: 'He had the entire audience on his side and if you weren't careful you came out of it looking none too dignified.'

On his travels as an official military showman, Sergeant Major Lowe visited Beirut and Lebanon. By 1944 the war was far, far away in Europe and his theatrical skills as a producer were much in demand as troops waited for their orders to stay put or return home. It was in Lebanon, however, that Lowe met Captain Martin Benson, who had been a professional actor before the war. They became friends and were posted with the unit to Alexandria in Egypt, which, although it had been hit by German bombing raids, remained far more cosmopolitan than Cairo. At least 10 per cent of its 100,000 population was made up of rich, aristocratic Brits who revelled in the sophistication imparted by the French ex-pats living nearby. The culture of Alexandria, with its museums, palaces and exotic dancers, was recorded in the beautiful glossy *Sphere* magazine, which was of the quality of *Tatler*.

What the city did not have, apparently, was a professional theatre and so Captain Benson, Sergeant Major Lowe and the No. 2 Field Entertainment Unit thought it was time to create one, and begin offering the locals and fellow troops a variety of performances. In August 1944, as the sun beat down on the hard-working theatricals, including several women volunteers from the Auxiliary Territorial Service and the Women's Royal Naval Service, a large empty room at 8 Rue Nubar Pasha, off Mahmed Aly Square, was turned into the Mercury Theatre. It is extraordinary to think the venue was created in just six weeks in temperatures of 87 degrees Fahrenheit or more. It was Lowe's job to paint the sets and look for costumes. He also had a raw set of amateur performers to get into shape before the opening night.

In an interview in 2000 carried out by Lowe's biographer Graham Lord, the theatrical veteran Captain Benson recalled how the Mercury Theatre was originally just meant for troop entertainment but soon enough the local civilians began to flood in through the doors to watch each show. When the plays got too intellectual, he said, the locals arrived more often, and the audience numbers wearing khaki dropped off.

According to records, there was always a variety of productions on offer, thanks to Lowe's diligence and intuition in regards to play selection. Benson recalled at least a new drama each week and both his and Lowe's association with the British Army became less and less. There was no let up from routine and discipline, however, as their theatrical endeavours saw them in action seven days a week and often rehearsals continued well into the night. They thoroughly believed in their duty to serve the troops by keeping up morale. With the Germans now far from North Africa, the city of Alexandria was at peace.

Benson recalled: 'We didn't live in barracks – Arthur lived in one room, as I did – and we wore uniform only because it gave you admission to the various clubs and discount shops. It was a holiday place!' Looking back, Benson and Lowe agreed how they 'virtually lived' in their little home-built theatre, and the regular calls for actors and stage management crew were placed around various military camps in the form of an eye-catching poster. Benson described Lowe as an 'odd' character and quickly added how they always got on:

Arthur was very quiet, almost dour. You didn't get much of a laugh out of him. He wasn't in the slightest the life and soul of the party, and he didn't seem to have much sense of humour, which is strange in the light of what he went on to do!

He was Mainwaring and Mainwaring was him; a little pompous, but you can't be too pompous in the army. He was a neutral man, neither likeable or unlikeable. He was subdued and unobtrusive, and struck me as being a typical engineer type, and he looked a little funny in his long shorts, and he was on the way to being completely bald. I don't think he had any girlfriends. There were lots of pretty girls around at the Mercury but I don't think Arthur was interested. He was just rather dull: a quiet, slightly introverted man who lived a secret life in his head, and no one would have known what that secret life was. I had no inkling that he might become famous.[13]

However, research carried out by Graham Lord revealed Benson wasn't that popular himself and during rehearsals often 'shouted at the enthusiastic WRNS' for being 'too wooden' on stage. Others remembered Benson as someone to be avoided if he was in a bad mood. Sergeant Major Lowe, however, obviously aware of his own fledgling career on the professional scene, could be extremely encouraging with the amateur actors and always told them 'they were doing a grand job'. Lowe's words of encouragement to young performers continued well into his career, as confirmed in the introduction to this book by actor Ian Lavender, who starred as Private Pike in *Dad's Army*.

However, when the curtain first went up at the Mercury on 9 October 1944, within just a few weeks of the crew receiving permission to convert the hall, the director's name on the billboard was given as 'Arthur Lowe' and the production of *Without the Prince* by Philip King was hailed a hit. It was the first time that Lowe's theatrical endeavours had been reported in a newspaper, *The Gazette*, and he was delighted with the positive coverage. *Without the Prince* – a three-act comedy – was astutely chosen to open the new Mercury as it was about a group of amateur players preparing to produce *Hamlet*. Lowe thought it was a guaranteed recipe for laughter – an accurate prediction if ever there was one. (Indeed, the records of the Royal Leicestershire Regiment reveal that the play was also a hit for ENSA when it was staged at the Garrison Theatre, Calcutta, on 22 October 1945.)

Philip King, actor and playwright (1904–1979), is best known for his comedy *See How They Run*, which took the West End by storm in January 1945. Yorkshire-born King served in the RAF and once gave a revealing insight into just what it was like for theatre-goers who dared visit the West End during the war. It was very different from Sergeant Major Lowe's experiences far away in the relative calm of Alexandria in 1945. At the time King was in the RAF and stationed at White City, Shepherd's Bush:

During my four years service I had risen from the rank of AC2 (the lowest rank possible) to AC1 (not the highest), but I was fortunate in as much as, owing to the shortage of accommodation at White City, I was allowed to 'live out' in civilian digs. By the grace of God the play went like a bomb – even three 'doodlebugs' dropped during the performance. George Gee, playing the leading part, swore that all three dropped as he was saying his funniest lines. No one left the theatre until the play was over.

The morning after the 'first night' I went down to Shepherd's Bush, bought every morning paper there was, and went to my usual workmen's cafe directly opposite RAF White City, and over a pint mug of tea and a Spam sandwich read the notices.

They were marvellous! But, as I read them, I suddenly remembered the pictures I had seen of Noel Coward sitting up in a wonderful looking bed, in an even more wonderful dressing-gown, a silver tray at his side, reading *his* notices! And here was I . . . a pint mug of tea and a thick Spam sandwich. But what the hell? I had a success. That's all that really mattered.

No doubt Sergeant Major Lowe and the hearty crew at the Mercury enjoyed the applause they received for their productions, which changed weekly. Entertaining plays by writers such as J.B. Priestley and Merton Hodge were in the repertoire, and another review by a former drama critic, David Scott Daniell of the *Manchester Guardian*, enthused how a particular show had been 'charming, unsophisticated and very wholesome' and 'would no doubt send people away very happy!' The great camaraderie among the actors and the stage crew was evident to one and all and the enthusiasm with which each production was staged was remarked upon again and again by reviewers. Even Benson, the ever-keen Lowe's theatrical cohort, was impressed with the 'esprit de corps' he witnessed between the troupers and remarked that Egypt had never seen anything like it!

Always backstage and keen to remain in control of each production, Lowe never cast himself in a Mercury Theatre play. There was, however, little doubt that the man who 'rather liked it in the army' would continue to stoke the flames of his ambitions to be a professional actor and all the experience he had gained during his time in Wales, Palestine and Egypt would serve him well. For the rest of his life the 5ft 4inch tall actor was proud to continue his membership of the Duke of Lancaster's Own Yeomanry Regimental Association. He was obviously keen to pay tribute to his valuable and formative years in uniform.

When the war in Europe ended, the 30-year-old, skinny, bald, short-sighted and knobbly-kneed Sergeant Major Lowe was posted back to Britain. His report card was marked 'exemplary', and Benson had praised his colleague's 'great appetite for theatre, use of imagination and complete reliability'.

Back in the north of England in 1945, and not much liking the idea of returning to his old job at the Fairey Aviation Factory, the confident Lowe strode out to achieve and live his 'actor's life'. Soon he was offered a chance to join the Manchester Repertory Theatre. It was the same year he met his true love, Joan Cooper (1922–1989), who became his wife in 1948. They would remain together until his death in 1982. Their son Stephen was born in 1953. From then until the 1960s he enjoyed success throughout the theatres of Britain and was a popular cast member with a variety of leading companies. In the West End he appeared with aplomb in *Call Me Madam*, *The Pyjama Game* and *Pal Joey*.

From 1960 to 1965 he appeared as a draper-cum-lay preacher by the name of Arnold Swindley in ITV's northern soap opera *Coronation Street*. In 1966, in a sit-com called *Pardon the Expression*, he worked with the actress Betty Driver, who in 1969 went on to appear as barmaid Betty Turpin in *Coronation Street*. Driver didn't enjoy working with her co-star and described him as a 'difficult man to get on with'. For one episode of *Pardon the Expression* she was required to pick up Lowe and throw him, and in doing so she hurt her back so badly she briefly retired from show business.

To any *Dad's Army* fan, the stories about the cast and crew during the creation of the show are legendary. This raft of popular anecdotes, so often recalled by the stars themselves, explains the rhythms of human nature in all its forms and how dynamically the actors' personalities melted into the characters. Wasn't it Einstein who said: 'Two things are infinite: the universe and human stupidity; and I'm not sure about the universe.' When it came to the peccadilloes and nuanced behaviour of actors like Arthur Lowe, then we can't help but be amused by his obsession for certain rhythms. It was the accommodating writer Jimmy Perry who had to wait behind at the Bell Inn hotel in Thetford each morning until Arthur had 'been'. Perry recalled that the rest of the cast would go on ahead to start a busy day of filming, but he might have to wait anything up to an hour until Captain Mainwaring could be driven to the set. 'Arthur,' he explained, 'wouldn't leave the hotel until he'd spent some time in the lavatory each morning!'

This habit, and Lowe's propensity to eat huge fried breakfasts, lunches, dinners and snacks – which had to be Mr Kipling cakes on pain of death to whichever poor runner got the wrong brand – were often remarked upon by other members of the cast. John Laurie

(Private Frazer) often described Lowe as a 'glutton'. Perry, who began to think of himself as Lowe's chauffeur, said the situation over the late morning start eased somewhat when he gave the actor a box of bran to help get things moving. 'At first he said he wouldn't eat the muck,' explained Perry. 'Then he tried it and told me bran had completely changed his life!'[14]

The skinny soldier who had once wowed the troops with his entertainment extravaganzas twenty-five years previously had now become the portly figure of the captain, a semi-pedant type of character who had inspired Perry during his own days in the Home Guard. Lowe's well nourished physique perfectly suited the character of Mainwaring, and his short height helped him bristle impeccably when he was, albeit gently, challenged by the languid upper-class Sergeant Wilson (John Le Mesurier), who played his chief clerk at the bank in Walmington-on-Sea.

When Lowe was finally offered the role that shot him to fame and fortune, the BBC's head of comedy Michael Mills was wary and unsure about an actor he described at the time 'as not one of us'. Mills did not think Lowe could play an officer as well as the charming Le Mesurier. A few months later, of course, in 1968 the proud Derbyshire actor proved Mills wrong and the dynamic between the characters of the uptight grammar school-educated lower-class, chip-on-the-shoulder Mainwaring and the former public schoolboy Wilson proved comedy gold.

During casting, Lowe was invited at first to the BBC to discuss the idea with Perry and Croft. They had lunch in the restaurant and Croft asked the actor what sort of comedy programmes he enjoyed. According to Perry, the indomitable Lowe said: 'I can tell you one I don't like: that thing *Hugh and I.*' Croft replied: 'I produce that.' After a slight pause Lowe blinked and said: 'This wine's not bad.'[15]

In an interview with Australian television in 1976, the earnest Lowe explained:

I first got involved in *Dad's Army* after 'the Swindley years'. I'd played this Swindley character in *Coronation Street* for six and a half years and it was time to stop so I decided I'd go back into the theatre for a year while the heat was off, television-wise you see? So I did but within nine months the BBC had offered me this *Dad's Army* thing, you see, and it was very strange because it came in a welter of other work. I suddenly had one of those spurts and work was coming for me from all sides and we were sorting it out, what to do, what not to do and in the back of my mind I sort of did a double take and I heard my agent say 'Oh, by the way, David Croft wants you have lunch with him at the BBC about a seven part series or something' . . . and I did this double take days after and I thought this is a man I'd go and see because I'd like to work for the BBC again and I went along and saw him with Jimmy Perry and he said 'We've got this idea and what do you think about it?' So I said I liked the idea and asked who they had in mind for the rest of the cast and when they told me of course I jumped at it as with a team like that I couldn't see how we could fail.[16]

Perry recalled how after the initial lunch and invitation to join the cast, Lowe gave him a lift home in his old Daimler, proudly explaining that 'they don't make cars like this any more', and then by accident Perry went to adjust the sun-shield which promptly broke off. 'I quickly put it under the seat and hoped Arthur didn't notice,' recalled Perry and then said years later: 'I then realised that a man who could be so naturally funny as this was a gift to any writer.'

When Lowe was asked about playing Captain Mainwaring, the character who catapulted him to fame and fortune, he described it as 'a wonderful part . . . a sort of military version of Mr Swindley' (the character he played in ITV's *Coronation Street*). Many believed Mainwaring had a great deal in common with Swindley, and Lowe's speciality was to play 'jumped-up types' who fill our civil service, banks and offices 'because they think they've made it', remarked one critic. Perry believed Lowe and the character of Mainwaring sort of 'melted into one another' and it was always great fun writing so intimately for him. 'David [Croft] and I took every little quirk of his personality, so that the man and the character became one,' Perry told *The Guardian* in an interview years later.

For each episode of *Dad's Army* Lowe was paid £ 210 (about £ 4,500 today) – the same as Clive Dunn (Corporal Jones). The BBC loved John Le Mesurier because of his upper-class mannerisms and paid him rather more, £ 262 a day (about £ 5000 today), and told journalists to pronounce Le Mesurier like 'treasurer'. When Le Mesurier arrived for his audition he made an impression by carrying his golf clubs in the back of his car.

In 1968 Lowe was 52 years old. Perhaps he realised at the beginning that he may well have landed the role that would ensure he would be remembered for ever as an actor. He was also aware he had joined a cast of notable actors just as good as himself, many of them well regarded war heroes and veterans.

But initially Croft was concerned that Lowe and other members of the cast were 'under-playing' their roles and not taking the show as seriously as they might. However, once the actors got used to the rugged countryside of Thetford and had begun to talk to each other off the set, the filming went more smoothly and Lowe soon realised the show would not be a one-minute wonder after all.

An army training base was the perfect location for *Dad's Army*, even though there were one or two incidences of real ammunition going off at the same time. Once too, the actors and crew discovered the army was about to blow something up in the area 'in ten minutes', so it was a case of 'Don't panic, Mr Mainwaring!' until word got through that filming was going on.

For the next ten years Lowe, often with his wife Joan, would travel to Thetford and check in at the town's historic Bell Hotel. Other popular accommodation with the cast and crew was the Anchor. The first series was shot over five days on location in black and white, and then recorded in a studio at BBC Television headquarters. Among the reviewers was the *Daily Mirror*'s Mary Malone, who described Lowe as 'superb'. In *The Times* the notable Michael Billington wrote: 'The one solid pleasure last night was watching the performance of Arthur Lowe.'

It was during the location weeks that other members of the cast noticed Lowe's tendency to exhibit fussy behaviour over the small things in life. For instance, he had a habit of carrying a radiator key in his pocket because he always said hotel staff never got the heating right. Lowe's son Stephen recalled how his father once approached a hotel receptionist and said: 'Our room commands the most spectacular view of the service well. Do you have one which merely looks over the sea?' And to another member of staff at a hotel he said: 'I didn't sleep so well. I believe we are next to the rooms of ill repute.'

Arthur and Joan Lowe would only smoke 'Craven A' cigarettes and only one teabag was allowed to go in the pot, but the coffee when ordered should be strong. More often than not, each obliging waiter would be questioned relentlessly about the ingredients of each meal on the menu, with Lowe needing to know how each item was prepared. Even the kippers came under his scrutiny. At one point he was overheard asking a waiter if the kippers were 'boil in the bag or real ones?!', then waggling his hand he said 'you know, swim-about-kippers?'

Sandwiches were described as 'jambons'. Lowe liked to be pretentious and declare his knowledge of the French language, possibly harking back to his wartime days in French-colonial Egypt. But despite all his sophisticated dietary requirements, there was no barrier to the size of each portion and Lowe as a gourmet had to buckle his belt around an ever-growing paunch.

Each morning on the way to a location shoot the coach trip was a hoot. According to the actor Bill Pertwee (ARP Warden Hodges), the 'Dad's Army Club' got off the ground like 'a schoolboy's holiday'. (During the Second World War Pertwee had been a member of the Air Training Corps, and worked in a factory making parts for Spitfire cannon.) The Dad's Army Club's adventures after a day's filming deep in the heart of Norfolk provided the opportunity for more stories to emerge about the cast. Just how starry Mr and Mrs A. Lowe behaved is probably no more opulent or ostentatious than anyone else associated with this famous show.

According to Pertwee, Arthur retained his penchant for military discipline. At 6 every night at the hotel he and Joan would take a bath, and at 7.30pm he would order two large gins in big glasses, a slice of cucumber in each, two bottles of tonic water, and a separate dish of ice. God help the waiter who misinterpreted such specific requirements and delivered the wrong drinks. Once the Lowes had reached the downstairs bar, another two large gins would be downed before dinner, where Joan ate little but drank a lot. Then came the red wine with the food and Joan's voice got louder. After liqueurs, it was time for the actor to help his wife get back to their room and into bed.[17] In Stephen Lowe's book about his father, he writes how while Joan was drifting off to sleep a cold beer would be ordered, which Arthur drank sitting on the side of the bed. It was a nightly ritual which continued, explained Stephen, for many years. If he wasn't too tired, Arthur would occasionally go with some other members of the cast to the cinema in Thetford around 10.30pm to watch the day's filming.

Was Captain Mainwaring sociable in real life? 'Not at first,' recalled former actress Caroline Dowdswell, who played bank clerk Janet King in the first series. 'I don't remember him coming to the bar with the rest of us. I knew very little about him or his private life. But later I learned he was a very warm and kind man.'

Other cast members including Bill Pertwee said Lowe was the kind of person who thought 'until I know you I don't want to know you'. And yet, after a couple of years working alongside the Dad's Army family, he showed his support in many ways. Ian Lavender (Private Pike) said that despite the thirty year age difference, Lowe was happy to make sure the younger man was always in shot even if he didn't have any lines to say. Lavender said: 'We worked together for ten weeks a year and saw each other two or three times a year, and that was it. But I liked him enormously, I really did. Yes, he and Joan sometimes ate separately in the evenings, and it did upset some people, but then we'd been in each other's pockets all day filming.'

Among the legendary stories about the cast is Lowe's allegedly irritating habit of not learning his lines and then making them up as he went along, thus throwing everyone else in the cast off balance. The producer David Croft approached Lowe about this practice and gave the actor two copies of the script – one for home and one to keep with him. Lowe retorted: 'I'm not having any rubbish like that in my house!' And so the paraphrasing continued on and off, and in hindsight Croft admitted it kept everyone on their toes and added even more spontaneity to each episode.[18]

Lowe's fussy behaviour often annoyed the crew, though, especially as the actor himself was impatient with anyone he thought was 'unprofessional'. Lowe earned the nickname 'Kitty' because everything, including his costumes, desk, mealtimes, even down to the precise placing of nail-clippers in his pocket, had to be just so. He was a stickler for timing, too. If dinner was at 8pm it was no good if it was 7.59pm or 8.01pm.

Imagine how his frustration boiled over into his character when dealing with Le Mesurier ('Le Mez'), who would amble around the set and exude a certain languid helplessness that had all the make-up girls rushing to his attention. Lowe complained that the women in the crew were always fussing around his co-star, yet if they offered to wash Lowe's hair for him he always felt uneasy and told them 'not to worry as Joan would do it'. It was noted that the actor was a prim, uptight sort of man with little or no sexual allure at all. The actress Pamela Cundell (Mrs Fox) never saw Lowe flirt with any of the girls around the set: 'I became close to him I suppose because I was jolly and made him laugh. He admitted to me himself he never had any sex appeal.' In contrast, it has been suggested that Joan Lowe could be bawdy and liked to guffaw at dirty jokes. Some friends wondered if Lowe's commitment to his life's work as an actor left his wife sexually unfulfilled.

Lavender remembers that the couple behaved lovingly towards each other, and he recalled how Lowe liked to spend at least one day a week in bed, and eat his meals there too. Both aged 60 by then, Arthur and Joan still had a spark of life between them, and Lavender remembered a funny evening when after dinner and before going up to bed at the hotel, they disappeared and then came back with a rose bush, two open bottles of Guinness and a piece of hosepipe. 'I guess it was their way of having fun,' explained Lavender.[19]

Then came Lowe's adamant refusal to wear long-johns in a scene, and/or have anything shoved down them so Laurie as Private Frazer could manhandle him near the crotch area. He remained uptight about the whole idea but only told Croft and Perry he wasn't going to 'remove his trousers or any other item of clothing' on the day of the shoot. In the show it was eventually Clive Dunn (Corporal Jones) who agreed to do the stunt with the bomb down the trousers. Lavender explained that Lowe was forgiven because he was such a brilliant comedy actor and never made an effort to be funny, 'which is death to comedy'. And it was what he left unsaid that made us all laugh.

Many of those who knew Lowe described how he instilled respect, not fear. He wasn't, they agreed, one of those 'stars' who would 'go ballistic' if their dressing room wasn't quite right, or there was a disagreement. He was often kind and tolerant of any children of the crew who might be around the set during filming. Many of his *Dad's Army* colleagues were astounded by the way he worked so well with Le Mesurier, as when they weren't filming they rarely spoke to each other. This was also strange as in real life the television captain and his sergeant enjoyed many of the same pastimes – jazz piano and cricket especially. It was suggested that Lowe bore a grudge because at the beginning of the series Le Mesurier earned more than he did. He also made it clear he disapproved of Le Mesurier's louche and bohemian attitude to life. Bill Pertwee (Warden Hodges) recalled how Lowe would appear irked when Le Mesurier rolled up to start work on the set after drinking and schmoozing at Ronnie Scott's jazz club in London until 5 that very same morning. Lowe soon realised, however, that the languid Le Mez had a photographic memory and did not need to stay up all night learning his lines.

The majority of the cast agreed that Lowe really *was* Mainwaring in many ways, the main difference being that Lowe often burst his own balloon and beneath any pomposity there was often nothing but kindness and consideration. Tales of the actor being mean with money filtered through the ranks too, although Joan always defended her husband by admitting he 'just didn't like waste'. He would always turn off the lights or take a packed lunch instead of dining out. Ian Lavender (Private Pike) explained:

> In a way we weren't actors. I think one of the reasons why *Dad's Army* made such an impression was that in a way we all played ourselves. If you look at the very earliest scripts, you'll see they are very different from the ones that followed. The reason was that the scriptwriters had got to know all of the actors and they started to write the scripts around our personalities.

One well known anecdote involved Lowe and his beloved Daimler car, which he named Henry. One day Lowe was driving in the countryside and ran over a cockerel by mistake. He carried the dead cockerel to a nearby farmhouse and promised the farmer he would like to replace the bird. 'Please yourself,' shrugged the gruff man. 'The hens are round the back!'

Best friends among the cast in a 'Three Musketeers' kind of way appeared to be Le Mesurier, Clive Dunn and James Beck, who enjoyed various adventures in the hotel involving young women, vast quantities of alcohol and late night parties. It wasn't unusual for Lowe to fling open the door of his room to see what all the noise was about along the corridor.

On the political front, Lowe appeared to be traditional Conservative and one floor manager reckoned the actor had something of Enoch Powell about him. Lowe couldn't abide hearing about a workforce striking and wasn't shy of letting everyone know his views. Sometimes he'd say something, but in essence it was just a jest and a wind-up for whoever may be listening.

One cast member who annoyed Lowe considerably was Clive Dunn (Corporal Jones) because he upstaged him and got more laughs. Pam Cundell (Mrs Fox) was good friends with Arthur and Joan. She recalled that 'Clive was an untidy performer and never did or said the same thing twice so he was difficult to work with.' She went on: 'Also Clive could be bossy and was always making denigratory remarks about *Dad's Army* and saying it was a load of rubbish, and that got up Arthur's nose too because he really thought they were a proper platoon and really believed in that blasted Home Guard in the end. It became a real thing.'[20] When Dunn was awarded the OBE in 1975 his co-star was reported to be 'furious', and is alleged to have accused Dunn of letting down the platoon by accepting the honour because he was strictly a Labour man. Cundell added: 'Maybe Arthur thought he should have got it, and he should have done. I don't know why Arthur was never offered anything and he would have been bitter. He would have liked an honour.' Lowe got his own back though, telling a friend: 'I'd never accept that bargain basement stuff . . . Only a knighthood would have been good enough.' John Laurie's reaction to Dunn's OBE was terse: 'Clive's been up [Harold] Wilson's arse for years!'

Any leisure time Lowe allowed himself beyond the swathe of work, including television commercials (Cadbury's chocolate was one of his favourites), he spent aboard *Amazon*, his houseboat. Stephen Lowe writes in detail about the holidays he spent with his parents aboard the 31m-long screw schooner, built in 1885 at Southampton as a 'fast and good sea boat'. The Lowe family took to her decks in 1968 after *Dad's Army* star Arthur Lowe had seen her advertised as 'a beautifully fitted ex-steam yacht, or permanent home. The vessel is capable of accommodating ten in comfort. At present moored London but alternative mooring available Norfolk Broads. Constructed from 2' Burma teak, sheathed in copper, the hull is practically maintenance free.' The actor fell in love with *Amazon* and paid the agent £ 2,000 for his dream. After extensive work, she was finally ready to take to the seas again in 1971 and Lowe was delighted. Stephen recalled the day they all set off for Cubbitt's yacht basin, near the rowing club at Chiswick, London, to inspect the vessel:

> *Amazon* was my father's romantic vision. But more often than not, it had to be consummated in the form of on-board dinner parties where the guests were asked to turn off lights to conserve the power, not to wash their hands under a running tap to conserve water, and to conduct themselves as economically as they possibly could, even though the vessel at the time never left the security of the jetty.[21]

But once the 'black velvets' (Guinness and champagne was a favourite tipple with Arthur and Joan) had been drunk during many a jovial adventure, and a hearty meal cooked by Stephen had been cleared away, the happy sea-captain Lowe tidied away his deck shoes, weighed anchor and returned to work on the television set. On occasion he was able to moor *Amazon* alongside a jetty in a town where he was appearing at the local theatre, and once the curtain came down returned happily to reside in his own floating home. Years later, as Stephen sat down to write his memoir about his legendary father, he described how the logbook still smelled of the old yacht and very much distilled his memory of that first summer on board her doughty decks.

The second series of *Dad's Army*, still in black and white, was broadcast in the spring of 1969. Audience figures that April leapt from eight million to twelve million, and finally the BBC conceded it had a brilliant success to shout about. 'Operation Kilt' and 'The Battle of Godfrey's Cottage' were two of the six episodes from the influential second series, which had disappeared from the BBC archives at one time. Thankfully they were rediscovered in the 1970s by a film fan casually looking through some rusting cans of film atop a skip outside Elstree Studios.

By 1970, and after the fourth series, the viewing figures for *Dad's Army* had topped sixteen million. Academics, including the esteemed Professor Jeffrey Richards, attributed the success of the show to its characters and humour being 'immortally English, just as those in Dickens and Shakespeare', and he cites the 'rude mechanicals' in *A Midsummer Night's Dream* as a good example. There certainly is a

Dickensian style in Arthur Lowe's performances as an actor, but as a private man too and it's little wonder he was such a success appearing as Mr Micawber in *David Copperfield* or Mr Pickwick (*The Pickwick Papers*) in television adaptations of 1974. Any actor of the time who reminded the British public of John Bull – a character full of pomposity and yet great incidental wisdom and stoicism – was and is still greatly loved.

When it came to explaining the success of *Dad's Army*, Arthur Lowe – war veteran, actor and sailor – had a theory. He claimed if a comedy show was going to become a hit that lived on for ever, then if the audience still laughed with the sound turned down, it was a sure sign of success. Asked about Mainwaring, he once said: 'It's a wonderful part. Mainwaring is prudish and pompous. He's an extremely brave little man who would gladly go through hell and high water for Walmington-on-Sea. He's also a very good bank manager – good for the bank that is.'

And even when the show closed, and the actor took off his khaki uniform and strode out of Walmington-on-Sea, he was seldom out of work. Fighting his regular bouts of narcolepsy, he appeared in *Bless Me Father* and *Potter*, and his legacy was affirmed again when he become the voice of the *Mister Men* cartoons, too. By this time, however, his health was beginning to fail and in 1979 he suffered a stroke. He then decided only to accept roles in productions that would also include his wife Joan. In April 1982 Arthur Lowe died, aged just 66.

One of the best tributes to this hard-working actor, who once revealed that he never went on stage expecting great stardom, appeared in a national newspaper. It said: 'Few can die and have it said about them that their passing caused as much grief as their living caused laughter.' Almost thirty years later, in June 2010, a life-sized bronze statue of him was unveiled in Thetford, Norfolk, where the classic sitcom was filmed between 1968 and 1977. It is a figure of the actor as Captain Mainwaring – it bears a facial expression of comical incandescence and frustration, and remains as recognisable as ever. No one who visits the *Dad's Army* Museum in the town can forget to be photographed alongside this wonderful tribute.

Today, in so many ways Arthur's legacy, especially his love of sailing, lives on too through the historically important work of his photographer grandson Jack Lowe. There's little doubt the *Dad's Army* legend would be most proud to learn that Jack tours the country recording the lives and times of all those past and present who maintain and operate Royal Navy Lifeboat Institute stations and vessels. For decades the much-loved actor supported the RNLI and encouraged many of his co-stars, including John Le Mesurier, Bill

Pertwee, James Beck and Clive Dunn, to help with charity events and various galas, as Jack's pictures in this book reveal. It was as if his heart really did belong to the sea and his beloved *Amazon* was never far from his mind.

Indeed, I was honoured when Jack agreed to let me include this poignant and treasured excerpt from his 'Lifeboat Photographic Project Logbook' entitled 'The Teddington Collection'. He has loved the RNLI since he was a child and has devoted several years of his life visiting all 238 lifeboat stations in the UK and making portraits of the Institute's coxswain, helms, mechanics and women crew members. His father Stephen is an experienced seafarer and introduced him to the wonders of the lifeboat. He writes:

On that April morning in 2015 before setting off to photograph five lifeboat stations along the Thames, *Neena*, a converted former ambulance, was just about packed and ready to go.

As I cast my eyes around the studio to make sure I had everything, I remembered at the last moment to dig out a treasured photo album from the 1970s that my late Mum put together when I was a baby. I was *so* pleased that I'd managed to remember it.

Why? Well, shortly after I was born, the three of us decamped from Scotland to live on the family boat, *Amazon*.

*Amazon* (no longer in our family) was and still is a 100ft-long Victorian schooner built by Tankerville Chamberlayne in Southampton in 1885. She was designed by Dixon Kemp as a private yacht and over the decades has been many things and sailed the world. My grandfather Arthur found her as a derelict hulk on the banks of the Thames in 1968 and made it his labour of love to restore *Amazon* to her former glory. She set to sea again in 1971.

Therefore, in essence, she'd become a houseboat and this is where we'd now live for the foreseeable future. At the time, she was still moored close to where she'd been discovered on the Thames at Teddington.

The last lifeboat station I'd be visiting on my Thames journey would, of course, be Teddington and the treasured album contained photographs of our lives from exactly that time. Having never returned since, I wondered if I could use the photo album to pinpoint exactly where we'd lived . . .

On the morning of Saturday, 2 May we pulled up outside the lifeboat station. I could see it was all abuzz. Indeed, I was all abuzz! Between us all, we'd been building up to the visit by email as well as on the social media.

You see, there's another connection: my grandfather, Arthur (who bought and renovated *Amazon*), also happened to be President of the Twickenham and District RNLI Branch in the 1970s, a branch that has now matured into Teddington RNLI Lifeboat Station. Arthur was a huge RNLI supporter and I'd already been taken aback at Cromer when the station's historian, Paul Russell, managed to unearth a newspaper clipping of a visit he'd made in 1973.

With Sheerness, Gravesend, Tower and Chiswick under my belt, I could now turn my attentions to a visit that I knew would be both special and emotional but little did I know how much.

As soon as I arrived I wound down the window of *Neena* to be greeted by a friendly face, the DLA (Deputy Launching Authority) Charlie Molloy: 'Good morning, Jack! Welcome to Teddington!'

A fine welcome it was too, full of warmth and high spirits that continued for the rest of the day. Unbeknown to me, the staff had unearthed a whole catalogue of photographs from Arthur's era. Not only that but they'd made a display of them for me to admire and enjoy.

We were so relaxed chatting in the crew room but, of course, we had some photographs to create. The crew started sweeping the launch ramp, making it spick and span for the plates I'd make of the view. Even the children grabbed a broom and mucked in. While they were doing that, it was a chance to collect my thoughts; I set up the camera and settled my emotions a little.

As the ramp-tidying neared completion, the 1970s photo album popped into my head – I'd nearly forgotten all about it! I stepped into *Neena* to retrieve it, opened it up and turned the pages. If my emotions had had any time to settle at all, imagine how I felt on seeing the photograph of me as a baby on the deck of the *Amazon* with Teddington Lock in the background. My family has always been really good at labelling photographs, so I slipped the print out of its sleeve to see if there was any information on the back. Another surprise was lurking: the date was written in my Mum's handwriting – 'May 9, 1976' – thirty-nine years ago, almost to the day!

With regard to making the day's photographs, time was rapidly slipping away. We snapped back into Project mode and, by the time the day was over, I'd made a set of five photographs of which I'm very proud. The full collection can be seen by visiting www.lifeboatstationproject. com and prints can be bought online.

The three plates I made of the river views from Teddington Lifeboat Station – the spot on the Thames that proved to be so nostalgic for me – combine to make a particularly personal and heartfelt collection. The support and enthusiasm shown by Teddington was simply fantastic and proved to be a momentous day for the Project. My sincere thanks to all the crew and staff at Teddington for making Saturday, 2 May 2015 such a special occasion that will live long in the memory.

Today it's apparent that devoted maritime photographer and storyteller Jack Lowe has inherited from his grandfather Arthur, sailor and comedy legend, a unique bond with the camera and of course a love of the seas and waterways of Britain. Jack's storming work behind the lens is enough to make even Captain Mainwaring bristle with pride.

# JOHN LE MESURIER

Darn it Lee Mesure! You're no soldier! You're more suited to life as an officer!

Royal Tank Regiment sergeant major yelling at a bumbling young recruit named John Le Mesurier in 1941.

JOHN Le Mesurier (pronounced as in 'treasurer') was easily among the most charismatic actors of his generation. Full of charm and good manners, he was top billing not only with friends and colleagues but with audiences too, and especially so during his later years as the loveable Sergeant Arthur Wilson in *Dad's Army*. Whether on stage, in a film or on television, the instinctive charisma of the star, who always described himself as 'just a jobbing actor', enabled him to come across as a noble gent who furnished his beautiful performances with a unique Edwardian style and panache.

Always excruciatingly polite in real life, and preferring to avoid conflict at all costs, John 'Le Mez' was 56 years old by the time he agreed to join the cast of the now legendary Walmington-on-Sea Home Guard platoon. He had endured an often tortuous personal life, and had been taking whatever work he could find, whether it was a cameo role in a black and white film or on stage with a repertory company. Long before he signed the contract with *Dad's Army*, he realised that his life's work was not about being a 'star' – instead, he was a reliable and fine actor, who always made the best of the characters in whatever script was placed before him.

Wearing a uniform for his character Sergeant Wilson was not unknown to the languid, good-natured John. During the Second World War he had been 'an officer and a gentleman' serving with the Royal Armoured Corps, firstly at home in Britain and then in India. Looking back into his Norman-French ancestry, it is apparent that his mother Amy's family, the 'Le Mesuriers', included several generations of men noted for their military achievements either in the Royal Navy or in the

British Army. There are records, too, of a familial link to the wonders of the Far East, especially India.

One such adventurer in John's background was Havilland Le Mesurier, who, after the War of American Independence (1774–1783), returned home to Britain to distinguish himself as Commissary-General of the Army. Another was a certain Colonel Cecil Brooke Le Mesurier, a highly decorated hero of the nineteenth-century Afghan Wars, who was involved in the invention of a new style of firearm. Another of John's ancestors on his mother's side was a Royal Naval lieutenant who was great friends with Lord Byron. Amy came from Alderney in the Channel Islands. Her parents John and Georgina had grown up near Bombay in India as part of the British military community and then returned to Britain not long after their marriage in 1868. It's fun to imagine just how Captain Mainwaring in *Dad's Army* might huff and puff with indignation on discovering that the man behind Sergeant Wilson's character boasted a steadfast and honourable military heritage that may have well outshone each and every man of the Walmington-on-Sea Home Guard platoon!

***

MANY decades before the hit television show rocketed its cast into the spotlight, Amy Le Mesurier gave birth to baby John Elton Le Mesurier Halliley in Bedford on 5 April 1912. John's father Charles Elton Halliley was a wealthy lawyer and successful Conservative Party agent, who in 1913 decided to move the family, including John's older sister Michelle and their nanny, to Bury St Edmunds in dreamy Suffolk. This was the same Nanny who tried to dampen toddler John's fascination with a group of flamboyant 'theatricals' he spotted one day spilling out onto the street. She told him never to be friendly with 'people like that'. Perhaps it was from that moment John knew he had bumped into kindred spirits, and Nanny's stern advice was not heeded, as time would tell!

Charles's own father, Charles Bailey Halliley, was born in Ceylon (Sri Lanka) under British colonial rule. The Hallileys were top-notch civil servants, with William Halliley (John's great-grandfather) serving as head of the Customs Department in Ceylon. By 1858, though, Charles (John's grandfather) had returned to Britain and in 1878 in Bedford it is recorded he married Emma Mary Elton. He spent many years regaling his own son Charles (John's father) about the lives of eminent Hallileys who held positions of power in government departments. In his own memoir, *A Jobbing Actor*, John recalled:

My grandfather was also a lawyer but his special interest was gambling, on which he spent a great deal of money. He and Granny used to come to stay with us from time to time. Grandfather was supremely confident and especially when it came to stories about racing. He would tell us with great authority about his winners but didn't say too much about the losers. He'd talk in a loud clear voice when he was talking utter rubbish. He wore an Edward VII beard and creased his trousers sideways, like pyjamas.

The way he told his stories always made me laugh, but the laughter was not always for the reasons he hoped! Sometimes I would have to hide under the table at mealtimes before my mother said, in desperate tones, 'Come out, John, and don't make things more difficult than they need be.' I was always slightly relieved when my grandparents left. But I missed Granny who was a dear and frequently gave me two-and-six or five shillings which I immediately spent on either whipped cream walnuts or on ten De Reske cigarettes – in that order.[1]

The actor always confessed he was closest to his mother, both in temperament and interests. She, he said, had inherited a small income from her own father, who was a general in the Royal Engineers – a formidable man by all accounts:

I remember my father telling me about the agony of asking permission to marry my mother. I gather my grandfather was madly efficient about everything. He could paint, build houses, ride horses – camels indeed; he had a curious affection for camels and rode them a lot in India. I am glad never to have come across him – I don't think I'd have survived the encounter!

From this comment it seems clear that even early on in life John was not one for the brisk one-two no-nonsense attitude of the successful military personality, and he had definitely not inherited the Halliley gene for being 'madly efficient' about life's practicalities. Already he realised the men in his family had created vast expectations for him to follow suit if he was to serve both sides of the family with honour. However, already feeling the shadow of such pressure to conform, he described himself growing up as a sullen, slightly spoilt child who never really got on well with his accomplished and popular sister, who rode horses, played tennis and 'flirted very well'. Michelle Halliley was far more suited to the regimental way of life and accordingly she married an army officer, whom John described as a man 'with a moustache that didn't grow very well'.

Charles Halliley was a man who followed the rules of the time when it came to raising his son John. He took advice from a Conservative Party colleague of the Greene King brewery family. This man recommended that when John was 9 years old his parents should send him to Grenham House preparatory school in Birchington-on-Sea, Kent, which had a good record for academic success under the stewardship of Bernard Ransome. The owner of the establishment was Henry Jeston.

So in 1921, dressed in his new sombre school uniform and with only the romance of the train journey to comfort him from not knowing what lay ahead, little John Halliley arrived at Birchington-on-Sea, where the bleak world of Grenham House – 'a red brick, turreted Victorian pile with scrubbed corridors that smelled of carbolic soap' – awaited him. It was, his father's friend assured him, 'a place that would knock the nonsense out of a boy'. Indeed, boarding at Grenham meant there would be no more trips to the cinema for the little boy who had got used to being enchanted by the films he saw on days out to the Bury fleapit with his mother and sister. It was then that he began to envision a future for himself as an entertainer.

Within days of arriving at Grenham, John sensed something was wrong. He realised he would hate every minute of the grim establishment, with its atmosphere of 'fear, blood, sweat and dread'. Over the years other notable actors and writers who were Grenham boarders have revealed how they despised the place – some even suffering a form of post-traumatic stress disorder at the memory of the 'hell-hole'. Ironically, the classrooms of misery were just a stone's throw from the house of Birchington-on-Sea's most famous resident, the glamorous actress Gladys Cooper, whose home was often full of fun and twinkling party-life. Little did she know how badly one of her youngest fans, in the form of little John Halliley, was suffering just down the road.

John recalled, however, the tiny instances of kindness that kept him alive during times of terrible beatings and sadistic activities at the school, which included naked swimming in the freezing North Sea – punishments dealt out by 'the bastards' who ran the place. It's worth remembering that in the 1920s it was difficult to find good and decent teachers as so many of them had been killed during the First World War.

One day, when a prank during a game of cricket backfired, the umpire grabbed him, took him into an office and whipped him six times with the cane. Shortly afterwards, as the sensitive and unhappy battered boy sat weeping, he was approached by the school matron, a woman in her late 20s, who arrived to tend his wounds – and promptly introduced him to his first sexual experience. For ever after, John was attracted to older women. Other pupils remember how the same matron took the boys swimming and often displayed her nakedness in front of them as she changed.

It seems John's time at Grenham was spent learning how to avoid confrontation and dodge as much cruelty as possible. It's no surprise he desperately counted the days until he could go home to Suffolk and see his mother again and of course visit the cinema – his one true joy apart from cricket. As a schoolboy he realised that being a loner meant survival, but the impact of enduring each day at schools run by dysfunctional, embittered and cruel staff left a terrible scar on his emotional health for the rest of his life. He grew up to be a kind and sensitive adult, but he lacked confidence and he suffered the pain of a broken heart during every one of his three marriages. He also did his utmost to avoid confrontation all his life. In many ways he lived the life of a crushed romantic. Whether or not he learned to manage the traumas he suffered at school is difficult to know but many boys who endured such places went through their adult lives with severe psychological damage.

Former public schoolboy and journalist Alex Renton revealed in his 2018 television documentary that boarding schools have been described by psychiatrists as places which practice on children the techniques of 'attachment fracture', which means they aim to remove early emotional ties in a bid to build *esprit de corps*. There is a distrust of women and minimal empathy for the weak and ordinary. He also looked at the behaviour of many senior politicians today who were brought up with these Victorian-style ethics and who now run the country.[2]

Another survivor of Grenham House is journalist John Suchet, who told a national newspaper he was sent there in 1953. From his comments, it's clear that even thirty years after John Le Mesurier's time there (1921–1926) the place was still just as brutal and sadistic as it ever was. Suchet, always a good scholar, described Grenham as 'monstrous'. He revealed:

> I have to remind myself all the time that in 1953 that was where you were sent as a boy if parents could afford to do so. My brother David (the actor David Suchet) followed me there two years later and hated the place as much as I did. If we were mischievous the headmaster, Denys Jeston (son of the owner), used to beat us with a long bamboo cane for breaking school rules. He'd move the desks out of the way so he could

run right across the classroom to give extra power to the whack. The sting was terrible and I can still feel it now. I'd tell David 'don't cry, don't cry'.[3]

Other former pupils of the time remember the twisted Jeston waiting with a towel to dry their bare backsides every time the swimming lessons in the algae-swamped school pool were over. The deputy headteacher Jack Liston, who had a false eye, was no better and liked to put his hands up the boys' short trousers and pinch their bums.

The writer Louis de Bernières, author of *Captain Corelli's Mandolin*, was another pupil at Grenham. He arrived there aged 8 in the 1960s. He said the place, which 'happily doesn't exist any more', was run by two bastards – a sadist and a paedophile. Both Jeston and Liston died before they could be brought to justice.[4]

Back in 1926, John Halliley's parents had begun to discuss his future and sure enough their son was desperately relieved to hear that his escape from Grenham, after five miserable years, was imminent. Firstly they thought the sensitive young man with a talent for cricket and a love of show business magazines might do well in the Royal Navy. An interview was arranged but alas, it wasn't a success. At the interview the melancholy John offered only bored and indifferent replies to the questions. He wasn't overly concerned that he'd messed up, as he knew in his heart that a life at sea wasn't for him at all. So that day he got the train back from the Royal Naval College at Dartmouth and his parents told him to return to Grenham and wait to hear from them.

Soon enough a date came through for another interview – this time for Sherborne School in Dorset and in May 1926, during the General Strike, the 14-year-old found himself in 'Lyon House' sitting on an empty bed in another cold, over-ventilated, unwelcoming dormitory – the air thick again with tears and misery. Sherborne by then had been publicly criticised by former pupil Alec Waugh, brother of Evelyn, who wrote a novel about his time there called *The Loom of Youth*. Published in 1916, not long after he had been expelled for 'kissing another boy', Waugh's book discussed the moral corruption of the main character and scandalised Sherborne. The book condemned any romantic notions associated with the public school system and described their very essence as 'wretched'. Waugh wrote:

> For the boy with a personality school is very dangerous. Being powerful, he can do nothing by halves; his actions influence not only himself, but many others. On his surroundings during the time of transition from boyhood to manhood depend to a great extent the influence that man will work in the world. He will do whatever he does on a large

scale, and people are bound to look at him. He may stand at the head of the procession of progress; he may dash himself to pieces fighting for a worthless cause; and by the splendour of his contest draw many to him. More likely he will be like Byron, a wonderful, irresponsible creature, who at one time plumbed the depths, and at another swept the heavens – a creature irresistibly attractive, because he is irresistibly human.[5]

This insightful and prophetic observation by Waugh provides us with an accurate description of the heritage inherited by John, the former Sherborne pupil who became one of Britain's best-loved actors. John was indeed more Byron than anyone else. He had, after all, an ancestor who was friends with the great poet. In his own memoir he recalled a particularly negative man in his life:

My housemaster at Sherborne (A.H. Trelawny-Ross) was a typical example of his breed – a rulebook teacher who confused discipline with bullying. He held to the therapeutic value of long country runs and cold baths in all seasons and urged us to adopt his fanaticism for rugger (rugby) – a game I loathed. Almost by way of retaliation, I accepted unquestionably a rumour that he had been turned down by the girl he wanted to marry. A sensible lady, thought I!

There was at least some opportunity for the teenager to explore his natural talent for mimicry. As a fan of the actor Jack Hulbert, he memorised a monologue made famous by Hulbert at a comedy revue and performed it to mystified classmates.

As a schoolboy John also collected autographs, mostly of actors, actresses, writers, painters and anyone in the arts who was popular at the time. When his housemaster discovered an envelope addressed to John containing a picture of Tallulah Bankhead, he was subjected to more violence: 'I had to show the housemaster my whole collection of film star photographs and he tore up the lot and beat me. More than anything else I resented Sherborne for its closed mind, its collective capacity for rejecting anything that did not conform to the image of manhood as portrayed in the ripping yarns of a scouting manual,' recalled the actor.[6]

Any chance of listening to music for pleasure was also ruled out at Sherborne. The housemaster's only choice of acceptable songs would be, for instance, something by Harry Lauder about 'keeping on until the end of the road'. On one occasion John managed to smuggle in a portable record player; sticking a sock in the speaker to muffle the volume, he listened to his own favourites, like Louis Armstrong or Evelyn Laye. Looking back on those days he described himself as resembling an MI5 agent crouched over the machine listening in secret!

Each day for the pupils was rigorously policed with a strict timetable of lessons. Without fail every morning they endured extreme physical education, as 'toughening up' each boy was of primary concern. Also at Sherborne, and suffering too from its steadfast adherence to obedience and threats of violence, was a bright, slightly built boy named Alan Turing, who often shared a classroom with John. Turing, described as 'scruffy and gauche', found himself hemmed in by the school's strict fences around scientific subjects, which Trelawny-Ross, a Latin master, had dismissed as 'low and cunning'. The same Trelawny-Ross would enter a classroom and growl about it 'smelling of mathematics' and comment that disinfectant was needed immediately to clear the air! It seems John's housemaster was allowed to be arrogant about the Classics being the best subject, as the headmaster for many years, Nowell Smith, was a cultured and artistic man who deemed the study of Greek history and myths as a top priority. When Smith hung up his mortar board for good and retired, Sherborne's new head was Charles Boughey – a man whose obsession with discipline was even more strident. John found himself facing even more rules, more difficult lessons, and with even less time to dream about a life on the stage. By the age of 15 John knew he wanted to be an actor, and yet he was fully aware his parents had plans for him to become a lawyer and for him to join an elite establishment enabling professional men to prosper together.

That said, he was always glad when it came to holidays from school as he returned home to Bury St Edmunds, which he always referred to as 'his womb'. Whenever he could, he would visit the theatre, either going to the Theatre Royal in Norwich or jumping on a train to get to one of the West End venues in London. Here, at the Aldwych Theatre he saw productions like *Thark, Plunder* and *A Cup of Kindness*. How he loved to revel too in the memory of seeing *Showboat* at the Theatre Royal, Drury Lane. And how his former neighbour at Grenham, the glorious Gladys Cooper, was applauded by John when he saw her in *The Secret Flame* at the Playhouse.

In Bury itself he had the opportunity to visit the ancient Central Cinema, with its lighting fuelled by gas and the screen images managed by an elderly projectionist. Here in the dark the teenager watched in awe the silent classics as their stories unfolded before him, including Alfred Hitchcock's 1927 thriller *The Lodger* and Fritz Lang's now legendary *Metropolis*. John certainly had good taste, as his fascination with acting seized his soul. Every moment he could he would watch his idols on the big screen – Ronald Colman in *Bulldog Drummond*, for example, or Gloria Swanson in Somerset Maugham's *Sadie Thompson*.

Returning to the rigours of Sherborne struck him with gloom. It wasn't as if he had any real friends there and it was difficult to be part of the in-crowd who ran the school dramatic society. On rare occasions he did have a chance to act, usually in a Gilbert and Sullivan operetta, or even a Shakespeare play. But any theatrical adventures were quashed by his overbearing housemaster, who was anxious about young men getting involved with roles for women performers. A Sherborne pupil who became a 'cissy' would not be tolerated at all!

According to John's biographer Graham McCann, there were rare occasions when youthful high spirits got the better of Trelawny-Ross, who was 'becoming more cruel and callous as each new term went by'. He even censored each boy's letters to and from home. One pupil, Claude de Crespigny, climbed the clock tower and wound the clock hand forwards by 20 minutes in a bid to play a joke on Trelawny-Ross. The enraged housemaster then lined up the boys in their shorts and inspected their knees for any scarring marks that would indicate the culprit. He was too late, though, as de Crespigny had scarpered out of Sherborne and fled Dorset for good. This story is also recounted in a letter by John to his dear friend Derek Taylor, the journalist and Beatles' publicist, in the late 1970s. It seems, claims McCann, that back in 1929 this small rebellious act by a fellow pupil had brought some sanity into John's life and in doing so had exposed even more the growing lunacy of the misguided and overzealous Trelawny-Ross.[7]

It's not hard to imagine John's delight when in 1930 he could pack up his trunk and leave the horrors of Sherborne far behind for ever. Not even the occasional times when he had enjoyed being a superior cricket player at the school could lighten the dreaded memories. As an 18 year old, he could only look back in regret at the time wasted living in fear of those in charge of his classroom education. (Decades later, when he had established himself as an actor, he happened to stay in a hotel near his old school in Dorset – and who should he bump into? The deranged old bombast of a housemaster A.H. Trelawny-Ross, that's who! John recalled how both men stared hard at each other before John walked away, overwhelmed with silent rage at the gruesome memories of the man who ruined his childhood.)

Back home in Bury St Edmunds, John's desire to become an actor gnawed gently at his heart. But he admitted, years later, that he didn't have the energy to go against his parents' wishes for him to settle down, take his place in conventional society and become a good lawyer: 'I allowed them to gently guide me into the legal profession and I became an articled clerk to a highly respectable local old firm of solicitors called Greene and Greene.' Mr and Mrs Halliley were obviously proud of their son, an 'Old Shirburnian', whose impeccable manners and sophisticated ways suited the steady life prescribed by good Conservative Party members. According to the actor, it wasn't long before he began to doubt the value of legal work and asked why success had to be measured by workload. He wrote: 'I was not easily persuaded that all the work was strictly necessary. Why did everything have to be written out at such laborious length and copied (in my best handwriting) quite so often? The purpose, I was told, was to make plain to the meanest intelligence the intricacies of the English law, which must have said something about me for the more I wrote the more confused I became.'[8]

Working at Greene and Greene (with, as he remarked, the perfect 'e' at the end of Green to make this notable family firm stand out as the best) was described as a 'delaying tactic', and illustrated John's tendency for procrastination, which was one of his faults in life. But however much he regretted his time in the law, he did occasionally learn from watching the artful barristers at work in the Assizes Court. Their performances and oratory skills impressed him as much as any theatrical performance by a well known stage actor of the day. He said: 'I attended all manner of trials, even murder, and always marvelled at the polished fluency of the barristers. Sometimes the accused weren't too bad either. And if their dramas failed to teach me about the law they certainly kept my interest alive in the theatre.'

After three long years of watching the clock in the office, playing golf and visiting the cinema or theatre on his days off, in various unsuccessful attempts to quash his passion to go on stage, he finally found the courage to face his parents and tell them the truth about his ambition. Charles and Amy Halliley were disappointed in his decision to leave Greene and Greene, but were realistic enough to know how important it was for their son to be happy. They obviously took into account that he had done things their way for all his life and now he should have the opportunity to find a profession that would engage him wholeheartedly. They also knew that as a young man of 21 years, their son had 'come of age' and if he wanted so desperately to follow his heart, then they would quietly accept his decision. (Ironically enough, in 1957 John did appear in a cameo role playing a barrister in the film, *Brothers in Law*. His legal background had not all gone to waste!)

By the end of the summer of 1933, with his heart full of hope, he began his training as an actor at the Fay Compton Studio of Dramatic Art, run by Fay's sister Viola, in Baker Street in London. The establishment was founded in 1927 by Compton, a leading actress of the day, who had worked with the likes of Noel Coward and John Gielgud, and John chose it because the classes were so professional that he discovered more than 90 per cent of students landed work after graduation. Until it closed at the start of the Second World War, the school continued to produce many excellent performers, including John's great lifelong friend (Sir) Alec Guinness, who always marvelled at John's great gift for 'comic timing'.

On his arrival in London in 1933, John rented a cheap room in Wellington Road, St John's Wood. How could he go wrong when the area shared his name?! For the first time in his life, he felt free and ready to make his mark on the world of stage and screen, and he was, of course, able to see whatever film or theatre production he so wished. According to his biographer, John saw a variety of films, ranging from German art classics starring Emil Jannings to the American screen giants at work, including Cary Grant and Carole Lombard in the wartime aviation drama *The Eagle and the Hawk* (1933). It's interesting to note that the first time he came across a future *Dad's Army* co-star was in a stage production of *A Midsummer Night's Dream* at the Botanical Gardens, starring a dour 36-year-old Scotsman and First World War hero called John Laurie.

Soon enough, John's life was becoming full of what he perceived as amazing opportunities and within a few months, with a good understanding of the Greek tragedies and the plays of William Shakespeare, and his skills in dance, deportment and stage fencing, he began to earn a living from his new profession. Soon John was offered a job at the Palladium Theatre in Edinburgh and he became a bright young member of the Millicent Ward Repertory Players. His confidence soared. He earned £ 3 10 shillings a week. Then, after some important and varied professional experiences, he moved on. This time, through his friend Alec Guinness, he landed a role with the Gielgud Company playing understudy to Anthony Quayle's Guildenstern in *Hamlet* when the play went on tour. John described the understudy's role as 'worrying', and he thought the part of Guildenstern was 'boring'. While he was always at the ready if needed to walk on stage, he recalled standing in the wings listening to Gielgud's cello-like voice as Hamlet, Prince of Denmark.

After his time appearing on stage in Edinburgh and also in Glasgow, he landed a job with Oldham Rep, yet he found himself strangely out of sync and didn't react well to the northern suburbs and its audiences. He said he 'didn't live up to their expectations'. Once he overslept because his landlady failed to wake him, and so missed his entrance in a play called *Up in Mabel's Room*. John recalled: 'Years later when I told Noel Coward about the disgrace of not turning up in time, he comforted me by saying "A very sensible choice of play to sleep through, dear boy!"'

Then came a spell with the Sheffield Rep, when he appeared as Malvolio in Shakespeare's *Twelfth Night*. But before too long he became desperate to get back to London's West End, or the south of England at least. Looking back on his career he revealed that if he'd known it would have taken so long to make a name for himself he would have 'given up!'

When he did return to the south in 1937, he had decided to make a few professional changes, the first being his name. Thus John Halliley became John Le Mesurier. It's difficult to discover exactly why he decided his mother's maiden name sounded more alluring in the show business world. Certainly he didn't seem to mind when many called him 'Le Mez' for short.[9]

The actor also pulled strings with people he knew from his former life in the legal field. Notably, he contacted J. Baxter-Sommerville, a former solicitor who was passionate about the theatre and by 1937 owned the lease at the Theatre Royal, Brighton, and had founded the Croydon Repertory Company. 'Croydon wasn't ideal,' explained John, 'but Croydon was closer to London than the premier cities of Scotland.' He earned £ 5 a week with Croydon Rep and described 'JB' as something of a 'Mr Pickwick' in his attitude to expenditure. 'When I asked JB for a rise, he threw back his head in laughter just like Mr Pickwick at the thought of it!' added John. By then he shared digs with several other young theatricals in Ebury Street, London, where the landlady was a small mousey woman with the extraordinary name of Olga Titoff.

Life was good for the young actor, even though he was still concerned his career wasn't moving fast enough. When there was time to socialise, he began to get to know many of his fellow company members, including of course Alec Guinness, Maurice Denham, Dennis Price, Carla Lehmann, Anna Wing and Pamela Ostrer, who married former Croydon Rep leading man, the film star James Mason. John was proving popular with anyone who knew him.

The women in the company described him as 'being divine' and 'absolutely stunning with his blue-black hair, beautiful dark eyes, and good looks'. The young actor, who was always happy to receive advice from more experienced colleagues, was often seen in the company of actress Carla Lehmann, who had flowing brown hair, a lively personality and a body as svelte as Greta Garbo. He used his new name for the first time in September 1937 in a production of *Love on the Dole* by Walter Greenwood.

However, when John became restless he took up the opportunity to join Ronald Adam, who ran the Embassy Theatre in Hampstead and major venues in Edinburgh and Glasgow.

\*\*\*

IN 1938 'Le Mez' appeared for the first time on television in a play called *The Marvellous History of St Bernard* by Henri Ghéon. In the following year, during the chill of mid-winter, on 31 January 1939 he landed a major understudy role at the Apollo Theatre in Shaftesbury Avenue in his much-desired West End, in Patrick Hamilton's brilliant psychological drama *Gas Light*. (This play was made into a blockbuster Hollywood film in 1944 starring Charles Boyer and Ingrid Bergman.)

The play tells the story of upper-middle class couple Jack and Bella Manningham, whose marriage is like an unexploded bomb. Jack plays mind-games with Bella around early evening tea at 'gas lighting up time' in a bid to convince her she is going mad and cannot trust her own judgement or even her memory. He regularly disappears from the house and when a police detective named 'Rough' informs Bella that Jack may have murdered a rich woman for her jewellery, she begins to reclaim her sanity and helps Rough gain the evidence he needs. The play ends with Jack arrested for murder.

For John, his understudy role meant a lot of hanging about and frustration because the star actor Dennis Arundell, who played the creepy Jack Manningham, never became ill. The actress who appeared as Bella Manningham was Gwen Frangcon-Davies. But hope was at hand as he had been promised that the lead role would be his when *Gas Light* went on tour from June to October that year and sure enough, soon after the eager young actor stepped out as Mr Manningham, his performance was hailed a hit. The production offered him the chance to play both sinister and charm, and showed off his gift of perfect timing. The *Guardian* revelled in the production: 'One may praise John Le Mesurier's portrayal for giving one a really uncomfortable feeling in the stomach or the boots, or where ever such feelings of apprehension reside.' During its tour *Gas Light* starred Winston Churchill's daughter Sarah, and her famous father went backstage to meet the cast: 'I was introduced to the great man but I am ashamed to say I can't remember a word he said to me,' recalled John in his memoir.[10]

When the final curtain came down on the tour of *Gas Light*, it was time for John to return to his digs in Ebury Street. Any alarming headlines in the national newspapers about Hitler's ambitions for Germany were soon forgotten when he opened a letter offering him the leading role in a touring production of the West End comedy *Goodness, How Sad!* by Robert Morley. John was perfect for this comedy, which was about an actor who was struggling to make a living working with a local repertory company. The comedic value of the play is drawn from all sort of mishaps, confusion and misinterpretations, and it provided its new leading man with a good salary and his name on the billboard. It also gave him the chance to show his versatility as an actor, too – a skill often overlooked by those who believed 'Le Mez always played one character and that was himself'.

*Goodness, How Sad!* marked a turning point in John's life as he fell in love and married the director June Melville, who hailed from an influential theatrical family with interests in the Lyceum and Prince's Theatre. The Melvilles also owned the Brixton Theatre and its repertory company. June's own dynamic personality and searing intelligence made her a pioneer of the stage, as it was rare in those days for a woman to be making important decisions about a production. John found 24-year-old June's good looks, keen mind and effervescent charm irresistible and he was knocked out too by her sense of style and grace. He recalled: 'I became close to June almost immediately. I think she found something to admire in my acting and there was a hint from her and her family that I introduced a welcome element of stability to her life.' What he did note was June's extravagance. She thought nothing of taking the company out to expensive London restaurants for lavish meals. As the play toured the north of England, their love deepened by the minute.

The only cloud in their dream-world was the outbreak of the Second World War. John recalled: 'On the day Neville Chamberlain told us we were at war with Germany on 3 September 1939, I was in the process of moving from Ebury Street to Smith Street in Chelsea, where June and I had taken a short lease on a house owned by Findlay Rea. Findlay was a good friend who had strong political and theatrical connections. The house itself was charming and there was room for my vast collection of records which I had built up over the years.'

Within days of war being declared, however, every man aged between 18 and 41 was liable to register for conscription into the armed services 'if and when called upon'. By 1940 John was 28 years old and there was no escape from the news headlines revealing Hitler's plan to invade Britain. Insecurity was rife as people's lives were put on hold and men stood in readiness to defend their freedoms. Theatres and cinemas closed, leaving actors, stage crews and staff suspended in a fog of anxiety and despair. The government believed the Germans would bomb anywhere that attracted large crowds. However, the decision to keep people out of entertainment venues was soon perceived as far too rash and it was overturned following a letter published in *The Times* from the influential impresario Sir Oswald Stoll, who wrote:

Entertainment is necessary to the morale of the people. Crowd psychology is a potent influence. Remember 'Are we downhearted?' Remember Sir James Barrie's 'Der Tag!' Remember the film, *Four Years in Germany*, initiated by the American Ambassador to Berlin. Remember the community songs and singers of soldiers and people. Remember, too, that it is not logical to close theatres and cinemas and to open churches to crowds. None can foresee where bombs will fall and whether by night or day. The people are willing to take them as they come, under ordinary precautions or intermittently extraordinary precautions.

While freely acknowledging the efficiency of our system of black-outs, as such, in hiding the country from air-raiders, I submit humbly but with conviction that complete black-outs, from sunset to sunrise, are excessive, that they should be imposed only when actual air-raids are signalled; that the conversion of semi-black-outs into complete ones is quick and easy work, if top lights are at all times obscured; that, without this necessary modification, no lives were lost in theatres during the last war.

Government ministers now acknowledged the power of escapism and its potential for positive propaganda purporting optimism and hope during the harrowing times now facing the population each and every day.

John's own recollections of the autumn of 1939 are among the most detailed and descriptive in his memoir. It's clear that by now he felt deeply he ought to play a real life part in the early years of the conflict known as the Phoney War – a period which in effect offered Londoners and the rest of the country a chance to prepare for the worst and get used to the idea of being braced for impact. The actor decided to become an ARP warden; he nervously signed on the dotted line and took up his post at Dolphin Square, Pimlico, in Westminster.

Such a role brought him face to face with the public, who when responding to a siren often asked him what was going on? In a firm but kind manner, he usually told them to stay calm and to trust all was under control. He learned in the early days of the war that sometimes the sirens would go off but no bombs were dropped. Such knowledge gave him the confidence to do his rounds, and when the danger seemed far off he spent time with other wardens at Dolphin Square learning how to apply bandages and dish out emergency first aid.

By the end of 1939, as bitingly cold temperatures left Britain wreathed in snow and ice, warden John began to feel that his acting career was going nowhere so he decided to join the cast on a tour of Terence Rattigan's comedy *French Without Tears*. First stop was at the Grand Theatre in Blackpool. Despite the popularity of the play, which first opened at the West End's Criterion Theatre in 1936, with its leading man played by Rex Harrison, it failed to attract audiences in the north of the country. In fact, John recorded that each time the curtain went up, whether it be in Hull, 'Hell' or Halifax, the theatre management's excuses about the poor audience figures were either weather related, put down to people feeling the pinch in wartime, or downright spurious. At one time the cast heard people had flocked to a local polo game instead of coming to see a comedy about a man attending a special school to learn to speak fluent French in a few days.

The great snowdrifts of late 1939 caused long delays on the railways and disrupted the working lives of many, including the cast of *French Without Tears*, who had plenty to weep about when their journeys across the country came to an icy halt. On 12 January 1940 the freezing temperatures at Kew Gardens in London reached a record minus 22 degrees. When John returned to the capital, hunched over in his big coat and woollens, he discovered a frosty and somewhat formal welcome awaited him in the form of a brown envelope. The letter inside summoned him to a room where he had to go through an Army medical and stand naked in a line of teenagers. That bleak day, standing among the perky firm physiques of British youth, he noted that, at 28, his knees were knobbly and his shoulders slouched in an ungainly manner. He then recalled being asked to 'piss in a pot' by a charmless medical orderly and was soon announced healthy enough to fight for King and Country.

All he could do at this point was await his call from the British Army, and in the meantime go back on stage. This time he was able to use a taxi to get to and from the Brixton Theatre from his marital home in Smith Street, Chelsea, to join the cast of R.C. Sherriff's excellent drama set in the First World War, *Journey's End*. The amiable John remembered how the noise of the anti-aircraft guns and 'bombs falling in the distance made the sound effects far more realistic than anything our stage management could muster'. One night, when the cast received a standing ovation from an audience who had decided to ignore the air raid sirens and instead stay and watch the performance, the actor explained how he was much cheered by the response and realised the utter joy of using his talent to captivate and entrance a crowd.

The courage of all those working in the theatre, who turned out on stage night after night, for matinees too, during the Battle of Britain and the Blitz, is highly commendable. And all those who took their seats in the auditoriums for a shot of escapism did so with stoicism, too. Remember, the risks they took were great, as by September 1940 London's neighbouring counties and airfields of Kent, Sussex and Surrey had already suffered months and months of repeated bombing attacks by Hitler's marauding Luftwaffe. London soon became a ready target. The brave men of the Royal Air Force and the women of the Women's Auxiliary Air Force lived each minute, each hour and each day with fortitude and trepidation, united in determination to drive Hitler's aircrews out of the skies over England for good.

By the early autumn of 1940 John still hadn't had his call-up papers. However, the war came to John and June Le Mesurier when they arrived back from the theatre to find Smith Street in ruins. Their rented property at No. 20 was a pile of rubble and the whole area was full of scurrying firemen, police and air raid wardens. The anxious couple began asking questions about neighbours and friends, and were told by a solemn policeman to visit the 'Hall of Remembrance in Flood Street'.

Every possession the couple owned had been obliterated thanks to one of Hitler's 18,000 bombs that tore into the capital city that day in September. The same night they discovered the Brixton Theatre was also now closed off as an incendiary bomb had hit it just seconds after the Le Mesuriers had left for home. John recalled:

> Bombs were falling as we drove along and the sky was lit up. It was like some hideous fairyland. It occurred to me a few days later that among my personal documents disposed of by the Luftwaffe were my call-up papers. I had in mind to report to a Royal Armoured Corps base in Tidworth on Salisbury Plain but for the life of me I could not remember when this appointment was due to take place. Enquiries at various recruitment offices were met with blank incomprehension. In the end, I said my farewells and took off at what I thought was about the right time.[11]

What was going through John's mind during that car journey to south-east Wiltshire must have sparked a mixture of emotions, which may well have included a strange relief to feel independent again. Whilst he had enjoyed working with and for his wealthy in-laws, he had begun to grow concerned about June's increasing dependence on alcohol. The sensible side of the actor had begun to admit feeling weary of his wife's delusional behaviour, and her attitude that everything would be fine after another bottle of gin. Indeed, there was only so much loucheness he could tolerate when the rest of the country was struggling to survive as Hitler's military forces continued to rampage across Europe. So in his philosophical way, I guess he approached his posting to the garrison town of Tidworth as he would a new acting role but with a very different kind of repertory company – aka the British Army and its newly formed Royal Armoured Corps.

Originating in 1939, the Corps was regarded as a special parent unit that supported individual regiments and former cavalry troops which had converted to mechanical military transport and weaponry in the 1920s. Included within the Corps was the notable Royal Tank Regiment. Imagine then just how much John had to embrace his delicious sense of irony in full knowledge that he was not the least bit mechanically minded. He must have smiled to himself and wondered just what use he would be to such a unit!

Soon after he had driven through the garrison barrier and parked his car, he was welcomed with smiles and laughter when it was noted his car boot contained his bag of golf clubs. His army number was 7918208 and he was issued with his kit, all of which had to be pristinely placed next to his neatly made bed. His Bohemian look and long hair were soon altered as a trip to the military barber left him with the traditional short back and sides. But try as he might, the sergeant in charge of the new recruits was unable to train John to be an effective soldier. In his memoir the actor explains that he didn't mind one jot, especially as this particular shouting sergeant, who used to call him 'Lee Mesure', suggested John might be more suited to the life of an officer!

Full of enthusiasm at the thought of wearing a 'more relaxed style of uniform', John, without thinking it through, suggested he might volunteer to join the Parachute Regiment, until a lieutenant advised him against the idea. That officer was Fulke Walwyn, who in civilian life was a well known British jockey and horse trainer. 'That man was something of a hero of mine,' explained the actor. 'On the Parachute Regiment idea he told me to step away and stop being a "silly c**t"!'

During his weeks breathing in the fresh air of Salisbury Plain John admitted to feeling much fitter than his usual self who lived the high life of theatre land, and he responded well to his training as a tank driver. By 1941 John had discovered he had a particular knack with the controls of a Bren Gun (Universal) carrier. This steady and staple vehicle of the Royal Armoured Corps not only accommodated human occupants but supported weapons too. It could also be rigged up to be used as a machine-gun platform. His affection for the Bren Gun carrier revealed how John always liked to feel a sense of security, achieved, of course, with style!

Such was John's confidence behind the wheel of this sturdy form of transport, which he claimed ate up the rugged miles across Dartmoor, that he confessed how he'd like to buy one to drive around London one day. He didn't need to be the least bit mechanical to do that! Of course, the biggest issue with that idea was the fact that the Bren Gun carrier of the Second World War did just 7 miles to the gallon, so it would be an expensive way of getting about in civilian life. Such a fanciful prospect of owning one, though, might have inspired a *Dad's Army* episode. Imagine Sergeant Wilson showing the platoon his 'new car'. And just how would Captain Mainwaring react?!

Soon enough John fell into the swing of army life and made new friends. When he met June during leave he had begun to find theatrical life somewhat dull and shallow. He wriggled out of many events with the excuse that he must return to the army for further training. It was only a half lie as he had indeed been posted to Blackdown Camp, near Camberley in Surrey (now Princess Royal Deepcut Barracks), which during the Second World War specialised in teaching young men to become officers. In truth, he dreaded the prospect – and soon discovered his worst nightmare had come true. Life was hard, unbearable at times, as he endured a series of physically and mentally tough experiences. John, however, ignored the little voice in his head telling him he'd rather go back to the ranks, and continued on towards gaining officer status. Undoubtedly his hideous experiences at public school had readied him to survive anything at all costs. But by the time he was in the army, he had gained some useful skills with which to win over his superiors.

For the men at Blackdown Camp John produced and appeared in the comedy *French Without Tears* – remarkably he could still remember his lines from the time he'd appeared in the same play two years previously. He confessed his hopes that his talent as an entertainer might divert any attention away from his failings as a military man. It must have worked!. He never did master the controls of a motorbike and nearly killed himself when the machine rocketed towards a brick wall. Nimbly he managed to remove himself from the seat in record time.

The idea of returning to his unit with his tail between his legs also pepped up his determination to win his officer's pips. When he finally took part in a passing out parade, he said 'a great weight has been lifted from my shoulders'. And while some of his fellow officers decided to strut about in their new uniforms and shining leather straps, the amiable John decided to get back into his civvies and head off to Coventry Street in London to meet June for dinner and celebratory drinks at the Café de Paris.

When his car wouldn't start on 8 March 1941 he called June to let her know he couldn't make the dinner appointment. The fact that his old Ford refused to start almost certainly saved his life as within hours the Café de Paris had been bombed, leaving thirty-four dead and eighty people injured. Dance band leader Ken 'Snakehips' Johnson was blown to pieces during the second chorus of 'Oh Johnny', and many seated at the tables were killed when two 110lb bombs fell on the famous London nightclub. The daughter of former prime minister Stanley Baldwin was among the injured.

Academic and historian Juliet Gardiner wrote:

> A dustman who happened to be passing stood with tears running down his cheeks as he watched young men in uniform carrying out their dead girlfriends. It was a hideous sight too, with the dead and injured lying among the rubble, twisted metal, glass and broken furniture. A misdirected call meant that some of those who were seriously injured had to wait more than an hour for an ambulance, and meanwhile looters stepped over bodies, emptying handbags, searching jacket pockets for wallets and wrenching rings from the fingers of the dead. Finsbury ARP warden Barbara Nixon described it as a 'gory incident'. In the same week as the bombing intensified another dance hall a mile to the east of the Café de Paris was hit, resulting in two hundred casualties.[12]

The grim news of the bombing at the Café de Paris was watered down in a bid to hide the extent of the death toll and devastation from the Nazis. When it was reported in *The Times* on the following Monday, the courage of the survivors and rescuers was highlighted, although the actual building was not named. It would be some months before a small item appeared in the newspaper revealing that the Luftwaffe raid had resulted in a direct hit on a restaurant in the capital on 8 March.

It seems that John, who had already been warned not to join the high-risk Parachute Regiment, had escaped yet another brush with death. When he finally arrived back at his mother-in-law's house in Highgate, as bombs rained down and the debris of destroyed buildings blocked the roads, he had seven days' leave with June ahead of him before orders arrived to report to the 54th Training Regiment at Perham Down, a couple of miles from his old base at Tidworth,

Wiltshire. There's little doubt the grim sights and sounds he endured in London during the Blitz had provided him with a solid reason to accept his new life in the military, and to understand why his efforts were needed even though he always confessed he wasn't a 'natural' at soldiering.

When John arrived in Wiltshire that spring he was given a batman whom he described as 'a sullen character' from Newcastle, with an accent no one could understand. It was this same dour man who woke him at 6am every morning and ensured he was on the parade ground to partake in strenuous exercises to 'improve mind and body'!

John's time as the officer in charge of air raid precautions involved him 'stumbling about Salisbury Plain' in a gas mask in case of enemy attack, and carrying 'the wounded' about on makeshift stretchers, a rehearsal experience which would come in useful when filming *Dad's Army*. The mockery that came with the makeshift scenarios he learned during his army years ensured his performances had a beautiful and yet genuine comedic edge. Like all good actors, he used every activity to his advantage.

The next time he returned to London, wearing his uniform and carrying his tin hat, it was early evening and he was on his way to meet his wife at a restaurant near the old Shaftesbury Theatre. En route he discovered a nearby street was in ruins following a bombing raid that had taken place only minutes previously. Volunteers were now urgently needed to help the injured, remove debris from the dead, and clear the area so ambulances could get through. John wrote in his memoir: 'I did not exactly fall down in a dead faint at the sight of death and mayhem, but I did vomit at one point when trying to attach the wrong arm to the wrong body. The poor man kept saying to me, "Go away for Christ's sake, go away".'

In some ways his return to Perham Down and some sense of order came as a relief and his job maintaining fire buckets, which sounded dull, helped calm his jangled nerves. His next posting was to Barnard Castle in Yorkshire, and his unit was marched into Deerbolt Camp by the 10th Hussars Military Band. Life became more sociable for the actor-cum-officer when he made friends with a military cohort named Neville Crump, whom he described as a 'large, volatile' type of character. It was Crump who encouraged him to think about presenting a show to the men. John chose J.B. Priestley's *I Have Been Here Before*, aptly set in the old Black Bull Inn on the Yorkshire Moors, in which the cast have weird confrontations with all the traits of déjà vu. The play, which premiered at the Royalty Theatre in 1937, had enthralled the young actor, and his choice to present it to an audience of army personnel proved a success.

A brief appointment to the role of orderly officer, and occasionally duty officer, put John in charge of mealtimes at the camp, and he was even sent on a cookery course – at which his half-hearted attempts to make a stew guaranteed him a mediocre 'pass', amid the certainty that he would only be called upon to be cook if his unit was desperate!

Next came John's time learning how to administer army wages – a role which perhaps his commanding officer believed would suit him. It wasn't long after passing his exam in accountancy – largely thanks to his actor's brilliant memory, which he applied to the routine questions on the test paper – that he received his posting to India. John, now a captain in the Royal Armoured Corps, made his way to a Royal Navy dock in Rosyth, Scotland, and boarded a robust troopship bound for Bombay. Captain Le Mesurier and his unit sailed in the early months of 1943. As they made their way towards the Suez Canal via the Straits of Gibraltar, he recorded in his memoir how his homesickness began to drift away when he suddenly felt the warm Egyptian sun on his back. Disembarking at Bombay, he was struck by the aromas of 'spiciness' in the air, and the 'kitchen odours of millions of curries being cooked over the centuries'.

In Poona he made his way to a British Army officers' club but any dreams of finding the roads as slick as those around the majestic Whitehall buildings à la British Raj style were soon dashed as he described the dangers of driving over rocks on dusty routes punished by potholes and other hazards. However, he did concede that Poona became 'rather magical' at night with the sounds of drums and the music of the sitar throbbing through the sultry air. His final destination, where he would remain for the rest of the war, was the Royal Armoured Corps/Indian Army Corps training base at Ahmednagar, some 120km north-east of Poona. Ahmednagar was the birthplace both of comedian Spike Milligan and of the great Malik Ambar, a Siddi military chief who led a successful war to defend the area against the aggressive Mughal Empire in 1604.

Here, the young captain became accustomed to the smell of muskiness on his uniform, the result of being in a country rich in flavours, sights and sounds. However, in contrast he became weary of the relentless instructions and drills he had to dish out to the men in his charge. He found many of his fellow officers boring because they only talked about technical matters. Doubtless during such times he must have contemplated his acting career and wondered if he would ever get back to the theatre at all.

As John's biographer Graham McCann points out in *Is That Wise, Sir?*, it was sad how all of the actor's duties were of a military nature when not too far away the likes of would-be actor/writer Jimmy Perry and other soon to be well known entertainers were in India creating morale-boosting productions for the troops and therefore keeping involved in their chosen profession. Likewise Arthur Lowe, who was in Egypt for much of the war, remained involved in a range of theatrical events.

However, during John's lonely spell as a British Army officer he was able to hook up with the Anglo-Indian communities, who welcomed him to their grandiose homes situated to the east of Ahmednagar. But before long he grew tired of sipping tea and listening to chitchat laced with nostalgia about the old days when the area had a British viceroy and his Lady, and the polo matches of old were a 'constant joy'. He recalled being startled by the sights of Indian men sleeping at night entwined and unshakeable in their slumber. When he tried to separate them with his swagger stick he was advised by a duty sergeant to 'leave them be' as they 'do it all the time' and 'it didn't matter'. John admits to having acted like a prude at the time.

Whilst John battled with the overwhelming sense of solitude, he always had the faithful Dohdiram to turn to for his meals, laundry and other domestic needs. Dohdiram, a noble Sikh, had been assigned to assist the young officer and on one occasion they visited Bombay, where at the Taj Mahal Hotel John could sip gin and tonics and listen to the band play Gilbert and Sullivan numbers, albeit a little too frequently. It was in this noisy city that he confessed to visiting a famous brothel at 4 Grant Road, only to discover the deed was to be a 'hurried' event of half an hour; the brutish pay-as-you-go fashion resulted for John in abject failure and a deflated ego.

He also sensed he was being punished for 'behaving unwisely', as the Army decided to send him on various courses to boost his skills. An aerial-photography course in Peshawar meant a tortuous and crowded train journey lasting four hours, and John commented that the train 'stopped everywhere all the way to Delhi'. He continued:

I found the heat appalling and the journey was somewhat of a nightmare. There was nobody in the carriage who spoke English, so I read A.G. MacDonnell's *England, Their England* and did a lot of staring out of the window. I saw the Taj Mahal as we passed through Agra. Unfortunately, it was not 'by moonlight' as Noël Coward had favoured in *Private Lives*. Still, it managed to look pretty breath-taking in the fading light, and seemed to have a pink-ish glow around it.[13]

The rest of his military days in India were to prove a frustrating waiting game. It was as if he was in a depressing kind of limbo, which he could only shake off when he'd had two or three decent drinks to quell what he termed 'boring' conversations about tanks and military events. There was also the perpetual hot climate, which sapped his energy too. All he wanted to do was sit in the bars in Peshawar, and then by the end of 1944 be at his usual watering hole in Ahmednagar so he could absorb his gin and dream again of the stage.

When VE Day arrived on 8 May 1945 he sat among the other officers, made a toast to the King with champagne and thanked God. Years later he wrote: 'Did I ever fire a shot in anger? Well, I fired a shot now and then, but couldn't say I was angry. I must say I found the whole thing very boring.'

Before he could be fully demobbed, he faced a long journey of 100 miles or so to Deolali, the transit camp made notorious for being one great dollop of tedium. Still, he knew he would be home within a few weeks. It was a blow that he didn't ever get to see the Royal Artillery concert party in action at a nearby venue, starring the one and only Jimmy Perry. They were, however, destined to learn that their ships, far from passing in the night, would certainly meet on another night twenty years later!

Back in England, having been greeted only by the grim, grey docks of Southampton, John was ecstatic to see his wife June and his in-laws. Soon he was back in his old haunts in London, wearing a classy brown demob suit and trilby hat. He was also relieved to find many of his friends had survived the war and like him were seeking a job on the stage or in front of the camera. His main intention and key focus was now to find some all-important work. Soon he found his domestic situation was becoming insufferable. Firstly, he felt compelled to leave the large Melville home owing to the surly behaviour of his brother-in-law, a rough-tough Canadian businessman who had married June's sister Sheila. John was also beginning to realise that June's drinking was becoming a serious problem. Work tethered him to sanity but he had no desire to work for the Melville Theatrical Company!

There were also the pressures of being 34. In a business obsessed with youth, he worried that he was past his prime and yet he remained desperate to go it alone. His escape plan came to fruition towards the end of 1946 and he set himself up with a bachelor lifestyle in an apartment in Gloucester Road. When he left June, he said she was hugging a gin bottle and refusing help from friends and family. But like her now estranged husband, she soon faced up to the idea that her wartime marriage was one of the many that failed. Within a matter of months, however, during a visit to the Players' Theatre in London, John met and fell in love with the awesome Kent-born actress Hattie Jacques (Josephine Edwina Jacques) and in 1949 they married and went on to have two sons, Robin and Kim.

The new Mrs Le Mesurier had experienced a busy war service. Soon after the conflict in Europe broke out in 1939 she became a nurse with the Voluntary Aid Detachment (VAD) and was posted to work from a mobile station in London, which was especially in demand aiding victims of the bombing during the Blitz. However, when her VAD unit was radically changed during a reorganisation of medical staff in 1943, she decided instead to be a welder in a factory based in the north of the capital. By early 1944, however, she had quit the boiler suit and protective goggles and was offered a role in revue with the entertainer Leonard Sachs, and film and radio work soon followed. Ironically, Jacques went on to find fame in the *Carry On* films and starred as 'Matron' in *Carry On Nurse* (1959). Her wartime experience proved of extra benefit no doubt when making her presence known as the top no-nonsense nurse on screen.

For her husband, the affable John, there were opportunities to work in various films, although he was terrified that his age (he was then 35) was against him. However, by 1956 he had been cast as a psychiatrist in *Private's Progress* – a Second World War comedy film directed by the great Roy Boulting and starring Ian Carmichael and Richard Attenborough. This movie affirmed John as a talented character actor and from then on he was rarely out of employment. The same year he took a minor role as the chaplain aboard HMS *Exeter* in the full-colour epic *The Battle of the River Plate*, written, produced and directed by the famous wartime propaganda filmmakers Emeric Pressburger and Michael Powell.

In 1957 he was offered a role in *High Flight*, a film about RAF pilot cadets. This movie was derived from a poem of the same title written by Royal Canadian Air Force aviator John Gillespie Magee Jr, who in real life died in 1941 when his Spitfire was in a mid-air crash with an Airspeed Oxford over RAF Cranwell training base. Actor John Le Mesurier appeared in the film as a commandant.

A year later, in 1958, he was back on the big screen in *I Was Monty's Double*, in a small role playing a Royal Army Pay Corps adjutant. This film focuses on a government misinformation campaign designed to spread rumours to the effect that the D-Day landings would not be staged in Normandy, with an actor employed to impersonate General Montgomery in North Africa in a bid to deceive the Germans. The screenplay of this clever film was written by wartime Intelligence Officer and Combined Forces Entertainment Unit operative turned actor and director, Bryan Forbes.

In 1959 the future *Dad's Army* star John had the opportunity to travel to Rome, having won a small role playing a surgeon in the epic *Ben-Hur*. He confessed in his autobiography how he loved to travel and work in different locations. John's next appearance that year was as the character of Colonel Janssen, a security force contact in the brilliant *Operation Amsterdam* – a film set in Holland in 1940 during the early days of the German invasion. John's minor role as a wartime British Army officer in the 1965 film *Operation Crossbow* was deleted during the edit and his appearance never made it onto the screen.

Three years later, however, he had landed his next and most fiscally advantageous part – as Sergeant Arthur Wilson in a new television series called *Dad's Army*. After negotiation, he earned a fee of £ 262 10 shillings per episode. Here was the proof that his insecurities about his age and the fickleness of the theatrical profession did not ring true. John was 56 and he was about to welcome fame into his life.

The writer Jimmy Perry once recalled that John, now known as the languid voice of sanity in the show, asked him for advice about how to play Sergeant Wilson. Perry's reply was to 'make the part your own'. John recalled: 'I thought, why not just be myself, use an extension of my own personality and behave rather as I had done in the army? So I always left a button or two undone, and had the sleeve of my battle dress slightly turned up. I spoke softly, issued commands as if they were invitations (the sort not likely to be accepted) and generally assumed a benign air of helplessness.'[14] The star also confessed how much he enjoyed making *Dad's Army*, in particular the times the cast spent in Thetford each year filming the outside scenes.

When the jazz-loving, piano-playing, three-times married comedy icon John Le Mesurier died in November 1983 at the age of 71, he was suffering with severe complications caused by cirrhosis of the liver. At his bedside in Ramsgate hospital was his third wife Joan. His last words were: 'It's all been rather lovely.' In tributes written after his death, it was suggested that the star's interactions with Arthur Lowe's character of Captain George Mainwaring were 'a memorable part' of one of television's most popular shows. And 'it was the hesitant exchanges of one-upmanship between Le Mesurier's

Wilson, a figure of delicate gentility, and Lowe's pompous, middle-class platoon leader Mainwaring, that added to the show's finest moments'.

Today, I like to imagine I'm relaxing with John over a few gin and tonics at Ronnie Scott's jazz club in Soho. He was described by his friends as having a naughty and wicked sense of humour, so I'd have to choose the right moment to ask him a serious question: 'Did he believe his own experiences in the Second World War had helped shape his eventual performance as Sergeant Arthur Wilson?' I know just how the actor would consider my enquiry most carefully, sip his drink, light another cigarette, there'd be a pause followed by a slow nod of the head, a thoughtful tug of the ear lobe, a charming chuckle, a glance towards the ceiling, and in that famous disarming voice, which always made me feel as if John was surrendering his words, he'd languidly confess his time in the military had taught him some 'jolly neat tricks'.

# CLIVE DUNN OBE

Working for Hitler became a game of bluff . . .

EVER one to observe and comment on the ironies of life, comic actor Clive Robert Bertram Dunn OBE (Corporal Jones) was born in the London of 1920 when the world was still in mourning for the dead of the First World War. In Britain grief was everywhere. It was as if the dreaded reaper had risen from his hellish cave to haunt every corner of every home, street and field. As one eminent historian wrote recently: 'What was different about the 1914–1918 conflict was the sheer scale of the trauma, the sudden deaths of so many. Around three million Britons lost a very close relative – a parent, a child, a sibling, a spouse. But many more, almost the entire population, lost a more distant family member – an uncle or cousin – or simply a friend.'[1]

And yet, despite the recurring despair of the population at that time, Dunn's musical hall comedian father Bobby Dunn, who had survived the horrific battlefields of France, returned to the stage fully believing he could engage with an audience again in the hope of offering some comfort in the struggle to believe in a future.

Baby Dunn's mother Connie was also a stage performer. She, too, was keen to use her talent to help lift the mood of the nation. Among Connie's claims to fame was the sound of her mellifluous voice dubbing that of the Hollywood star Mary Pickford in a silent film. The purposeful Connie also toured as far as Africa to thrill the crowds with her song and dance routines. The heat and passion of the theatrical world was truly in Connie's blood. Her father was British music hall star Frank Lynne, popular in the 1890s. However, as with so very many families, the Lynnes experienced great sorrow during the 1914–1918 conflict when Connie's youngest brother Bertram was killed in action on the Western Front. Connie went on to ensure her brother's name lived on in her baby son Clive, whose middle name she recorded on the birth certificate as Bertram.

More often than not, Connie was able to continue her career and leave her toddler with his doting grandparents on the Dunn side of the family in Portsmouth, Hampshire. By 1926 she had become a star of the burlesque and was top billing across the south of England, her heart soaring at the sound of rapturous applause at venues like the Floral Hall, Westcliff-on-Sea, Southend. Holidaymakers adored her shows. Indeed, if people turned to anything for relief from the suffering of war, it was often to theatres and pavilions to witness the magical live performances of Bobby Dunn, Gracie Fields, the comedy eyebrowed George Robey and cheeky George Formby.

It's easy, then, to understand how the little Clive Dunn – that future star of television's *Dad's Army* – was greatly influenced by the power of entertainment and its force as a healer of troubled hearts and minds. No one knew this more intensely than the musical hall stars of the 1920s, whose luminosity and boisterous displays of colour, fury and fun provided much of the therapy of its time. As often seen in *Dad's Army*, Dunn was always up for the 'Fols de Rols' musical hall-style performances, and often expressed to the show's writer Jimmy Perry that he wanted the 'Joey' parts – Joey being a theatrical term for 'clown', stemming from the great Victorian genius of violent clowning, Joe Grimaldi.

Remember the episode where Corporal Jones is mounted on a white horse floating on a raft along a river, and then leaps up to grab hold of an overhanging branch to escape his predicament? Acting up and acting out was in Dunn's nature. The fact that he really did have to seize onto that branch in a hurry is brilliantly transformed into comedy, helping to establish the legend of his character in *Dad's Army*. Dunn went on to reveal later that the horse was in fact as terrified as he was during the river scene, so he decided to jump first while the cameras were rolling!

Decades before he became a comedy star, however, Dunn discovered that schooldays were far from fun and not half as roly-poly as the calamitous world of his theatrical family. He was just 6 years old when he was sent to a strict boarding school in Eastbourne. It was a gruesome establishment, and he later described in his memoir how a particular schoolmaster used to molest the small boys. This horrific episode is written quietly and merely as a mention, a simple 'by the way this happened to me'. And yet behind that sentence sits a traumatic childhood event which he unconsciously dealt with throughout his life with remarkable and admirable displays of resilience and fortitude. Dunn, of course, wasn't the only one of the *Dad's Army* cast to suffer at the hands of sadistic, abusive schoolteachers. As a boy his great chum John Le Mesurier endured a similar fate of abuse and misery at school.

By 1929 Dunn found himself sitting at a small desk in a classroom at his new school in Sevenoaks, Kent. It was here – when not feeling bullied or left out because he was smaller and younger than many of the other boys – that he learned to love the classics, including Kenneth Grahame's *The Wind in the Willows*, Charles Kingsley's *The Water Babies* and Henry Williamson's *Tarka the Otter*. He professed an aptitude for English, history and geography, but subjects such as physics, chemistry and mathematics left him 'truly stumped'. He explained:

> So I turned to sport for success, and by the time I left school I had been in the rugby team, the boxing team, the gymnastics team, the tennis team, and the cross-country team. The business of winning was instilled into me, and encouraged continually, but you were expected at the same time to be a good sport. You could still be a good sport if you put on some padded gloves and smashed your friend in the face, giving him a black eye or a broken nose![2]

On the subject of religion Dunn cast a cynical tone. At school he discovered that praying in church was not really his favourite way of coping with the ill winds of fate. 'Appeals to God can be a comfort in the face of disaster, but practical benefits – forget it,' he said, then added:

> Many years later, during the Greek campaign in 1941, I was watching a dead soldier being lifted out of a tank onto a stretcher, while in the sky three hundred Luftwaffe bombers swept overhead like a great cloud on their way to knock hell out of some misbegotten town. The padre was looking at the soldier's corpse saying: 'Poor old boy,' when someone nudged his arm and pointed to the aircraft in the sky. We waited for some words of comfort. 'Oh, my God!' he said. We all looked away in embarrassment for him, and then got on with the war.

Dunn admitted to joining the Christian Scientist movement as a teenager, especially when his theatre-loving headmaster explained it would mean a free high tea every Sunday with cake and all the trimmings. (Years later, during his time as a prisoner of war, the young entertainer was overjoyed to receive parcels of food and clothing from the Christian Scientists. It meant they had remembered him, and their packages often beat the arrival of any official Red Cross essentials.)

During his school holidays he either spent much of his time watching his mother Connie appear on stage across the south-east of England, or he stayed with his Uncle Gordon (Connie's older brother) and his fiancée Primrose who took him out to Ascot Races, and fed him salmon and cucumber sandwiches.

By the mid-1930s the spiteful influences of Germany's far right politics were seeping into Britain, with certain factions at Dunn's school, as with many others, falling under the influence of Oswald Mosley's British Union of Fascists (known as the Blackshirts). Dunn later confessed how for a brief time he joined in various goose-stepping marches around the playground and even paid a subscription to Mosley's gang. In his memoir he explained: 'When I read how in the East End of London, Mosley's bully boys had beat up any stray Jewish lads in the street, it all had a sinister and frightening ring about it. I thought my dad looked rather Jewish and he might get hurt. I wanted there and then to tear up that little blue BUF membership card but couldn't find it. Fifty odd years later I discovered it in a scrapbook where it sits as a reminder of that disgraceful period.' Within weeks, however, the hideous BUF fell into disrepute across the country and its menacing ethos was expelled from the school and 'never mentioned again'.[3]

As he began enjoying his young life again, free of evil politics, his father Bobby was working as stage manager and producer at the Aldwych Theatre in London's famous West End. Bobby then managed to find his son a small role in a Will Hay film, *Boys Will Be Boys*. What with the money Dunn received for this appearance and a generous donation from a grandmother, he was persuaded by his father to pay to stay on at school in Sevenoaks and pass his exams. However, too much larking about, repeated thrashings for misbehaviour and a problematic French test result left the teenager failing to achieve a School Certificate. Years later he confessed: 'I left Sevenoaks after seven years, with an injured pride, a sore bum, no certificate and regrets.' In those first few weeks after school he admitted 'feeling free'. He accompanied his mother during a music hall tour of the Isle of Wight, and met people who later became big names in Hollywood, including the suave David Niven, the comedian Tommy Trinder and the film star Mona Washbourne.

When Bobby Dunn was hired by British Movietone News, he landed his son a job as a 'clapper boy', which led to lots of travel to various locations and training, of course – with the ultimate goal in life to become a cameraman. At this time young Clive was able to work in the studios where the great and the good of the 1930s film world were in action on set, including the actors Robert Donat, Marlene Dietrich and Elizabeth Bergner. However, Dunn's professional ambition to get behind a camera never materialized, as the film company planning to employ him went broke. It was then that his parents asked him if he wanted to apply to the school-cum-theatre of the great Italia Conti in Holborn, London. Italia Conti and her sister Bianca (Mrs Murray) had trained some of the greats – Jack Hawkins, Noel Coward and Freddie Bartholomew. Dunn was accepted and found himself in a dance studio rehearsing with the handsome and talented (and future Second World War hero) Richard Todd, as well as the actors Graham Payne and Michael Derbyshire. He wrote too how he soon found out about girls, who expected 'something of him' – so he spent most of his time ignoring them, especially at first, choosing instead to befriend Richard Todd, who had 'short legs, no breasts, and didn't expect anything! . . . Michael [Derbyshire] on the other hand, had very long legs and a thin, sad face and was known as 'Happy'. We became close friends and the three of us would go merrily from class to class as we gradually lost some of our schoolboy gaucherie,' explained Dunn.[4] It was a highlight of his year when the young Princesses Elizabeth and Margaret watched a jaunty Dunn and his pals appear in a musical produced by Italia Conti at the Holborn Empire. His future looked bright and his drama training would ensure he could work in the world of professional entertainment.

By 1937 Connie Dunn had decided to retire from her physically demanding theatrical vocation. Her son, meanwhile, did his best to find work in the West End, and at one time in Abergavenny in Wales – where he recalled how any play 'delivered by Londoners' was always well received. He even mentions that the first time he got a belly laugh was from an appreciative Welsh audience. The family then moved to a small flat in Barnes, London, and Dunn soon discovered that much of life revolved around 'who you know' and not 'what you know'. On 3 September 1939 he was living alone beneath a dog parlour, with a puppy as his companion. He recalled: 'War had been announced on the radio. After what seemed like only seconds, the wail of a siren sent some people into the coal cellars, some under the pavements, some under the stairs, some under the bed, and some under the wife! . . . I had no intention of being buried in the basement so I looked for company and with my pup I wandered into Crawford Street, Marylebone, looking up at a surprisingly empty sky!' That day there were no hordes of Nazi bombers and everything seemed as regular as ever until he was approached by a warden in a gas mask who yelled at him in a 'muffled blurt' to 'get down into the shelter'.[5]

Soon enough Dunn felt he wanted to join the armed forces and fight Hitler and his fascists. But which military service should he aim for? First he tried to join the Royal Navy but was told by an officer from the Admiralty Office that he would have to sign on for eight years. He shrivelled at the thought of such a long time away from show business, and instead decided to try for the Royal Air Force. On the way he was told by a stranger that this option was only open to candidates who had passed their Matriculation examinations. Dunn didn't even get to the door of the RAF recruiting office as he remembered he had no school certificate because he had not achieved the grades in his French tests.

Aged 19, he walked around with his head down, wondering what to do. Soon enough he found his way to an ambulance station that was looking for recruits who could also work as mechanics. The pay was £3 10 shillings a week. So for the next few months he learned first aid and enjoyed working with the raft of volunteers who were on call to help those in need on and off the streets.

It was with absolute clarity that he recalled a day in the spring of 1940 when 'a little buff envelope arrived from Mars, the God of War'. His future destiny as a soldier had begun as he packed his meagre belongings and made his way to Wool Station, Dorset, on 2 May. He was to report to the headquarters of the 52nd Heavy Training Regiment at Lulworth – a military base first established in 1918 and still in operation today, used by the British Army's tank and armoured fighting vehicle regiments. In 1940, however, Dunn found the train journey there from London was full of gungho raw recruits and he chummed up with another lively teenager named David Bradford. 'I was now out of the phoney war where nobody got killed but merely stared at each other across no girl's land, into a proper war where anyone could get killed,' recalled Dunn.[6]

And it is with great poignancy that the future *Dad's Army* star remembers his youthful initiation into soldiering. Lying in a trench on a Dorset beach, wearing a tin helmet and swimming trunks, chatting to his pal David, and talking about their rifles with only four bullets each to kill any Germans who should fall from the sky or advance out of the sea in their direction. Then there were the jam sandwiches munched in haste in case the invasion started. Ever ready to defend Britain's shores, so noble and so patriotic in the summer of 1940, the two pals witnessed one of the heaviest days of the Battle of Britain in the skies overhead. That day they saw Hurricane fighter aircraft roaring straight for the clouds, only to be met by swarms of black German bombers, Dorniers most likely, full of deadly explosives and machine guns to blast the RAF out of the sky.

No parachutes descended, though, and both squaddies watched pop-eyed and 'shit scared' at the action taking place over the sea, not fully realizing or appreciating how the mere push of aircraft gun buttons could mean death and destruction. How proud the two soldiers felt of the RAF pilots who flew into the swarm of Luftwaffe fighters and bombers, and the sudden cheers that rushed from their throats when an enemy aircraft went tumbling down, down, and down in flames into the sea, leaving just a brief trail of smoke scattering into the breeze only to disappear as quick as a waking thought. 'We read later that this day had been one of the main showdowns of the Battle of Britain, and it impelled the Prime Minister Winston Churchill to make his "Never in the field of human conflict . . ." speech,' added Dunn.[7]

From there on, Dunn's training continued. It included arduous exercises with bayonets at the ready, and it was during one of these physically exhausting experiences that he ran for cover as a huge German aircraft loomed overhead and suddenly a raft of bombs rained down. Along with the men around him, he heard their sergeant yell: 'Break ranks!' Dunn described the experience as a 'Dunkirk moment', as when the explosives hit the sand great clumps of sand and metal pieces went flying in all directions. One soldier was killed and another was wounded by shrapnel. This close encounter with death left each man with a sense of dread, and the bleak realization that any day might be his last. Definitely, remembered Dunn, it was time then for a cider or two, fish and chips and a walk about the town and a lark or two with the local characters at a pub. So off he went with his chum David to the bright lights of Lulworth to escape the fears that threatened everyone's sense of security and sanity.

But within a few months of that happy night out in the sleepy hallows of a Dorset inn, the young entertainer would find himself playing out the biggest role of his life – this time he was about to discover just how little the theatre of war had in common with his civilian life on the professional stage. Dunn and his pal David received their orders to report to East Anglia. It was serious. They were now called upon to serve in the 4th Queen's Own Hussars, which had as its colonel-in-chief no other than Winston Churchill – a Second Lieutenant in the regiment back in 1895. Formerly known as the 4th (The Queen's Own) Regiment of (Light) Dragoons, it was in the second line of cavalry on the right flank during the famous Charge of the Light Brigade at the battle of Balaclava in 1854. At the outbreak of the First World War the 4th Hussars fought in the first and second battles of Ypres. The regiment also played a major role in preventing the German advance during the battle of Moreuil Wood in March 1918. Three years later the gallant Hussars were posted to India. By 1936 their horses had been replaced by mechanised vehicles and back in Britain the regiment was transferred to the Royal Armoured Corps in 1939.

Dunn recalled: 'David and I felt the difference immediately! The normal gap separating the officers from the men in the average British regiment was magnified tenfold in the old cavalry regiments. We were now away from the big barrack atmosphere of the training regiment and were billeted in country houses. Our new regiments had been deprived of their horses and had instead been given small tanks to master.' As a novice driver in 1940, Dunn was ordered to drive a fifteen-hundredweight truck carrying passengers to a dental clinic in Newmarket. Nerves were shattered on the trip as he fought to control the monstrous vehicle and its power. 'After a hair-raising return to headquarters, the men who were on board went ashen-faced to the sergeant in charge of transport and begged that I should be relieved of my potentially death-dealing vehicle,' he said. However, the drama of Dunn and his lorry did not end there! When he went to find the field where he'd parked it, the vehicle had disappeared. After walking for miles looking for it, he returned to headquarters 'haggard and humiliated' to await a court martial. But his fears of severe punishment were unfounded as a soldier calmly informed Dunn the truck had been discovered and he just needed to hand over the key.

Instead of driving, he was tasked with painting camouflage over the tanks as part of the preparations for a big mission. Dunn observed how 'the sergeants barked orders, and the officers walked about waiting for their dinner', and remarked that 'contact with these elegant personages was rare, which was not surprising as most of them were so rich they could hardly speak!'

Soon enough, on the day the regiment learned it was to be sent overseas, Churchill arrived, wearing his prime minister's hat to wish them well. In Churchill's honour that day a display of marksmanship was arranged. However, the so-called crackshot sniper chosen for this exhibition was unable to hit the bullseye, and clipped the bottom of the target instead. Churchill, ever the optimist, declared: 'At least he hit the target!'[8]

For Dunn and his mates there was a brief leave to say goodbye to family and friends. With him went his tin hat, rifle and kit bag as word was out there was always an enemy invasion expected at any moment. He travelled first to London with his pal David and remembered seeing the sky over Soho peppered with German bombers, and how the sound of the ack-ack guns was fast and frequent. Next stop was Sheffield, where he visited his parents Bobby and Connie, by then busy staging entertainments in local factories and camps. 'Both', said Dunn, 'had suffered the First World War, and now were going through the horrific routine of sorrowful farewells again.'

At the end of December 1940 the 4th Hussars arrived in Market Harborough for a final few drinks, a regimental dance and a chance to say goodbye to their home country. Ever the entertainer, the young uniformed Dunn managed to visit the local variety theatre, absorb the atmosphere, and feel the warmth of its lights and its audiences, and he questioned whether he would ever see or experience any of it again.

Indeed, the sharp cold winds blowing across the Liverpool docks on 31 December confirmed the grim fact that he had no control of his future at all as Dunn and his regiment boarded the SS *Orcades* bound for the shores of Africa. It was dusk and drizzling as the troopship pulled away from its moorings. A former cruise liner, built to carry 750 passengers and 300 crew, the 700ft-long *Orcades* was built in 1937 by Vickers-Armstrong in Barrow-in-Furness for the Orient Line. She was requisitioned by the British Admiralty in 1939 to be converted into a troopship.

Dunn, on his first sea journey, recalled sharing a cabin on the 'luxury liner' with three other men, and soon enough they got their sea legs despite the churning waves of the Atlantic Ocean. The trip took three weeks, their route including a detour towards the USA to confuse the enemy about the ship's actual destination. There was opportunity for the squaddies to watch the escorting naval vessels protecting the *Orcades* and its precious human cargo in case Nazi U-boats came in to attack. (In October 1942, less than two years after the ship had successfully carried Dunn and the 4th Hussars to North Africa, the heroic SS *Orcades* was torpedoed by a German submarine around the waters of Capetown. She sank with the loss of forty-five lives.)

For Dunn and many men in January 1941 the time aboard ship went slowly. Daily exercise routines were arranged and ribald lectures were offered about how to survive life in Egypt. As a very young man he admits he felt 'immortal' and ready to take on the world. Comically he recalled how once the SS *Orcades* arrived to dock in Durban, its passengers walked down the gangplank in long shorts and solar topee hats, their knobbly knees on show to 'frighten' the local residents! Durban, however, was not a happy place. Just before the 4th Hussars had arrived, there had been uproar in the city, caused by rowdy Australian troops who had petrified the 'posh' white South African population. Dunn soon noticed to his horror the appalling notices in parks and buses which segregated black from white: 'I could hardly believe that one set of human beings could restrict another, in such an insulting way,' he wrote.

Soon enough the soldiers set sail again, their destination Egypt. The stark, ramshackle, mysterious and heat-soaked city of Cairo soon enveloped Dunn into further youthful adventures. Not long after arriving in the busy sand bowl of activity, like so many other

British and Australian soldiers he began making the best of life with a military tent for shelter. On discovering he was to be left at the base as 'reinforcement' when orders came through to move on, he protested and reminded his commanding officer that his skills learned with the ambulance service could be of use. Sure enough, he was given the role of sole stretcher-bearer – which made him laugh as usually they worked in pairs. Being assigned to assist the medical officer made Dunn feel proud that he could be of use, especially as his new chief was Captain Eden, cousin of the politician Sir Antony Eden. Dunn remembered how the men were most impressed with his first aid skills, and he learned even more useful knowledge from his conscientious MO.

However, the lure of the twisting lanes, smoky bars and beautiful long-lashed women soon proved too much for the sex-starved bandsman Dunn had chummed up with in recent days. Now, in spite of the warning signs urging soldiers not to venture along the narrow streets, the two squaddies did just that. They paid a random boy who was 'offering them girls' and all they had to do was follow the young man to see these ravishing beauties. But this young pimp did a runner – straight into the arms of the police. Dunn and his pal were then escorted to the police station, where Dunn got half of his money back – the other half was now in the pocket of a police officer who suddenly decided to let the soldiers return to their barracks!

Not to be put off their forays into Cairo's forbidden zone, Dunn and the boisterous bandsman returned again looking for female company. When two young women beckoned them into a doorway, Dunn handed over 'some ackers' (money) and they were led into a tiny room. A naked girl appeared from behind a curtain and performed an exotic dance, then proceeded to insert a lit cigarette into her vagina! Shocked at first, then highly amused, both men dashed out, much to the dismay of their female entertainers. Another adventure along the sultry lanes of Cairo saw them getting tipsy in a sleazy bar. When Dunn's pal realised his wallet had been stolen, they asked an Egyptian man in a suit and fez if he could give them directions back to barracks in English.[9] They told him that they had to be back in the desert by morning, and the man obliged by calling a carriage for them. But when it stopped, they were nowhere near the barracks – instead they appeared to be in the middle of a Cairo backstreet, where the man beckoned them to follow as they might like to join an orgy!

Soon Dunn and his friend were introduced to a sleepy young Egyptian woman in a tiny room. She was given the impression by the man in the suit that Dunn was King Farouk, and if she slept with both soldiers one of them would marry her! Within minutes of Dunn's pal taking up the invitation to join the woman in bed, they both fled the squalid scene. Out in the street, Dunn asked: 'What's up?!' His pal replied: 'I've just remembered the wife!'

Back at the El Tahag base, Dunn took his turn at guard duty. Within a couple of days he noticed more officers walking about the camp and amused himself by wondering if they'd run out of polo matches. He described a scene of everyone 'running about and taking tents down'. Gallons of reserve fuel was burned too, as the regiment was unable to transport it to their next destination. He recalled: 'A trooper in the army would never be told where he was going or why, and when we moved to a transit camp west of Alexandria we guessed we would be moving into the Western Desert. Not at all. We were taken to the port of Alexandria and onto the cruiser HMS *Gloucester*. At dusk we set sail in a north westerly direction.'[10]

***

ON 28 October 1940 the fascist Italian leader Benito Mussolini ordered his armed forces to invade Greece – an action driven by egomania and which was to prove one of the most careless military campaigns ever launched. Weeks beforehand, the Italian leader had been keen to invade Yugoslavia and Romania but his plans were vehemently opposed by Hitler, who wanted Yugoslavia's raw materials and Romania's oil for the German war effort. So instead Mussolini turned his attention to Greece. He sold the idea of an invasion to Hitler by claiming it would form part of a double attack on Britain's position in the eastern Mediterranean. This, argued Mussolini, would enable complete Italian supremacy over the Aegean. However, as leading military historian Anthony Beevor suggests, 'Hitler had not fully appreciated the Italian regime's talent for disaster.'

The reaction in Greece to the arrival of the Italian jackboot in the autumn of 1940 proved explosive. The Greek president, General Ioannis Metaxas, fascist, philosopher and a deeply patriotic man, was at home in Athens when he was suddenly woken at 3am by a furious banging on his front door. Still in his pyjamas, the annoyed Metaxas found Emanuele Grazzi, an Italian minister, standing in front of him to declare that Italian troops had crossed the Albanian border and were on their way to march into Greece. Metaxas had one word for Grazzi to report to Mussolini: 'Ochi!' ('No!') Metaxas loathed Mussolini, a character he described as a 'theatrical windbag'.[11] Next day, the population of Greece united behind their leader and emotional demonstrations erupted across the country. Suddenly the

Greek Venizelist anti-monarchist liberals and socialists forgot the president's steadfast royalist leanings, which they once argued had corrupted the Greek constitution and banned opposition. (Today an annual 'No Festival' is hosted by residents in western Crete around the village of Elos, and 28 October, Ochi Day, is a public holiday to commemorate the occasion when Metaxas gave that now famous one-word response, 'Ochi'.)

What Mussolini did not appreciate at the time was the strength of the tough Greek militia, undoubtedly motivated by ancient myths and the great battles of Marathon and Thermopylai, and by the heroics of Alexander the Great, of whom Winston Churchill was a great admirer. Ever artful, and well aware of the long-standing alliance that ensured Britain would send military aid to assist Greece in its hour of need, Metaxas made it clear to the world he was keen to retain this diplomatic situation, as laid out by a Declaration made by the British Parliament on 13 April 1939, which stated that in the event of a threat to Greek or Romanian independence, 'His Majesty's Government would feel themselves bound at once to lend the Greek or Romanian Government all the support in their power.'

Personnel at the Royal Naval base in Souda Bay to the north of Crete and at a site at Lemnos welcomed in the newly arrived British forces as guards on 31 October 1940. Souda Bay's previous resident troops, the 5th Cretan Division, were then deployed back to defend the mainland. Royal Air Force squadrons led by Air Commodore John D'Albiac flew to Greece in November 1940.

Much to the arrogant Mussolini's surprise, the determined Greeks successfully and aggressively fought off the Italian invaders and pushed forward to set up a serious line of defence in the mountains of Albania. To this day the Greeks' indefatigable stance and victory retains a somewhat mythological status, as remarkable as other ancient tales of Grecian valour. Now it is referred to famously as the Greco-Italian War.

Greece, it should be remembered, had been a neutral country until Mussolini's impulsive action muddied the waters for Hitler, who by November 1940 had realized that German troops and his Luftwaffe needed to join the Italians and secure a victory in Greece if he was to continue his own aggressive march through Europe. Hitler was also terrified that the British Royal Air Force squadrons would bomb valuable German-controlled oilfields in Romania and thus hamper his invasion plans even more.

By mid-January 1941 Churchill, under the impression that if the British were in Greece, then Turkey would join them, had instructed his Middle East Commander-in-Chief Archie Wavell to send in as many troops as possible. Years later Wavell expressed regret about this decision, as he realised all efforts should have been concentrated on driving the Germans out of North Africa.

Morale among the Greeks had begun to suffer around this time, especially when the newspapers announced that Bulgaria and Turkey had signed a non-aggression pact with Hitler. Then, on 22 February 1941, a delegation from Britain arrived at the Greek royal palace at Tatoi in Athens to campaign for a common stand against Hitler and his armed forces. This visiting party of British 'big guns' included the Foreign Secretary Sir Anthony Eden, with his 'film star good looks', the Chief of the Imperial Staff Lieutenant General Sir John Dill, General Wavell and Air Chief Marshal Sir Arthur Longmore.[12]

When this news was made known to Hitler, he became even more determined to speed up the Axis invasion of Greece. On 6 April 1941, in a bid to rescue his Italian ally from more humiliation, Hitler ordered his soldiers, supported by the Luftwaffe, to march through into Bulgaria on their way to Crete and Athens, which would within weeks suffer from a deadly blitzkrieg.

The doughty 4th Queen's Own Hussars arrived in Piraeus harbour, the chief sea port of Athens on the south-east coast of Greece, in February 1941. Resources, however, were scant for these valiant men. The ever-observant Dunn remarked upon the 'light, out of date armoured vehicles, a battalion of the Royal Tank Regiment, a few Australian and New Zealand troops, plus a handful of Hurricane fighter aircraft, several Blenheim bombers and a small selection of temperamental Gloster Gladiators', and he questioned privately how they would ever defeat the advancing and aggressive enemy with its seemingly endless supply of military equipment.

The decision to send in a token military aid force, including support from the RAF and Royal Navy, had been inspired in part by Churchill. He had expressed great admiration for the Greeks' hearty and early victorious challenge against Il Duce's Italian militia. The BBC's Richard Dimbleby was among a small group of journalists reporting from the front line. He soon let the world know Greece was facing a David and Goliath situation, and remarked that every sinew of every Greek man was being put to the test against the Axis powers. At first, cynical American reporters told their readers how Greece's President Metaxas' little army had no hope and God only sided with big united forces. But once the British had agreed to assist General Metaxas, the US reportage became more respectful of the Greek fighting man.[13]

By the time Dunn and the Hussars arrived in Athens, the RAF had already added much-needed support to the slender numbers of the Royal Hellenic Air Force and successfully bombed Italian shipping at Vlore and Sarande in Albania. However, the RAF attack on Vlore on 6 November 1940 had proved expensive. Three Blenheims of 30 Squadron were challenged by the Italian Fiat fighters of the 364 Squadriglia. Captain Nicola Magaldi, the flight commander, fired at a Blenheim and killed its upper gunner, Sergeant John Merifield. But despite suffering serious damage, all three RAF bombers made it back to Eleusis. Merifield was honoured with a hero's funeral in Athens. The event was filmed by various newsreel camera crews. One Greek newspaper reporter wrote 'The coffin was covered with two crossed flags – the flags of Greece and Britain. The procession was filmed by Pathé News and shown in cinemas throughout the British Commonwealth. As the first casualty of the battle, the Greek sculptor Phamyreas proposed making a symbolic bust of Sgt Merifield in Pentelic marble, the same stone as the Parthenon.'

Despite the RAF's resolve to keep the Italian air force out of the skies, the fighters of 364 Squadriglia were back in action on 7 November, attacking 70 Squadron's Wellington bombers over Vlore. Two of the RAF aircraft were shot down by Fiat CR.42s and Breda 65s. Among the men killed that day were Flight Lieutenant Alan Ellis Brian and Sergeant Pilot George Newcombe Brooks. Less than a week later, on 12 November the Royal Navy's Fleet Air Arm pilots flying 'Stringbag' Fairey Swordfish bombers over the Italian port of Taranto victoriously torpedoed the bulk of the Regia Marina's big vessels. There were other triumphs, too. Greek anti-aircraft fire rattling into the skies on 9 November shot down and killed Second Lieutenant Pietro Janniello of 363 Squadriglia. RAF Blenheims of 84 Squadron also dropped bombs on the squadriglia's base at Gjirokaster and flew away before the Italian fighters could scramble into action.[14] Dunn recalled that there was 'such a little lot of RAF and Fleet Air Arm to defend the northern borders of Greece, adjoining Yugoslavia and Bulgaria, from the entire German army and air force'. He described how: 'Within a few hours of leaving the sunny Athenian atmosphere we were among snowy hills and mountains, then later we went through villages and towns and down into the Macedonian plain. The residents were sweet and friendly, throwing into our lorries flowers and great round loaves of bread like small cartwheels.' Certainly the welcome offered to the British troops by the Greeks was astounding. They believed real help had arrived at last as they watched the cheerful young men in khaki with their cigarettes and backpacks move deeper into the wild terrain of the countryside on their way to a headquarters further on.

Dunn noted the weather was beginning to get warmer, and he was chosen to be the medical orderly for two groups of men. However, as he points out in his memoir, his job was mostly dealing with hangovers, sprained ankles, cuts and bruises. Nights out in local small towns thronged with drunken British soldiers spilling out of brothels ruined the peace and quiet for the residents. The joke was over for Dunn when he watched an inebriated army pal threaten a Greek army officer with a gun: 'I told him quickly to put the revolver away as the Greeks were our friends.' The incident culminated in the two friends throwing punches at each other, and Dunn's 'puny fists' managed to knock his friend-cum-opponent out. When the man awoke in a heap the next morning he had bruises all over his face – but couldn't remember a thing about how they got there![15]

On 6 April 1941 the Germans crossed the Bulgarian border and invaded Greece to shore up the Italian efforts, and began to creep further inland on their way to reach the Balkans and march into Russia. The German aim was to prevent the British from disrupting their advance on the southern flank of Greece. By 15 April the small British forces had begun to retreat, along with the Australian-New Zealand combined forces.

First, noted Dunn, the Germans completely demolished the tiny Yugoslavian Air Force, and then came in strength to beat the stoic British forces into the ground.

By 20 April the Greek army was in tatters. Its field commanders went to the Germans and requested an armistice. It was agreed that the Greek forces would still oppose the Italian invasion as a matter of 'honour'. But all the Greek supply lines had been destroyed, and the Italians kept marching forward, and the longer the Greeks waited to surrender, the more of them would die. The head of the Australian forces in Greece, Field Marshal Thomas Blamey, made wise and rapid plans to evacuate his troops of the 6th Division. He had realised from the start that the situation in Greece was one massive minefield waiting to explode into a humiliating defeat for the Allies. (Blamey was later criticised, however, for allowing his son Tom a seat beside him on a seaplane out of the war zone.)

Dunn recalled the time when he first realised the big retreat had begun: 'We were being pummelled by the German dive-bombers and following Field Marshal Erwin Rommel's arrival in the desert General Wavell could only spare a token force to help defend Greece. Sadly, we turned out to be the "token force". It certainly concentrated the mind.

Troopers sat in ditches awaiting orders, while high-ups worked out the next move.'[16]

From here on in it was a waiting game. Small groups of British soldiers moved about the countryside and further into the hills, doing their best to hide from any German marching parties. At times from camouflaged ditches Dunn could actually see the boots of enemy soldiers stomping by and around him. Any plan to get men down to the coast to be picked up by the Royal Navy had been thwarted. Most of the British tanks had broken down or had been decimated by bomb blasts or machine-gun fire. Poor decision-making by 'the high ups' led to British armoured vehicles gathering on a hillside – more destruction ensued as the German Luftwaffe and troops just blew the whole lot to smithereens.

'I now worked as a full-time stretcher-bearer with Captain Eden during the days men and lorries were just being blown up,' said Dunn. 'My work took place on a rocky hill but there was no way an ambulance could get through to get the injured to safety.' One of the most frightening memories which haunted the future *Dad's Army* star was the time a Stuka attack left a badly injured soldier stranded on a plateau beneath the heavy debris of a wrecked army truck. Dunn ran into action but as he was treating the man's wounds and talking kindly to him the dive-bombing started again. 'I held the patient's hand and pretended we were immortal as the ground seemed to lift us up. Suddenly the bombers were gone, and in the silence I still held his hand and could hardly believe we had survived.'[17]

In those early days of April 1941, stranded in the Greek hills, slippery with snow, yet searingly hot beneath the sun, Dunn and many around him were left baffled by the lack of direction from senior officers. No one supposedly in charge seemed to be making any sense. The High Command didn't seem to understand the speed of the German advance. One particular memorable experience during this period was when Dunn and another soldier chanced upon a big abandoned machine gun lying on the ground. He rapidly loaded it and yelled 'Fire!', aiming at a Stuka heading ferociously in their direction. Both Dunn and his comrade felt strangely thrilled to be in direct action against the Luftwaffe. But after one shot the gun jammed and both men dived over the edge of the hilltop to take cover. It could have been a scene straight from *Dad's Army* but in real life in 1941 the fear of getting killed left no opportunity for mirth. Dunn recalled: 'This particular incident made me lose confidence as a fighting soldier. I worried I had loaded the gun wrongly and puzzled over it for thirty years.'

After this lucky escape from the enemy dive-bomber, Dunn learned that the decision had been made to move back towards the 4th Hussars' original camp near Piraeus. There the men waited around. There was little else to do. The sight of so many broken lorries and tanks and other equipment did little for their fading morale. At last the major drafted in as their temporary leader arrived with news. Dunn hoped to hear that an evacuation was imminent, especially when the officer spoke loudly of how HQ had 'suggested the 4th Hussars should now be used to escort German prisoners of war to India'. However, the dreams of a sea trip to India, then Gibraltar and finally home via Southampton were dashed when the major continued monstrously: 'But I told them at HQ that after all you men had been through recently at the hands of the Germans, I could not trust you to guard the enemy. Therefore, I told them that I have volunteered on your behalf to engage in a rearguard action. You will now be issued with suitable arms and ammunition and the regiment will move off this afternoon to take up positions.'[18]

Dunn's memoir doesn't record his disappointment at the announcement made by the self-serving over-ambitious major but it does describe in detail how a rifle was added to his kit along with a belt of ammunition; then, as an infantryman, he joined the regimental tanks to head out of Athens towards the southern beaches of the Gulf of Corinth. The aim? To defend the Corinth Canal from German troops. He writes of journeying at night, driving along the narrow roads in lorries with the headlamps covered. (It turned out, however, that blanking out lights was not necessary as in Greece the Luftwaffe did not fly after sundown.) Soon enough into the journey, though, they discovered that once-friendly villages were now draped in white flags of surrender and their reception was much changed from a few weeks previously. Instead of being met with flowers and food, the retreating British soldiers faced hostility – bricks were lobbed at them and they were subjected to random gunshots.

Each man, still hoping for some sort of positive direction, believed and hoped they would be in a position to escape from Greece. But in reality many, including Dunn, wondered if a British Navy destroyer would seriously be put at risk of enemy fire and shelling just to rescue a 'hodge podge' of stranded soldiers. All around, each day and every day, the sound of explosions ruptured the air. Dunn saw a massive inferno out to sea – a ship on fire. Then came the distant sight of troops pouring in to the mainland across the water. It was some while before Dunn and his comrades discovered the advancing soldiers were Germans.

Meanwhile, the men were becoming depressed, and the lack of food and clean water was beginning to accelerate the drop in morale. One day, in his guise as a medical orderly, Dunn was called to climb into a lorry to help a soldier whose legs had been smashed to bits by a bomb blast. The injured man's friend insisted Dunn do something to save the man and they drove rapidly to a village to find a doctor. It was clear early on that the patient had already died of his wounds but his companion refused to take Dunn's word for it. As soon as a qualified doctor was found, confirmation of death was recorded.

Avoiding the Germans was the main focus of each day. Dunn walked about, often bent over to dodge enemy bullets, searching and scavenging for food. Water was often a problem. Drinking old water from dirty wells led to stomach cramps and other gastric ailments.

One day, during an evacuation plan to reach Kalamata, a captain told the men to hide and keep watch on a mass of German tanks heading their way. No other orders were given and confusion reigned. No one had been ordered to take a shot. When the captain reappeared, he realised a Bren machine gun had been left near the top of a hill and he ordered two men to fetch it back. They didn't seem keen so to 'end this embarrassing situation I went, not out of bravery but out of pure embarrassment for the captain,' explained Dunn. Once recovered, the weapon was placed in the back of a lorry – the plan being for it to be fired at any Germans who gave chase.[19]

What followed was an intense game of catch-me-if-you-can. The road along which the British soldiers in Dunn's group were travelling petered out into a narrow dusty track until the lorry could go no further. They saw the Germans advancing towards them. After grabbing a few items, Dunn and the rest of the men around him scattered into a nearby forest to regroup and make another plan of escape. He recalled seeing a British army captain run by him. This harassed, red-faced officer told Dunn that more than half of his own field squadron of troops had been captured.

The original seventeen soldiers of Dunn's group were soon joined by other stranded comrades. Soon the party numbered forty, and it continued to grow as stragglers came out of their hiding places and joined in. The new plan was to reach Crete, which they desperately hoped was still occupied by the Allies. But they needed food and water. Hunger and thirst diverted their ambition, which morphed into a regular hunt for sustenance. A shepherd here and there might give them some milk or salty cheese, and once the men pooled their money and bought an old goat to slaughter and boil for its meat. Occasionally a Greek orthodox priest would give them black bread. Dunn comically revealed that this bread, once digested, resulted in terrible attacks of flatulence so woe betide any man who walked behind someone who had eaten it.

At one point they bought a mule to carry their kit. Suddenly it stumbled and rolled and rolled down a deep ravine. 'We watched horrified, shedding its load as it went,' he recalled. 'When it stopped this animal, which should have been dead nine times over, got to its feet, shook itself and went gaily off into the scrub land, free as a bird.'

Now forced to move by night, the men were led through the hills by a trusty Greek known as Peter. They stumbled and trudged along in single file and then waited at certain places where local women would bravely bring them food out of the darkness and then disappear again.

Dunn remembered once seeing a fiery battle taking place at sea. A few of the Cypriot men in the group had managed to locate a rowing boat and reached Crete by 'island hopping'. The rest were now based around a small cove and facing the clear blue ocean, so there was at least a chance to swim. More than once Dunn swam over bright blue sea urchins. He admitted he didn't know at the time these sea creatures could have been brought to shore to be eaten for nourishment.

One day, out on the hunt for food, he met a Greek woman who kindly gave him two fresh eggs. He put them in the top pockets of his tunic. When he returned to the hideaway, a captain informed him that the Germans were close by so everyone needed to disperse into small groups. Dunn was to join a sergeant who had a badly injured knee and was stranded among the shrubbery. But as the gunfire increased all around them, the injured sergeant told Dunn to keep moving as he couldn't help him 'by hanging about'. Dunn took note and decided to disappear into the hills again. Still the explosions continued nearby. Suddenly, as he approached a corner, there was an enemy soldier standing in front of him, pointing a rifle at him; then he saw another German with a machine gun aimed directly at him and ready to fire. Dunn said:

> I was still armed with a pistol strapped to my leg and an egg in each breast pocket. Feeling glad I was still alive, I half raised my arms in surrender, and that was that. Behind me two British corporals who had followed me did the same. At this point in the game my mind was busy: I had managed to lead two men into captivity and I wondered how the injured sergeant had fared. A German advanced and took my pistol, waved it in the air and said, 'Mr Churchill, ja?' I agreed, as I was in no position to argue. Anything to keep them talking and not shooting.[20]

Dunn was forced to hand over his personal items, including the gold locket containing photographs of his parents, Connie and Bobby. The German kept the locket but returned the pictures. The two eggs were then cracked and swallowed whole by Dunn's captor.

By now the whole regiment of 4th Hussars had been forced to surrender after being overrun. Dunn was among 400 men, including senior officers, who were now in enemy hands. Life as a prisoner of war was about to begin.

*** 

THE first realisation of his new status as a captive arrived soon after Dunn was ordered by a young German soldier to carry a heavy machine gun. Walking for miles, seriously under-fed and forced to shoulder the weighty weapon without a break, left the starving Dunn near to collapse. He finally arrived at a farming village, with the rest of the exhausted troopers. Waiting until nightfall, he thought seriously about sneaking out and making for the woods. Suddenly two shots rang out – and he realised two men who had the same thought were no longer alive.

The only food offered to the prisoners was dry water biscuits. The men were then squashed into a lorry and taken to Argos, an historic city in the Peloponnese. When Dunn arrived there, he was dumped onto a dock in freezing weather. By now most of the men were ravenous and suffering from gastric issues, including severe diarrhoea. A few more days of suffering led to another journey. This time they were driven almost 30 miles to a former Greek army barracks at Corinth, and it was here that Dunn endured constant prods up the backside from bayonets wielded by cruel German SS guards on a sadistic high from exerting power over the prisoners. Brief respite arrived when he was woken at one point by the sound of laughter. It was his old friend David Bradford, and the pair shared the remains of an old cigarette and reminisced together.

In his memoir Dunn is candid about the horrors he suffered, especially at the beginning of his life in German hands. He describes how men were forced to queue for hours for a 'drop of infected water', lice were rampant, and the only place to sleep at the Corinth barracks was in a slit trench. Food like bread could only be bought with gold.

Soon, another march lay ahead for the prisoners, whose only sustenance was some salty oily fish, which led to an outbreak of desperate thirst. In a single day, suffering in the heat of 27 degrees Celsius/80 degrees Farenheit, they walked, stumbled, fell and staggered 30 miles along the roads and plains that led to the city of Lamia. If anyone dropped out of the line for a pee, they were shot. If anyone needed to relieve themselves, they had to drop behind the formation and squat in the middle of the road. The sun's rays were so relentless that even some guards dropped dead.

When the desperate prisoners reached Lamia, Dunn recalled that: 'The sight of those sick and wounded soldiers trying to survive that march is beyond description.' At one point they were herded into a cattle truck with only a can between them to use as a latrine. When they arrived at a city called Salonika (now Thessaloniki), they were 'driven like cattle' through the streets. Any resident who threw them food was ruthlessly beaten back by the German guards.[21]

A week in the Salonika camp weakened the prisoners even more, as their food consisted only of a small lump of bread. Back in the cattle truck, they were left to lie on a floor covered in 'spilled germ-ridden liquid faeces'. There was no opportunity to pour the muck out of the slit in the carriage which acted as a tiny window. Blow back was a terrible problem and the poor man trying to empty the bucket was drowned in the grisly contents of everyone's bowels. Recalling the horrors later, though, he added: 'This was tragi-comedy at its most potent and a sight I remember clearly. How different, twenty years later, when travelling first class on British Rail on the way to appear in a series called *Escapers' Club*, I saw in the loo the notice which read 'Gentlemen, Lift the Seat.'' But during his wartime suffering as a captive he had no option but to lie with his face to the floor of the cattle truck and nibble on three grains of wheat he had found and dug out from between the floorboards.

Soon after this pitiful scramble for crumbs of food, the train pulled up at Belgrade station in Yugoslavia, before continuing its hideous stop-start trek towards Austria. It halted only when the guards shot those fighting men, often driven mad with hunger, who had tried to escape by carving holes in the bottom of the carriage. Some prisoners died when they dropped onto the tracks, having misjudged the speed of the train.

Dunn said:

As our deprivation increased, I was feeling really ill and weak. When eventually the wagon ground to a halt somewhere in Austria, the doors slid open and we were counted by the track side. Over the next four years we would be counted again and again and again. We staggered on under guard for half an hour and reached our camp, which turned out to be a lot of wooden huts on land surrounded by barbed wire.[22]

More humiliation was imposed when the starving men were forced to remove all their torn clothes and ordered to run naked into a hot shower – which without soap did nothing to remove the grime and filth. Outside again, the men discovered their ragged uniforms had disappeared and been replaced by clean cast-off garments such as Dutch-style calf-length breeches, worn out tunics, caps and clogs. Despite the torment, and often experiencing stomach pains, Dunn managed to keep hold of a small bottle of water-purifying tablets. He described this little bottle as 'like a talisman' against the bad times.

When the Germans asked their captives about their civilian life, most replied 'butcher' or 'farmer', in the hope they would be given jobs working near food sources. Trooper Dunn, however, came clean and revealed he was an actor in real life. The German officer asking the questions gave him a quiet smile and gently took the long-grasped charm away from Dunn, explaining that the water was clean where he was going.

More than fifty prisoners were then herded back into the train and after a short journey arrived at a wooden cabin where they were allowed to rest. Later on they examined their new home. There was enough room for twenty-five men to lie next to one another, and it was equipped with a stove and what turned out to be a toilet – two planks of wood with a hole in the middle above a cesspit. Dunn and his pals were now residents of Pruggern in Obersteiermark, a small town nestled at the bottom of a mountain. Work started quickly and each man was put in the charge of Herr Fischelschweger. Dunn's new role was to work as a navvy up the mountainside. He wrote: 'I was given a pick that would have made a suitable anchor for the Queen Mary. My job was to widen the path enough so a cart could get through.'

As life began to settle down in their new camp, there was still a serious lice problem and the pathetic supplies of foam-less soap did little to ease it. Finally, after Dunn yelled at the guards about 'not liking' creepy crawlies, more soap was provided and more washing time was accommodated on the strict rota. Each day provided opportunity for the men to toil extra slowly in an act of self-preservation: 'Working for Hitler became a game of bluff; from a distance a man could flap his elbows up and down to look as if he were "bumping" the road surface level. We took comfort in thinking this road we learned to hate would never be finished, and the Germans who plodded up and down to watch us were smug about not being on the Russian front.' The guards in their arrogance also took great pleasure in spreading German propaganda about how many British ships had been destroyed, and how the Luftwaffe was dropping bombs all over Britain and winning the war.

Most prisoners realised that humour helped get them through the day, and many an hour was spent chuckling and making jokes about their German captors. One guard earned the name 'pissholes' because of his small red eyes. The object of their fun also had a habit of continually fiddling with his rifle and blowing into his mittens in an attempt to keep out the perishing cold.

As Dunn had a small dictionary and was able to communicate when any of the men were sick ('krank'), he was appointed by the sergeants in the prisoners group as medical orderly, which mostly meant he had permission to dish out a couple of plasters here and there. However, there was little to stem the pungent gastric issues caused by a diet of ageing potatoes. Anyone suffering serious health issues was escorted to see a doctor in the local village of Gröbming. Dunn once visited the real medic for himself; the doctor lanced a large painful boil under his arm which had swollen to the size of a ping-pong ball. Meantime another soldier developed a skin condition that prompted the panicking Germans to believe that bubonic plague was sweeping through the camp. Dunn was left to assist the suffering man and managed to help heal him using ointment and paper bandages. He also witnessed several cases of severe frostbite. One soldier's ears were so badly frozen they were covered in blisters and flapping to and fro 'like an anxious elephant'. The sub-zero temperatures of Austria took their toll on many men forced to work in the freezing air.

Occasionally Red Cross parcels arrived, and luxuries like cigarettes, prunes, chocolate and porridge oats were smoked or wolfed down all at once by the starving and needy recipients. Rarely, they had permission to send a card back home to console families anxious for news of their welfare. It was a big day when new British Army uniforms and sturdy footwear turned up in brown boxes – a donation that helped to improve morale and instill a sense of dignity: 'One of the guards remarked on the amazing change of personality that came over most of us. He put it down to the possession of boots. German soldiers were obsessed with boots, the jackboot being, presumably, their symbol of superiority over the conquered,' he recalled.

\*\*\*

SO feeling more presentable and morally in tandem with the rest of his workmates, Dunn learned they were to travel again. This time a billet 20 miles away at Liezen beckoned. The living quarters were different there as the men found themselves jammed up against one another in an old schoolhouse which had only three floors. Here they felt imprisoned at night, once the guard had locked the door, but struggling and surviving had become ingrained into their souls and so they embraced their new surroundings with as much cheer as could be mustered. They were given manual labouring jobs in the area but were forbidden to talk to or acknowledge the local residents. Talking to women and girls was a definite no no. Not only was Dunn the appointed medical orderly, he was also the camp leader and interpreter – so his job as chief communicator became implicit to maintaining good relations between friend and foe. This led to a collection of mirthful anecdotes in his autobiography. His pals would ask him to call a guard 'a prick' and the baffled German would enquire 'What does this mean?' The Germans also had no idea what the word 'fookink', or 'fockink', meant. When Dunn attempted to translate the word, the guards became even more bewildered as he mimed the act of sexual relations!

Compared to Pruggern, Dunn describes Liezen as more 'relaxed'. Even visits to the town to watch a film were permitted occasionally, and thanks to Dunn's persuasive efforts the German sergeant in charge of their camp allowed games of football to take place. Money for their work was also paid to the prisoners in a bid to prove to the Red Cross that the men were not being treated as slaves. Trouble flared up, though, when one captive set light to a large Nazi flag that had been hung outside the building in support of a visiting senior German official. Terrifyingly, the guards lined up the men and threatened them all with execution unless the guilty party stood up and confessed. When a man named George collapsed in shock, it was assumed that he was the culprit and he was carted off to receive the dreadful punishment. The real perpetrator then told Dunn that he had put a match to the giant cloth German swastika because he'd had a bad day and felt oppressed about their situation. George was returned to camp and Dunn watched the Germans lead the culprit away to a cell. There followed a meeting with a German captain. Dunn told him what the man had said about his part in the burning of the flag. A document was compiled and all parties had to sign it.

From the memoir it is difficult for the reader to ascertain what happened to the prisoner who dared denounce Nazi idealism but Dunn revealed he felt so sickened about 'saying goodbye to his mate' that all he could do was go back and 'lay down in a shattered lump'. The following day he stepped down from his role as camp leader, having realised he was not emotionally strong enough to cope with its demands. He did, however, remain as interpreter and chief cleaner in charge of keeping the rampaging fleas and lice under control.

The rules of the Geneva Convention meant the soldiers ranked corporal and above were not required to work, unlike those of the rank of private. With time at night to think, two pals and Dunn hatched a plot to go into town and meet friendly women. Dunn devised a way to make a replica key to one of the doors leading out of the building. This ruse worked well until one temporary escapee returned from his midnight activities at the same time as a guard. Fortunately they were able to bribe the German to keep quiet with cigarettes, but the next day the lock on the door was changed.

As the war progressed, more German soldiers were needed on the Russian front. This became obvious when the guards at Liezen were replaced with old men. Many of them were retired schoolteachers or gardeners, gentle characters who seemed to resent the conflict as much as their captives. However, any whiff of too much chumminess with the prisoners and any German of whatever age could still find himself dispatched pronto to the horrors of the war in the East, and certain death.

Despite the age of these new captors, Dunn remained steadfast in his complaints about the facilities and they had no choice but to march him off to see the camp commandant. According to the future *Dad's Army* star, the washing facilities at Liezen were poor – a situation that didn't help the perpetual struggle to keep lice and fleas at bay. At one time a fellow prisoner learned there was a woman living on the mountain who would deal with the laundry in exchange for cigarettes and soap. There's something very comical in his description of the dishevelled bunch of prisoners piling their clothes in a toboggan and then watching it slide by accident all the way down the mountain into the village, where it nearly ran over a German SS officer. A quick 'Heil Hitler' from the men to the surprised Nazi smoothed away any threat of punishment. The deal with the woman did not work out, however, as the miffed prisoners discovered that their garments, although clean, were always still ringing wet – and no one wants to wear wet pants.

Socks and underwear were occasionally included among the goodies in Red Cross parcels, which arrived sporadically. A three-month wait was nothing unusual, but it offered the hard-working men some hope. The idea that someone somewhere was thinking of the prisoners' welfare helped them through the ordeal of hard labour, including the time they were ordered to wade into a bitterly cold river to extract the ice for the hosts of local hotels and bed and breakfast establishments. As the medical orderly Dunn was kept busy helping those who caught chills and fevers or developed flu-like symptoms.

A moral battle ensued when a German officer decided to send the Liezen prisoners to carry out war work in a factory. The men refused absolutely, despite the risk of execution, still bravely quoting the Geneva Convention at the Germans. The factory owner told the Nazi officer he did not want any mutiny to cope with and so soon enough the plan for free labour from the British captives was abandoned. They had taken a risk in disobeying, yet had triumphantly returned to the camp where Dunn was waiting with tea for everybody to toast the victory.

Other courageous acts of defiance in regards to the heavy work load ensued and the prisoners' strike actions were proven to be effective, even though the threat of execution was ever-present. At one time a Hungarian-Austrian guard with a moral conscience gave the prisoners some leeway – but he paid a terrible price for his kindness. The German camp commandant sent him to the Russian front.

It was in the chilly conditions at Liezen that Dunn's stomach condition – colitis – began to worsen. It took its toll not only on his physical health but on his mental abilities too. He explained:

> I was sent down the valley in Rottenmann and a guard accompanied me on the train, and after a mile walk at the other end he left and handed me over to a nun. Two nuns guided me up the corridor, undressed me and stuck me in a warm bath – my first for three and a half years. The luxury of this dazed me. After ten minutes the heavily costumed Christian lady beckoned me up and out to smother me in a large bath sheet. She was so gently spoken and had such wonderful grey eyes, exactly the same colour as my Auntie Lydie's, that for a moment I thought I had arrived in heaven and that my present guardian angel would excuse herself to nip down to the corner shop to place a bet.[23]

Fed on a diet of semolina and foods gentle on the digestion, the rapaciously thin Dunn began to recover. He made friends with his fellow prisoners, and mentions in particular an Italian funnyman in the next bed who was full of lively, earthy anecdotes about nuns cuddling him after an operation on his lung. For the future *Dad's Army* star, it was the horror of having a rubber tube put down his throat to enable the doctors to withdraw fluids that proved the worst he had to endure during his hospital stay.

After a a recovery period lasting almost a month, Dunn was soon on his way back to the Liezen camp. Within a few days of getting back into the chilly rigours of a captive's life, it was a thrill to watch formations of US aircraft pouring across the skies overhead. Was freedom near?

He noticed the Germans were 'jumpy' and Austria was beginning to shift its allegiance away from Adolf Hitler and the Nazi tyranny. Suddenly more Red Cross parcels and letters began to find their way to the camp. Sadly for Dunn, the new influx of charitable delicious food could not be enjoyed as the rumble of his colitis took its toll. Whilst this condition was agonising for Dunn, it did provide an opportunity for him to insist on seeing a military doctor – an English one at that, based in the town of Wolfsberg, almost 100 miles from Liezen. For the ailing Dunn, however, his transfer to Wolfsberg was a hopeful sign that he might be sent home to Britain. In his memoir he writes with his usual acute sense of observation about some old women on the 20 hour train journey from Liezen to Wolfsberg staring at his British battledress uniform, whispering about him, and yet noting he was travelling with a German guard.

It's not unusual for train journeys to conjure up thoughts of the past. Dunn says while gazing out of the window at the passing scenery, he thought about the time he laughed and laughed one night at the camp when he was high on 'phong' – a moonshine-type beverage brewed from all manner of old bits of fruit and other goodies. 'Once I started talking that night I couldn't stop and rambled on and on, thinking I'd truly turned into some comic genius – and I'd discovered the true secret source of comedy. We laughed ourselves to sleep,' he recalled, indicating that his life in captivity had not destroyed his passion to eventually get back to work in the theatre.

Arriving at Wolfsberg brought him some cheer, as he met his old pal David Bradford and some other troopers from the 4th Hussars who had been with him in Greece. Life seemed easier here, with the German guards trusting the prisoners to run their own routines, as long as the correct amount of men reported for work duties. Any medical men, including dentists, were farmed out now and then to assist at other camps. For entertainers, there was a system of being hidden from the labour list, enabling them to take up the role of keeping morale afloat among the men. Within weeks of arriving at Wolfsberg, and despite the exhausting game of hide and seek he played with the knowing guards, Dunn was invited to join in the camp's next theatrical production. He said: 'I was the only pro in the outfit and played a bumpkin in a production of John Galsworthy's 1920 play *The Skin Game*.'

Being an entertainer and a good all-round sort encouraged his new friends to trust him. Dunn himself, however, was terrified after he was shown a crystal radio set hidden in a library book. The device enabled the prisoners to hear the latest BBC news in secret. 'I don't know why

I was let in on this,' he wrote, 'as I didn't think I'd be much good if caught and put under torture . . .'

Some weeks before droves of US military aircraft began to roar over the camp at regular intervals, Dunn was on stage again, this time playing the female lead in Ivor Novello's *Glamorous Nights*. The experience of recreating the role of a gypsy princess – using rolled-up socks for imitation breasts, a jaunty wig and a tight dress made of curtain material – proved fascinating, as he explained:

> It's a great challenge for actors to perform as a member of the opposite sex; drama schools should always include it in their curriculum. No one ever laughed at you in a prison camp for taking on this exacting role. To convince an audience of hairy prisoners I was a glamorous gypsy girl demanded the conviction of an Edith Evans (a famous actress of the time). The whole experience was rewarding, and as the audiences left the theatre to go back to their scratchy palliasses they were inspired to get through some more dreary months of captivity.

Getting hold of a joke book from a pal helped motivate Dunn to think of his theatrical future when he got back home, and yet his mood shifted when suddenly he had to jump out of bed when the camp was bombed. That day forty bombs hit the huts at Wolfsberg. A number of prisoners were killed or, as Dunn put it, 'wiped out by a confused wing of an American bomber force'. At one point Dunn, now much in demand as a medical orderly, helped save a man trapped beneath the debris of a hut. The man turned out to be a German guard, who 'never said thanks'. And then came the grim tasks of burying the dead and assisting in the operating theatre. Many men asked for his advice on how to keep their wounds open in order to escape the work rosters. Soon enough the bombing raids intensified, and the men at the Wolfsberg prisoner-of-war camp found themselves living in trenches they had built to shield them from the explosives.

When Dunn and a few other men expressed a wish to be transferred to the countryside to do farm work, they were put on a train, accompanied by a guard. First they stopped at the city of Liebnitz, then moved on to Gündorf, where there was a chance of some work opportunities. Then came a long walk with the guard dropping off what men he could at various rural homesteads. Dunn was finally taken in by a family who agreed he could bed down with eleven other workers in an old barn. He was fed well, but within a short time the guard appeared again to move him and the other prisoners of war on again as the Russians were closing in. It was during this march to what Dunn believed was another farm job that the guard suddenly left them on top of a hill, and said goodbye. 'Here was one of Hitler's soldiers who'd had enough and was actually deserting,' explained Dunn. 'We cheered him, and he turned to wave before he disappeared out of sight.'[24]

From that day the group of prisoners began to grow. They decided to embark on the long march towards the Allied-occupied territories, and within days they were joined by peasants and families left homeless by the Nazi aggressors. The never-ending hunt for food was exhausting and there were some days when there was nothing to eat but sugar and boiled leaves. At one point they were captured by the Germans again. Nervous Nazi officers, twitching to escape themselves, put everyone behind a barbed wire fence at Markt Pongau in north-west Austria, close to Salzburg. A message rang out, recalled Dunn, telling everyone to stay in the camps. Anyone, including the fleeing German guards, who left the area to board a train was killed. The US bombers saw to that.

After a week US military vehicles began rolling in. One by one the bedraggled prisoners were showered with delousing powder, given food and drink, and put into lorries. Once Dunn arrived in Salzburg, he was given a new uniform and was asked formal questions by a British officer in order to confirm his identity. Out on the nearby tarmac waited Dakota aircraft ready to fly the thankful former captives home. Dunn landed first in Belgium, and then from Brussels – and after a 'booze up' with pals and a friendly woman! – he caught the next flight back to England. He recalled: 'We landed in Stomping in Sussex where we went through more questioning. I was then told that due to my age group my expected release from the army was a long way off.' Full of dread, he timidly asked how long it would be before he could go back to civvy street. He was told it depended on the war against Japan. And with that dark cloud in the back of his mind, he waited patiently to return to London to see his much-missed family.

However, his fears of being shipped out to the Far East eventually came to nothing and instead he was able to celebrate his homecoming with his parents Connie and Bobby. He remained on leave until he was called to join a unit in the north of England. His job? Picking up rubbish. He expressed in his memoir how deeply disappointed he was at not being selected to join a victory parade through Newcastle.

The future *Dad's Army* star now relied on his debilitating colitis to persuade army doctors that he should be discharged from military service. Quite legitimately, he pointed out that he had already sacrificed his health for King and Country. What else could he offer? For so many young men called up to fight during the Second World War, the conflict exacted a serious toll on their bodies; but where their bodies healed, their psychological torment would often last a lifetime. Instead of being discharged, however, Dunn was informed that his experience as a medical orderly would be most useful and he was assigned to work in a packed Nissan hut treating painfully thin and sick men who had been subjected to the horrors of Japanese prisoner-of-war camps. Many of those he treated in 1946 had suffered brutal conditions while slaving on the Burma railway. At the end of the year he welcomed the news that he was about to be demobbed, and sure enough it wasn't long before he was back on the professional stage.

\*\*\*

IN 1947 Dunn was thrilled to land a role at the Palace Theatre in the West End as a singer in a long run of a musical called *Goody Two Shoes*. His memoir, candid, heartfelt and humane, reveals a young man determined to put the horrors of his war experience behind him. He showed the world he was the original comeback kid. And he bought a new jockstrap to celebrate! From here on in, he was on the road back to a full-time life on the professional stage. Auditioning here and there, he won parts in the West End and on tour, in radio, television and film. In 1959 he married Patricia Pughe-Morgan, his second marriage, and they would have two daughters. He was 48 years old when in 1968 he was offered the role that would rocket his career into the stratosphere of fame.

At the time Dunn was working in television with comedian Spike Milligan, doing parts he confessed weren't really his scene, when he bumped into old family friend David Croft. (Dunn's mother Connie once had an affair with Croft's father.) Croft, who was on the lookout for actors for a new series called *Dad's Army*, decided there and then that he had found his perfect Lance Corporal Jones. Yet despite Croft's enthusiasm, Dunn took a while to make up his mind about joining the cast of the show. In his memoir he revealed that he was busy at the time and had tired of the 'ups and downs' of the profession. However, he began to warm to the character of Jones after reading about his background as an old soldier who had served in the bloody battle of Omdurman in 1898. Dunn also read about Jones's job in later life running a butcher's shop in the mythical Walmington-on-Sea and how he had a steadfast determination to get his rank back as a lance corporal in the fight against Hitler's armed forces.

Dunn had not worked with many of his soon-to-be co-stars and was anxious about the anonymity of Jimmy Perry as a writer, but he did like the idea of a show about the Home Guard, and also took comfort in the knowledge that his old friend John Le Mesurier was debating Croft's offer to play Sergeant Wilson. Le Mesurier was in fact holding out for more pay, but it wasn't long before he found himself in Thetford, Norfolk, with Dunn beside him, filming the outside scenes for the pilot episode of *Dad's Army*. Dunn recalled:

> David Croft assured me I would be given the principal 'Joey Joeys' – clowning in the series. This was all-important to me – I felt secure in physical comedy, if not always in the spoken word. I wanted to exploit my ability in this direction and not have to stand around and watch other actors performing the best bits of comedy business. I thought that I was first choice for Lance Corporal Jones, and that my mother's ancient romance was the cause. In fact, as I discovered many years later, the part had first been offered to Jack Haig, who then turned it down for another job![25]

About his *Dad's Army* co-stars and the making of the programme, Dunn offered a raft of memorable anecdotes. One included the concern of BBC bosses about the original opening titles showing the German army marching into Belgium and the Netherlands. They believed the images might upset the Jewish community and the decision was taken to turn the opening scenes into the comedic, jaunty map and arrows we know today.

In his memoir he writes about the joys of working with the oldest member of the cast, Arnold Ridley ('sweet-natured' Private Godfrey), who was then in his 70s, and recalls that David Croft was most courteous to the elderly actors who might want to leave a shoot early. Ridley liked to be sure to attend his Masonic meetings when required, and was also allowed access to a chair to save his legs from tiring out – but it made for some amusement when Ridley, a former rugby player, recovered his ability to run when the bar opened at the hotel! Dunn also mentions the times when Ridley irritated his elderly co-star John Laurie (Private Frazer, ex-Navy and undertaker), who was also in his 70s, by telling everyone during filming to 'hurry up' and 'get on with it'.

According to Dunn, his co-stars Ian Lavender and John Laurie got on tremendously well because they shared 'bright, lively minds'. They often completed crosswords together and exchanged jokes. Soon enough Dunn, whose catchphrase 'Don't panic!, don't panic!' is still repeated by fans to this day, relished the joy of working with a cast of actors with whom he could perform without being anxious they would misbehave by upstaging him or playing in an over-dramatic fashion.

He had great fun working with Ian Lavender and recalled a time they sang a song together at a country club do in Somerset. Dunn prides himself on helping to develop Lavender's comedic talents. He also described how writer Jimmy Perry wrote each script with a certain actor in mind and distributed the best lines fairly. Jimmy Beck (Private Walker) he hailed a party man with a fine sense of fun and a brilliant talent. 'I know John Le Mesurier and me were crushed when Jimmy died so young at just 42,' added Dunn, who also talks about his family holidays in Portugal with Le Mesurier. He recalled too how he would sit and listen to Arthur Lowe (Captain Mainwaring) talking endlessly about his boat *Amazon*, into which he poured thousands of pounds to make her seaworthy. In 1977, two years after Dunn was honoured with an OBE from HM the Queen, the peeved Lowe remarked how the only honour worth receiving was a knighthood!

It was also in 1977 that the cast and crew met at The Bell Hotel in Thetford to toast the success of the show and say their farewells. It was over, and it was time for everyone to move on to other projects. 'The last few episodes were fun, tinged with regret; added to which, people kept on throwing farewell parties. At one stage I got the feeling I was attending my own funeral. The biggest splash was made by the *Daily Mirror* group, who organised a sort of last supper. It was quite a jolly evening at the Café Royal,' added Dunn.

For the next thirty years Clive Dunn, the man who went down in global entertainment history as the well-meaning and determined comedy character of Lance Corporal Jones, spent a happy retirement in Portugal, focusing on his new life as an artist. He died in 2012 at the age of 92. Frank Williams (The Vicar) said his co-star was always 'great fun' to be around. 'Of course he was so much younger than the part he played,' he told BBC Radio Four. 'It's very difficult to think of him as an old man really, but he was a wonderful person to work with – great sense of humour, always fun, a great joy really.'

The star's own memories of his wartime experiences provided an inspired thrust to this book. Authentic, candid, painfully honest and poignantly descriptive, it is the story of a man shaped by war. Indeed, his extraordinarily detailed record of the wretched and terrifying experiences during the Greek campaign that led to him becoming a prisoner of war is among the most important ever written. Dunn was a survivor. He lived off the fragile embers of his indefatigable human spirit and became a quiet hero, who, like all of his lice-ridden prisoner-of-war pals living off scraps of black bread and infected water, learned to duck and dive around the German jackboot world of authoritarianism. He admitted, too, how the cheeky 21-year-old soldier boys who sailed from Liverpool in 1940 changed significantly after their capture in Greece. His descriptions of being bombed and strafed by the German Luftwaffe, nursing desperate comrades whose legs had been blown to bits, and almost starving to death while lost in the hills during the humiliating retreat, all reveal how the war left deep scars in the hearts and minds of so many of his generation.

# TALFRYN THOMAS

**The mystery of an RAF crash**

THE real war years of John Talfryn Thomas, who appeared in *Dad's Army* in 1973 and 1974 as the *Eastbourne Gazette* photo-journalist Mr Cheeseman, are shrouded in confusion. Despite extensive research, there is little evidence to support the numerous theories about the actor's service with the RAF.

Talfryn was born on 31 October 1922. His father was a road turner by trade, but the Thomas family also had a butcher's shop and worked as farmers, too. As a boy, Talfryn lived with his aunt and uncle, following the early death of his mother. When the Second World War broke out he joined the local ARP as a messenger boy. On the night of the Blitz a bomb hit the family home but he escaped unscathed.

As a young man he developed a passion for acting and joined the Llandow Players, appearing in many local theatrical productions. His chosen profession was that of an instrument mechanic and he worked at a weights and measures office until his call-up during the Second World War. As the war continued, he joined the RAF and it is believed he went on many bombing raids over Germany. It is unclear if he trained as a pilot or gunner or both. It was during this time that he inadvertently made his debut on the big screen by making an appearance in a services newsreel.

In 1945 Talfryn was allegedly invalided out of the RAF, having survived an air crash and subsequently going missing for several weeks. He was, according to the National Archive, badly injured, with some suggestion that the tragedy which killed the rest of the crew happened in Britain during a training flight, especially as Talfryn was not listed as a prisoner of war. He was flying in a Halifax bomber as tail-end Charlie (rear gunner) when the aircraft went down. The aircraft is believed to have flown out of RAF East Kirby that day.

In September 1950 Talfryn joined the London Academy of Music and Drama and studied there alongside such luminaries as Margaret

John and Emlyn James. The big screen also beckoned, and *Worms Eye View* (1951) was one of his earliest film appearances. He later appeared opposite Richard Attenborough in *Only Two Can Play* (1962), with John Le Mesurier also in the cast.

Probably one of Talfryn's best-known roles was as Pugh the Poisoner in Dylan Thomas's *Under Milk Wood*. By the 1960s he had appeared in various supporting roles in television shows, including *Emergency Ward 10*, *The Avengers*, *Ghost Squad*, *R3* and *The Saint*. Talfryn also worked on *Doctor Who*, *The Onedin Line*, *Doomwatch* and *Survivors*.

In 1973 the actor was invited to appear in an episode of *Dad's Army* as the bumbling Mr Cheeseman of the *Eastbourne Gazette*. He was only due to appear in one episode, 'My British Buddy', in which the platoon constantly came into conflict with visiting US troops. However, after James Beck (Private Walker) died in August 1973, Jimmy Perry and David Croft decided not to replace the much-loved actor but rather to bring in a new element to the show. Talfryn then returned in the following series and Bill Pertwee later remarked that Talfryn's contribution to the series 'hit the right note'. But when *Dad's Army* returned in 1975, the character of Mr Cheeseman had been written out.

Talfryn went on to record *Under Milk Wood* for BBC Radio 4.

Two of his last comedy appearances included an episode of Perry and Croft's hit show *Hi-De-Hi!* and an episode of Frankie Howerd's wartime sitcom *Then Churchill said to Me . . .* He was due to appear in an episode of the classic BBC Wales series *Welsh Rarebit* when he suffered a heart attack and died at the age of 60 in 1982.

# THE *DAD'S ARMY* MUSEUM

**An experience surely not to be missed**

AS we drive through the old market town of Thetford in Norfolk on a mild day in early autumn, we prepare to reconcile with those irrepressible characters in khaki who march through our lives with noisy booted gusto, shuffling, loitering, laughing and japing in their everlasting guise as rare stars of the British cultural firmament.

It's along Cage Lane at the back of the stoic old Guildhall building where we conjure up the true hauntings which remind us somehow of having been here in this illuminating portal before . . . it is our ultimate Waterloo of déjà vu . . . so look, is that Captain George Mainwaring adjusting his officer's cap, polishing his spectacles and making ready to proclaim an order for us to stand to attention? Did we really see the lithe figure of Private Frank Pike in his military green denim uniform slip through a doorway with that immovable blue and maroon coloured scarf wrapped around his delicate teenage neck? And was that the beguiling Sergeant Arthur Wilson pulling at his earlobe deep in thought while standing idly by Lance Corporal Jack Jones's van?

Oops, look out, here comes our favourite doom-monger Private James Fraser, rolling his dark Celtic eyes in derision at the sight of the aged Private Charles Godfrey doddering about in the Marigold Tea Room and handing around his sister Dolly's upside-down cake. And quickly, oh so quickly, we catch a glimpse of the artful spiv Private Joe Walker, ready on the make and take with his latest line in ladies' stockings and black market whisky.

But we're not panicking, oh no, as we spy Jonesy lurking at the ready nearby on the pavement with his bayonet of steel glinting dangerously in the mid-morning sun. He can stand down, though, as we pose no threat and he can after all stroll along to the banks of the Little Ouse river and share a sausage roll with his wondrous darling Mrs Fox.

As visitors to this hallowed place of British comedy heritage, we have only a big welcome for the ghosts of *Dad's Army* as they are all here on this day and every day in and around this hearty old town and its army-camp/film-ready forest. And where else would enthusiasts be making ready to challenge the bombastic Chief ARP Warden William Hodges than at the *Dad's Army Museum*, which is housed in a building still oozing with the same eminence it had during the Second World War?

Let's be ready then to go inside and prepare to meet the doughty Captain Mainwaring. We find him seated loftily before us at the desk in the creaky office with its whiff of old damp, yellowing books, ledgers and wartime hair oil. It is the official room which the vicar, the Reverend Timothy Farthing, reluctantly shares with the captain because, as the vicar had to be reminded, 'there's a war on, don't you know!'

The captain invites us to be interviewed about joining his Home Guard platoon. He suggests we try on a British Army tin helmet for our 'little interrogation to check you're both not Nazi spies'. He looks at us suspiciously. We're not in 1940s dress, although as most visitors do, we unconsciously carry our ancestral memories of the war on the Home Front. I am prompted to recall the story of how my own maternal grandfather and First World War soldier Sergeant Charles Read became a proud member of the East Kent Home Guard in 1940. There are photographs of him looking earnest and every bit the part in this book.

Meantime, as we palely loiter and marvel in this hallowed volunteer-run museum of comedy greatness, we discover Captain Mainwaring is played by a lookalike called 'Mick', who has the gift of espousing the original Arthur Lowe style of pomposity for authenticity's sake. Mick is of the philosophy that 'if the tin hat fits one can join the ranks', and we joke about him 'saying *that* to all the girls!' But there's no parade drill for us. It's all a hoot. Just a few photographs and a chuckle before we continue our walk through this epic home and tribute to important television comedy history.

In a labyrinth of rooms we see rafts of exhibits, props, scripts, the village hall stage, autographs, photographs, screenings and much more depicting the eighty episodes spanning 1968–1977, and films which continue to be broadcast across television networks to this day. There's Warden Hodges' uniform and helmet to enjoy, and Jonesy's red uniform tunic, helmet and medals from his alarmingly brutal 'don't like it up 'em' military experience in the Sudan, all carefully curated inside a glass case.

Trot along the road to the impressive Charles Burrell Museum nearby and glory in the sight of the butcher Jones's dark blue and white van, symbol of all things laughable. It is surrounded by a crowd who jostle and peer in wonder and we all listen intently as a guide informs us this famous vehicle was bought by the Dad's Army Museum in 2012 for £ 63,100. In the BBC documentary *Don't Panic*, filmed in 2000, we recall how comedy star Victoria Wood drove Jonesy's van around Thetford as she talked about her adoration of the show and its characters. Then in 2018, to mark the 50th anniversary of *Dad's Army*, we learn how a set of commemorative stamps were issued, with some commentators cheekily suggesting that the collection includes some hidden reference to Brexit.

Today, more than fifty-five years since Thetford, in its guise as the fictional wartime Walmington-on-Sea, first began relishing its stardom, we find ourselves among the more than 100,000 enthusiasts who have made a pilgrimage to the museum since it was opened by the show's producer David Croft in 2007. Three years later, in 2010, he unveiled a full-size bronze statue of Captain Mainwaring. How could we resist, then, making our way towards the riverbank to snap photographs of ourselves with the captain, despite his stony-faced oblivion to our friendly poses by his side. Perhaps he took umbridge about us putting our hands upon his knee! What would his wife Elizabeth have to say about that? We doubt she'd even care!

Back at the museum a volunteer dressed as a lookalike Sergeant Wilson tells us how it was the success of *Dad's Army* that sparked the idea to take visitors on a long trail around the local sites featured in the show. The creation of the museum (once home to the old fire station) soon followed. 'It just had to,' he explained. 'The most natural thing to do as the show's popularity continues to grow and grow all these decades later . . .' Who could argue with this? It has to be one of the world's most unique visitor attractions, with the rarest of artefacts and the most perfect tea-room.

Once outside, we couldn't refuse a visit to the leaning medieval Bell Inn near the corner of King Street. Here we lounged with pints of local ale at the bar where back in the 1970s the resident cast had their parties and where John Le Mesurier (Sergeant Wilson) and James Beck (Private Walker) stayed up until the early hours downing fine wines and spirits and laughing at the day's high jinks. There's also the story of how Bill Pertwee found himself half naked and locked out of his room one night. James Beck, who was renowned for playing jokes on the show's cast and crew, is believed to have been the culprit who caused Bill's red-faced shame and embarrassment.

By chance at The Bell we found the opportunity to talk to a young chap who revealed how his father was barman in the 1970s when the stars were in situ either making merry or nursing a hangover.

'My dad served them breakfast every morning and remembered all their requirements. They'd all be ready and prepared to film in their uniforms. They all looked very 1940s and yet it was the 1970s – very much two eras for the price of one! My father remembered how Arthur Lowe ate the most and was tremendously fussy about his food!' he explained.

After lunch it was time for us to march about Thetford and see the murals and multitudes of reminders of its famous association with comedy phenomena. There's even a real 'J Jones Family Butcher Shop' at 38 King Street and a board outside advertising the best-ever Walmington sausage. Thetford is and always will be *Dad's Army*. There's certainly no place like it.

Melody Foreman and Christine Bailey
September 2023

# NOTES

## Introduction

1. 'The humour in *Dad's Army*': in Summerfield & Peniston-Bird, *Contesting Home Defence*.
2. 'the authors of the series': Nigel Grey, correspondence, quoted in Summerfield & Peniston-Bird, *Contesting Home Defence*, pp. 228, 229.
3. 'the researchers of that show': Bill Trueman, correspondence, quoted in Summerfield & Peniston-Bird, *Contesting Home Defence*, p. 228.
4. 'old fashioned BBC standards': Tom Sloan, *BBC Lecture 1969*, quoted in Summerfield & Peniston-Bird, *Contesting Home Defence*, p. 184.
5. 'Sons of the Sea': Jimmy Perry, quoted in Summerfield & Peniston-Bird, *Contesting Home Defence*, p. 184.
6. *Whisky Galore* (1949): 'the main theme is not to deride the Home Guard', quoted in Summerfield & Peniston-Bird, *Contesting Home Defence*, p. 173.
7. 'When the series was first aired', Stubbs, *Different Times*, p. 133.

## Jimmy Perry OBE

1. 'born with an erection': Perry, *A Stupid Boy*, p. 8.
2. 'bullied': Perry, *A Stupid Boy*, p. 35.
3. 'too common': Perry, *A Stupid Boy*, p. 9.
4. 'a bomb blew out all of the windows': Perry, *A Stupid Boy*, p. 90.
5. 'marrying an old man': Perry, *A Stupid Boy*, p. 19.
6. Hylda Baker, *Guardian*, 11 February 1965.
7. 'telling jokes': Perry, *A Stupid Boy*, p. 88.
8. 'so many people ask me': Perry, *A Stupid Boy*, p. 90.
9. 'I'll never forget the day': Perry, *A Stupid Boy*, p. 92.
10. 'this CO gave us a lecture': Perry, *A Stupid Boy*, p. 93.
11. 'When I joined the Home Guard': Perry, *A Stupid Boy*, p. 92.
12. Battle of Omdurman: Perry, *A Stupid Boy*, p. 96.
13. Court of Enquiry: Perry, *A Stupid Boy*, p. 127.
14. 'talk to the chaps about . . . sex': Perry, *A Stupid Boy*, p. 133.
15. 'I was 19 when I joined the ATS': Brenda Usherwood, interview with the author.
16. 'those wonderful women': Perry, *A Stupid Boy*, p. 135.
17. 'how the hell should I know?': Perry, *A Stupid Boy*, p. 138.
18. 'show some aggression': Perry, *A Stupid Boy*, p. 144.
19. 'home can't be that far away': Vera Lynn, *Keep Smiling Through*, p. 55.
20. *Burma 44*: James Holland.
21. 'a single Japanese aircraft': Perry, *A Stupid Boy*, p. 155.

22. Anne Callender and David Croft: Perry, *A Stupid Boy*, p. 101.
23. 'miserable lot of old sods': Perry, *A Stupid Boy*, p. 103.

## David Croft OBE

1. 'a complicated dance': Croft, *You Have Been Watching*, p. 63.
2. 'such thin slices': Croft, *You Have Been Watching*, p. 50.
3. 'a stew of some sort': Croft, *You Have Been Watching*, p. 62.
4. 'a team of ten men': Croft, *You Have Been Watching*, p. 64.
5. 'barely holding Rommel': Croft, *You Have Been Watching*, p. 65.
6. 'sinister': Croft, *You Have Been Watching*, p. 65.
7. 'no talent whatever to be uncomfortable': Croft, *You Have Been Watching*, p. 68.
8. Bône Airfield and the North African Campaign: Dwight Eisenhower, *Crusade in Europe*.
9. 3rd Parachute Battalion and No. 6 Commandos seize Bône Airfield: Hilary St George Saunders, *The Red Beret, The Story of The Parachute Regiment at War*.
10. German air raid on Bône in Algeria, North Africa, during the Second World War. Critical Past film footage.
11. 'from our gun site': Croft, *You Have Been Watching*, p. 74.
12. 'nothing wrong with this patient': Croft, *You Have Been Watching*, p. 77.
13. 'I knew absolutely nothing about infantry': Croft, *You Have Been Watching*, p. 81.
14. 'renamed 2nd British Division': Croft, *You Have Been Watching*, p. 89.
15. 'It was an ugly scene': Croft, *You Have Been Watching*, p. 90.
16. 'we did a certain amount of land training': Croft, *You Have Been Watching*, p. 92.
17. 'I had gone inadvertently': Croft, *You Have Been Watching*, p. 99.
18. 'it was a welcome departure': Croft, *You Have Been Watching*, p. 169.
19. 'Hodges makes a steady stream of mockery': Simon Morgan-Russell, *David Croft and Jimmy Perry: The Television Series*, p. 48.
20. 'If all this sounds like pure chaos': Croft, *You Have Been Watching*, p. 170.
21. 'Jimmy and I were filled with a high level of excitement': Croft, *You Have Been Watching*, p. 174.
22. 'Arthur would never take his script with him': Croft, *You Have Been Watching*, p. 175.
23. 'Teddy was the most worrying driver': Croft, *You Have Been Watching*, p. 178.

## Arnold Ridley OBE

1. 'One-two-three-four': Ridley, *Godfrey's Ghost*, p. 75.
2. 'I had always shown a marked individuality': Ridley, *Godfrey's Ghost*, p. 106.
3. 'I succeeded in imperilling my scholastic career': Ridley, *Godfrey's Ghost*, p. 64.
4. 'Youth regarded war as a great adventure': Ridley, *Godfrey's Ghost*, p. 65.
5. 'My friends were all sent on garrison duty': Ridley, *Godfrey's Ghost*, p. 65.
6. 'That day we were cursed at length': Ridley, *Godfrey's Ghost*, p. 67.
7. 'One evening and feeling wretchedly homesick': Ridley, *Godfrey's Ghost*, p. 67.
8. 'That day on my walk': Piuk and Van Emden, *Famous 1914–1918*, p. 61
9. 'One lost one's sensitivity': Piuk and Van Emden, *Famous 1914–1918*, p. 62.
10. 'The men had gone over the top': Piuk and Van Emden, *Famous 1914–1918*, p. 62.
11. 'Flers, a small, insignificant village, had fallen': Piuk and Van Emden, *Famous 1914–1918*, p. 55.
12. 'We in the ranks had never heard of tanks': Piuk and Van Emden, *Famous 1914–1918*, p. 55
13. 'If you've ever tried to keep awake': Piuk and Van Emden, *Famous 1914–1918*, p. 53.

14. 'We were told that there was a pocket of resistance left over': Piuk and Van Emden, *Famous 1914–1918*, p. 55.
15. 'Every officer in the battalion who had taken part in the attack was killed or wounded': Piuk and Van Emden, *Famous 1914–1918*, p. 57.
16. 'I was quite certain my hand would be amputated': Ridley, *Godfrey's Ghost*, p. 69.
17. 'He woke to the sound of appalling screaming': Ridley, *Godfrey's Ghost*, p. 69.
18. Arnold Ridley OBE. Ridley, *Godfrey's Ghost*, p. 70.
19. 'I was hurrying over the pages': Van Emden, *The Quick and the Dead*, p. 53.
20. 'My wife, my kiddie, oh God!': Van Emden, *The Quick and the Dead*, p. 54.
21. 'I wondered whether people at home': Van Emden, *The Quick and the Dead*, p. 41.
22. Lance Corporal George Taylor, Somerset Light Infantry. Author interview, Dr Julian Brock.
23. 'How did you do this? Jack knife?': Ridley, *Godfrey's Ghost*, p. 71
24. 'My father felt, I believe, the aching guilt': Ridley, *Godfrey's Ghost*, p. 78.
25. 'I always feel they were planning the best way to get rid of me': Ridley, *Godfrey's Ghost*, p. 107.
26. A.E. Filmer: Bishop, *Barry Jackson and the London Theatre*, p. 61.
27. Spanish 'flu: de Bernières, *The Dust That Falls From Dreams*.
28. 'somehow I managed to leave my digs in Birmingham': Ridley, *Godfrey's Ghost*, p. 108.
29. 'sorry to see you go': Ridley, *Godfrey's Ghost*, p. 109.
30. *The Ghost Train*: Ridley, *Godfrey's Ghost*, p. 123.
31. HMS *Keith* or HMS *Whitshed*: Ellis, *The War in France and Flanders 1939–1940*.
32. Murland, *Retreat and Rearguard: Dunkirk 1940*.
33. Harry Leigh-Dugmore, British Legion website.
34. 'One morning in June', Ridley, *Godfrey's Ghost*, p.146.
35. Nicholas Ridley, exclusive reminiscences of his father.

## John Laurie

1. Pertwee, *Dad's Army The Making of a Legend*, p. 55.
2. Perry, *A Stupid Boy*, p. 28.
3. National Archive: First World War Medical Records.
4. Dunn, *Permission to Speak*, p. 200.
5. Powell, *A Life in Movies*, p. 445.
6. Pertwee, *Dad's Army The Making of a Legend*, p. 57.
7. Croft, *You Have Been Watching*, p. 177.
8. Lowe, *Arthur Lowe, Dad's Memory*, p. 122.
9. Perry, *A Stupid Boy*, p. 103.

## Arthur Lowe

1. 'Like the great comic creations of Shakespeare and Dickens': Richards, *Films and British National Identity*.
2. Author interview with Stephen Lowe, 2021.
3. Lowe, *Arthur Lowe: Dad's Memory*.
4. Rusholme & Victoria Park Archive: www.rusholmearchive.org.
5. 'landed a position at the Fairey Aircraft Factory': Lord, *Arthur Lowe*, p. 18.
6. 'sleeping on a concrete floor': Lord, *Arthur Lowe*, p. 21.
7. Arthur Lowe interview – Australian Television, 1976.
8. 'We had a six-inch Howitzer gun': Lord, *Arthur Lowe*, p. 24.
9. Doreen Herring recalls Manchester in the Blitz on 'Greatest Hits Radio', December 2015. www.planetradio.co.uk.

10. Lord, *Arthur Lowe*, p. 27.
11. Lord, *Arthur Lowe*, p. 31.
12. 'A room in a Derna hotel in Libya': Lord, *Arthur Lowe*, p. 33.
13. 'Arthur was very quiet, almost dour': Lord, *Arthur Lowe*, p. 37.
14. Perry, *A Stupid Boy*.
15. Perry, *A Stupid Boy*.
16. Arthur Lowe interview – Australian Television, 1976.
17. 'Once the Lowes had reached the downstairs bar': Lord, *Arthur Lowe*, p. 157.
18. Croft, *You Have Been Watching*.
19. 'I guess it was their way of having fun': Lord, *Arthur Lowe*, p. 57.
20. 'Clive could be bossy': Lord, *Arthur Lowe*, p. 155.
21. '*Amazon* was my father's romantic vision': Lowe, *Arthur Lowe: Dad's Memory*.

## John Le Mesurier

1. 'whipped cream walnuts or ten De Reske cigarettes': Le Mesurier, *A Jobbing Actor*, p. 6.
2. Alex Renton, 'Fear, Lies and Abuse: the Private School Cover Up', *The Times*, 3 April 2017.
3. John Suchet, 'Oh no, another rotten caning coming up', *Daily Mail*, 6 March 2009.
4. de Bernières, 'Author describes "hellish" prep school ordeal', *Independent*, 31 March 2021.
5. Waugh, *The Loom of Youth*.
6. 'More than anything else I resented Sherborne': Le Mesurier, *A Jobbing Actor*, p. 16.
7. McCann, *Do You think That's Wise?*, p. 41.
8. 'I was not easily persuaded': Le Mesurier, *A Jobbing Actor*, p. 18.
9. Le Mesurier, *A Jobbing Actor*, ch. 2.
10. 'I was introduced to the great man': Le Mesurier, *A Jobbing Actor*, p. 36.
11. 'Bombs were falling as we drove along': Le Mesurier, *A Jobbing Actor*, p. 43.
12. 'It was a hideous sight too': Gardiner, *Wartime Britain 1939–1945*, p. 428.
13. 'The train stopped everywhere all the way to Delhi': Le Mesurier, *A Jobbing Actor*, p. 57.
14. 'I thought why not just be myself': Le Mesurier, *A Jobbing Actor*, ch. 7.

## Clive Dunn OBE

1. 'What was different about the 1914–1918 conflict': Prologue, Sackville-West, *The Searchers: The Quest for the Lost of the First World War*.
2. 'So I turned to sport for success', Dunn, *Permission to Speak*, p. 14.
3. 'When I read how in the East End of London', Dunn, *Permission to Speak*, p. 26.
4. 'short legs, no breasts, and didn't expect anything!', Dunn, *Permission to Speak*, p. 32.
5. 'War had been announced', Dunn, *Permission to Speak*, p. 55.
6. 'a little buff envelope arrived', Dunn, *Permission to Speak*, p. 57.
7. 'We read later that this day', Dunn, *Permission to Speak*, p. 59.
8. 'At least he hit the target!', Dunn, *Permission to Speak*, p. 61.
9. 'some ackers', Dunn, *Permission to Speak*, p. 68.

## Greek war

10. Carr, *The Defence and Fall of Greece, 1940–1941*, Preface.
11. Carr, *The Defence and Fall of Greece, 1940–1941*, p. 145.

12. 'big guns', Dunn, *Permission to Speak*, p. 70.
13. Carr, *The Defence and Fall of Greece, 1940–1941*, p. 59.
14. Carr, *The Defence and Fall of Greece, 1940–1941*, p. 59.
15. 'I told him quickly to put the Revolver away', Dunn, *Permission to Speak*, p. 71.
16. 'We were being pummelled by German dive-bombers', Dunn, *Permission to Speak*, p. 73.
17. 'I held the patient's hand', Dunn, *Permission to Speak*, p. 74.
18. 'But I told them at HQ', Dunn, *Permission to Speak*, p. 75.
19. 'I went not out of bravery', Dunn, *Permission to Speak*, p. 77.
20. 'I was still armed with a pistol', Dunn, *Permission to Speak*, p. 83.
21. 'The sight of those sick and wounded soldiers', Dunn, *Permission to Speak*, p. 86.
22. 'As our deprivation increased', Dunn, *Permission to Speak*, p. 90.
23. 'I was sent down the valley in Rottenmann', Dunn, *Permission to Speak*, p. 112.
24. 'Here was one of Hitler's soldiers', Dunn, *Permission to Speak*, p. 123
25. 'David Croft assured me', Dunn, *Permission to Speak*, p. 198.

# BIBLIOGRAPHY

Carr, John, *The Defence & Fall of Greece 1940–1941* (Pen & Sword Books, 2020)

Croft, David, *You Have Been Watching . . . The Autobiography of David Croft* (BBC Books, 2004)

de Bernières, Louis, *The Dust That Falls from Dreams* (Harvill Secker, 2015)

Dunn, Clive, *Permission to Speak, An Autobiography* (Century Hutchinson Ltd, 1986)

Ellis, Major L.F., *The War in France and Flanders 1939–1940*, edited by J.R.M. Butler (Naval & Military Press 2009)

Holland, James, *Burma 44* (Penguin, 2020)

Le Mesurier, John, *A Jobbing Actor* (Sphere Books, 1985)

Lord, Graham, *Arthur Lowe* (Orion Books, 2002)

Lowe, Stephen, *Arthur Lowe, Dad's Memory* (Virgin Books, 1996)

McCann, Graham, *Do You Think That's Wise? The Life of John Le Mesurier* (Aurum Press, 2010)

Murland, Jerry, *Retreat and Rearguard: Dunkirk 1940: The Evacuation of the BEF to the Channel* (Pen & Sword Books, 2016)

Perry, Jimmy, *A Stupid Boy* (Arrow Books, 2003)

Pertwee, Bill, *Dad's Army, The Making of a Television Legend* (Pavilion Books, 1998)

Piuk, Victor, and Richard Van Emden, *Famous 1914–1918* (Pen & Sword Books, 2008)

Powell, Michael, *A Life in Movies, An Autobiography* (William Heinemann, 1986)

Richards, Jeffrey, *Films and British National Identity* (Manchester University Press, 1997)

Ridley, Nicolas, *Godfrey's Ghost, From Father to Son* (Mogzilla Life, 2009)

Sackville West, Robert, *The Searchers: The Quest for the Lost of the First World War* (Bloomsbury, 2021)

Saunders, Hilary St George, *The Red Beret, The Story of The Parachute Regiment at War 1940–1945* (Michael Joseph, 1950)

Spinney, Laura, *Pale Rider, The Spanish Flu or 1918 and How it Changed the World* (Vintage, 2007)

Stubbs, David, *Different Times, A History of British Comedy* (Faber & Faber, 2023)

Summerfield, Penny and Corinna Peniston-Bird, *Contesting Home Defence: Men, Women and the Home Guard in the Second World War* (Manchester University Press, 2007)

Van Emden, Richard, *The Quick and the Dead, Fallen soldiers and their families in the Great War* (Pen & Sword Books, 2012)

# INDEX